OKANAGAN UNIV/COLLEGE LIBRARY

P9-EJI-559

K

RG 133.5 .F46 1998
Private choices, public
Fenwick, Lynda Beck

02487353

DATE DUE

NOV 0 4 1998	
DEC - 3 1998	
FEB - 8 1999	
MAR - 4 1999	
MAR 2 6 1999	
DEC 1 4 1999	
MAR 3 0 2000	
NOV 2 2 2000	
APR 2 2 2001	
JAN 3 0 2002	
FEB 1 6 2002	

| BRODART. | Cat. No. 23-221 |

PRIVATE CHOICES, PUBLIC CONSEQUENCES

Also by
Lynda Beck Fenwick

SHOULD THE CHILDREN PRAY?

OKANA... ...
...LIBRARY
BRITISH COLUMBIA

PRIVATE CHOICES, PUBLIC CONSEQUENCES

REPRODUCTIVE TECHNOLOGY AND THE NEW ETHICS OF CONCEPTION, PREGNANCY, AND FAMILY

LYNDA BECK FENWICK

A DUTTON BOOK

DUTTON
Published by the Penguin Group
Penguin Putnam Inc., 375 Hudson Street,
New York, New York 10014, U.S.A.
Penguin Books Ltd, 27 Wrights Lane, London W8 5TZ, England
Penguin Books Australia Ltd, Ringwood, Victoria, Australia
Penguin Books Canada Ltd, 10 Alcorn Avenue,
Toronto, Ontario, Canada M4V 3B2
Penguin Books (N.Z.) Ltd, 182–190 Wairau Road,
Auckland 10, New Zealand

Penguin Books Ltd, Registered Offices:
Harmondsworth, Middlesex, England

First published by Dutton, an imprint of Dutton Signet,
a member of Penguin Putnam Inc.

First Printing, January, 1998
10   9   8   7   6   5   4   3   2   1

Copyright © Lynda Beck Fenwick, 1998
All rights reserved

 REGISTERED TRADEMARK—MARCA REGISTRADA

LIBRARY OF CONGRESS CATALOGING-IN-PUBLICATION DATA
Fenwick, Lynda Beck, 1944–
    Private choices, public consequences : a personal look at how reproductive technology has
affected the legal, moral, and ethical decisions we make about life / Lynda Beck Fenwick.
      p.   cm.
    ISBN 0-525-94263-7
    1. Human reproductive technology—Moral and ethical aspects United States.
  2. Human reproductive technology—Law and legislation—United States.   3. Human
reproductive technology—Government policy—United States.   I. Title.
RG133.5.F46   1998
176—dc21   97-28712
                                                                                                                    CIP

Printed in the United States of America
Set in Adobe Garamond

WITHOUT LIMITING THE RIGHTS UNDER COPYRIGHT RESERVED ABOVE, NO PART OF THIS PUBLI-
CATION MAY BE REPRODUCED, STORED IN OR INTRODUCED INTO A RETRIEVAL SYSTEM, OR
TRANSMITTED, IN ANY FORM, OR BY ANY MEANS (ELECTRONIC, MECHANICAL, PHOTOCOPYING,
RECORDING, OR OTHERWISE), WITHOUT THE PRIOR WRITTEN PERMISSION OF BOTH THE COPY-
RIGHT OWNER AND THE ABOVE PUBLISHER OF THIS BOOK.

This book is printed on acid-free paper.

FOR MY HUSBAND, LARRY

ACKNOWLEDGMENTS

Because I set out to combine the common sense of individuals who have faced the issues presented in this book with the experience and study of professionals, I could not have succeeded without the willingness of a range of people sharing their opinions and personal accounts with me. I thank all those people who contributed both personal and professional information, not only those who are identified in the book but also those who enriched my research with background information and private confidences.

I thank my family and friends, the people who have encouraged me with their interest as I worked on the book and who have helped shape my own thinking about these issues. Particularly I thank my husband, Larry, who has been my harshest critic and my loving supporter for so many years.

Many people assisted with the survey, some of whom I know and others of whom remain strangers to me, and I thank each one. For participants, I appreciate the time and the thoughtfulness devoted to answering so many complex questions. For those who administered the surveys, I appreciate how much effort was required.

I thank my literary agent, Sally Hill McMillan, for helping me find the right publisher. At Dutton I thank my editor, Deborah Brody, for her positive encouragement toward making the book even better; Jennifer Moore, for her insightful editorial comments; and my copy editor, Amy Robbins, for her sensitive attention to detail.

For all the people who trusted me with the accounts of such intimate decisions, I thank you for your generosity. Your personal stories illuminate the issues and allowed me to write the book as I felt it should be written, stimulating both the minds and hearts of readers.

CONTENTS

INTRODUCTION

At first it was the headlines—sensational accounts of surrogates, frozen embryos, and genetic engineering. Next it was the news photographs of the babies—not just the abandoned crack babies but also the low-birth-weight babies with anxious parents keeping watch over their incubators. These reports convinced me that reproductive technology was out of control and that regulations were needed. But another set of headlines, appearing primarily in women's magazines and warning against the dangers of a bureaucratic pregnancy police with the power to control the conduct of women, raised equally convincing arguments. How could we protect against reproductive abuses without allowing government to push too far into our private lives?

I began this book with a bias in favor of the babies. It seemed to me that regulations were needed to protect the babies from the selfish decisions of too many adults. The consequences of that selfishness in matters of conception, pregnancy, and birth were being magnified by technology, and I lacked confidence in the will of medical professionals and individuals to curb the abuses.

These concerns differed from my attitude toward abortion. Like so many others, I am unsure whether an abortion would ever be appropriate for my own family, but I am certain that no stranger should ever have the power to make that decision for me, or for any other family. The inconsistency between my opinion about abortion and my willingness to regulate other reproductive choices troubled me, and I wondered if others shared my discordant views.

The rhetoric of abortion activists and the politicians who cozy up to one side or the other in the abortion debate made it sound as if all reproductive issues fit neatly into one of two boxes. Those who oppose abortion should also oppose assisted conception and unorthodox family planning. Those who trust a woman to make her own choice about an abortion should also trust her to achieve and conduct her pregnancy as she chooses. Since my own opinions could not be categorized that neatly, I suspected that the opinions of others might also crisscross erratically back and forth on such issues as fetal tissue research, genetic screening for diseases, and infertility treatments. Rather than trying to develop a consistent analysis, I began to extricate my preconceptions about abortion from my consideration of other reproductive issues. Certainly abortion remains a significant element of some of the issues, like prenatal screening for genetic traits or using fetal tissue in research, but it is not necessarily the sole element dictating the conclusion. Even within the abortion debate itself, people see different moral issues, such as whether the termination of the pregnancy has occurred because of rape or incest, gender preference, or a genetic disorder, and those moral distinctions alter their attitudes. If that is possible, then separating abortion opinions from other reproductive issues should also be possible for most people.

For those absolutists at either end of the spectrum who have determined to protect either the woman or the fetus, all reproductive matters may be bound together. For the rest of us, I doubted that it was so simple.

As I began to ask people their opinions, I discovered that how they characterized their views on abortion was no basis for predicting how they might feel about other issues we discussed. Contrary to what politicians believed, or at least what they told us, neither pro-life nor pro-choice positions dictate public attitudes, if policy were allowed to reflect the views outside Wash-

ington. I decided that any strategies for confronting the reproductive dilemmas raised by our growing prenatal access to the
fetus for information and treatment prior to birth and our increasing technological intervention in conception and birth can
succeed only if we set aside abortion rhetoric.

Without directly realizing it, the Americans with whom I
spoke have already done that. How they feel about a particular
reproductive issue probably relates to a personal experience in
their lives rather than to any political viewpoint. A grandmother whispered to me the story of how her daughter's prenatal test results showing the possibility of a genetic disability
had shaken the pro-life stance the woman had always taken.
"The follow-up test revealed that the trait was not present," she
confided, "but I am no longer so certain about my views on
abortion."

Similarly, my own experiences in talking with people who
had actually faced the reproductive choices that I had only read
about in print made me reconsider my views. For one thing, I
was impressed with the thoughtful evaluation of consequences
most of these people expressed, and while I did not always agree
with the conclusions they reached, I found a new respect for the
reasoning behind their decisions.

I also spoke with experts—bioethicists, fertility specialists,
and judges—but I often found that the common sense expressed by ordinary people had as much merit as the educated
opinions of the experts. One troubled father described the way
experts see these moral issues as "ivory-tower theories," and his
own struggles exemplified the fact that parents do not often
enjoy the luxury of being sequestered in ivory towers to ponder
their decisions. I knew that any book on the subject should
include not only the objective viewpoints of professionals but
also the very subjective wisdom of parents who live with the
consequences of their decisions every day.

The collective common sense of generations of parents
created taboos and moral codes to guide the reproductive decisions of their descendants, but two decades of technology have

muddled these social mores. Stripped of the wisdom of our ancestors, we seemed to be proceeding with the use of the technology without taking time to evolve new mores to guide us. I began asking people how they felt about changing reproductive options, trying to discover if any popular consensus was forming. For example, when relatives or friends provide the womb or the egg, are the taboos against incest and adultery irrelevant? When a wife bears another man's child with donor sperm, is marital fidelity breached? When a single woman goes to a sperm bank to conceive a child, does she impose a stigma on her baby?

I formalized questions about changing reproductive options into a survey, and the responses from people of all ages and backgrounds reveal what I had suspected. Technology has blurred long-standing definitions of what is acceptable, and without a universal moral code to guide us, many people have substituted economics and legality as their new guides. If we can afford it and it is legal, most of us would at least consider the option.

This openness has led many of the women with whom I spoke to employ unorthodox means to have their babies. As one of them told me, "You want to have a baby so much that eventually you are willing to try just about anything." These women described similar medical journeys to me, often beginning with their family doctors and proceeding from one specialist to another until they were led, one procedure at a time, far from the traditional conception and birth they had originally envisioned for themselves. "I had been so careful not to get pregnant during my twenties," one woman told me. "I never imagined that I would have trouble conceiving when I was finally ready. By then, I didn't have much time left and I was ready to try whatever the doctors suggested."

Slowly my feelings began to shift. I had begun with a bias in favor of the babies, whom I saw as innocents in need of protection from selfish adults. I was beginning to see that often the parents were nearly as vulnerable as their babies, made so by the same longings to have children that other people satisfy through traditional conceptions and births. The medical professionals who were employing all the space-age technology were only trying to help their patients achieve what most couples accomplish for themselves. But even as I became less judgmental in assessing the motives of the adult participants, I remained just as concerned about the methods we are seeing brought into mainstream obstetrics.

For many people the answer to my concern lay in the babies. "Look at this baby," they would say. "This beautiful child is proof enough for me that what we did was right." Yet we have never allowed the births of beautiful babies to justify rape or incest or motherhood for very young girls. Without condemning the babies, we have condemned those things as wrong. We must not excuse ourselves from examining the new ways in which babies are being conceived by cloaking every unorthodox conception and birth in the innocence of the children that result.

This book is not only about whether the technologies are appropriate. It is equally about what should be done if we decide that some of the practices employed in technologically and third-party-assisted conceptions, and certain prenatal behaviors, are wrong. Just as my definition of what was inappropriate underwent changes, my thinking about the need for new laws to regulate those that we conclude are inappropriate began to shift focus.

For one thing, I found that the state legislators who have attempted to draft regulations seem either to exhibit the intransigence characteristic of abortion politics or to reflect the same perplexities of the rest of us, lacking a public consensus to guide the political process. Legislation that has been passed in several states, when applied to real-life situations, often seems cumbersome and punitive.

For another thing, I discovered that professionals have recognized many of the problems and have prepared guidelines through their various medical associations to encourage their members to avoid the practices that led to earlier abuses. While these guidelines do not have the enforceability of laws, most ethical professionals follow them.

The most significant thing to cause my shift in focus, however, was my renewed confidence in people's desire to do what is right. Even the women with whom I spoke who had used cocaine during their pregnancies had wanted what was best for their babies and had sought help in battling their addictions. Clearly, abuses exist, but the world of selfish parents and technocratic medical specialists that I had imagined from reading the headlines was not what I found. That gave me hope; yet I also saw that the desire to have a baby can overwhelm individual moral reservations unless clear social attitudes are in place to help individuals hold to their values.

While the bioethicists, lawyers, religious leaders, and politicians argue endlessly, babies are being born as a result of the very practices the experts find so morally troubling. In a country founded on the principle of protecting the rights of individuals, perhaps no personal right is more private or more precious than the right to bear or beget a child. Uniquely, however, it is the one individual right that can never be practiced in solitude and without altering forever the lives of others. In developing the focus of this book, I finally realized the necessity of discarding the single-lens approach and utilizing a faceted lens capable of focusing at the same time on multiple priorities—not only the baby but also the mother, not only the mother but also the father, not only the family but also the greater community, not only the present but also the future. In the case of many of these practices, the multiple lens must also focus upon the consequences to gamete donors, infertile spouses, same-sex partners, siblings, surrogates, and society in general, all of whom are being affected by these reproductive choices.

There are two questions that weave the parts of this book together. First, even if I can have a child, should I? Second, who should decide? Technology and the assistance of third parties as donors and surrogates allow births that would never have occurred a generation ago. The fact that these births can occur must not excuse us from considering whether they should, when all of the emotional and financial costs are considered. Next, because the consequences of the decision may touch so many lives, it has become important for us to reconsider who has the wisdom to be trusted with deciding.

You may want to turn to the back of the book before you begin reading in order to take the survey and test your own opinions without being influenced by the ideas you will discover within the book. You might even find it interesting to keep a record of your responses and compare them with your feelings after reading the book. Just as my opinions were modified by exposure to the ideas you will be reading, I expect yours will be affected as well.

The book is enriched by the voices of individuals who disclose very personal experiences, as well as by the knowledge of experts who share their broader and more objective points of view. These individual voices reveal the emotions that shape the opinions they express.

While I will lead you among these divergent views, you will be challenged to absorb or discard the ideas you encounter according to your own moral compass. I warn you at the beginning that my own journey in researching the book has turned me aside from my initial pursuit of greater regulation. That change in heading includes, however, my belief that the greater reproductive options available to us today demand a higher level of moral accountability than any that has been faced by previous generations. No longer does conception necessarily involve only one man and one woman. No longer are a baby's traits matters of random chance. No longer are the nine months of gestation a complete mystery. Dealing with these realities requires more wisdom than coping with the problems of the past which we had no power to change. Turning to government to regulate our responses to the technology may be a tempting way to excuse ourselves from the responsibility, but it takes away a precious freedom that our Constitution protects.

Absolutely rejecting technology and whatever is unorthodox may also be tempting, but that false approach pretends that what we have already adopted into widespread use is essentially beneficial while the new technologies we reject are inherently corrupting.

The better strategy, I believe, is to accept for ourselves the responsibility of assuming not only the right but also the full consequences of our decisions. That would require that we be willing sometimes not to conceive or give birth, even though it may be possible, because the choice does not seem conscionable[1] or because the costs or the risks seem too high. In other words, I believe we should nurture personal conscience as the source for making appropriate reproductive choices rather than legislation that absolves individuals from responsibility. By sometimes answering "no" to the question of whether we should conceive a child, we can best ensure that the power to decide will continue to be entrusted to each of us. Reproductive options would be narrowed not by laws but by our own exercise of procreation in a way that respects the impact of our choice beyond ourselves.

If the news reports of turkey-baster inseminations, post-menopausal pregnancies, and criminal prosecution of mothers for prenatal conduct have set your moral compass spinning, I hope this book can help you to get a clear heading. The need for us to head in the right direction, especially for the sake of the generations that will inherit our judgments, is urgent.

CHAPTER 1

THE STORY OF MARY SHEARING

Despite her temporary celebrity status when the nation's press headlined the news that a fifty-two-year-old, menopausal woman was expecting twins, Mary Shearing is today a very typical mom. Ask her to tell you the most positive thing about the technology that allowed her to give birth to twin girls after seven years of trying, and she answers, "I've got two babies!" But she can't resist adding, "However, I would not give that same response at two a.m."

Like many other infertile couples in the vanguard of reproductive technology, Don and Mary Shearing did not suddenly decide to try some new procedure. Even before their marriage, they knew they wanted to have children together, although the twenty-year age difference between them meant that special considerations were involved. Prior to the wedding, Mary consulted a doctor and was told to "proceed with all haste because of my age," and upon her doctor's advice, she consulted a fertility specialist.

Looking back, Mary feels that the fertility treatments may not have been sufficiently aggressive for someone her age. After about two years, she and Don stopped the treatments, and without the benefit of any technology, Mary became pregnant. When she miscarried, they began to lose hope that she could ever carry a baby to term. With the onset of menopause, it seemed impossible, until Mary saw an article in the paper about a new procedure that might allow even a menopausal woman to become pregnant using someone else's eggs. The doctor named in the article was David Diaz, and Mary went to see him.

She was given a thorough physical, including a treadmill, blood work, and an examination by a cardiologist. Mary explains the purpose of the extensive tests to which she was subjected before being accepted into the program. "Why do the procedure if it is going to put me at so much risk that it is not going to succeed? Dr. Diaz's primary concern is that the procedure succeeds, and if he were to help me get pregnant and then I started having severe health problems, that is not success. That is stupid!"

Seeing Mary today, it is no surprise that the testing found her to be physically fit for the pregnancy. Her body looks toned and strong, and while it is apparent that she is older than Don, it is easy to see why she captured and held on to his heart. Although she has had little time for it since the twins were born, the years of bodybuilding still show in Mary's trim figure. Mary did not object to the physical testing she underwent, but would have adamantly opposed challenges to the wisdom of her decision. She explains Dr. Diaz's role in the decision whether she should be allowed to receive the donated eggs this way: "He did not play God. It was strictly whether I was physically capable of handling the pregnancy."

The technology involved would not have been considered particularly newsworthy had it been used by someone younger. Eggs were donated by another woman, they were fertilized by Don's sperm in the laboratory, and the resulting embryos were transferred into Mary's body. For many menopausal women, their other reproductive organs are perfectly capable of pregnancy even after their ovaries have stopped producing eggs. The successful use of donor eggs and in vitro fertilization with postmenopausal women was first reported by Dr. Mark Sauer of the University of Southern California in 1990, but Mary was almost a decade older than even the oldest of Dr. Sauer's pioneering patients.

Having passed the physical evaluations, Mary was accepted

into Dr. Diaz's program. "Everything was just so incredibly successful. It wasn't a case of trying and failing. We tried it and it worked and we had babies. It was just meant to be," Mary believes.

Because the technology was not new, the public attention that her pregnancy and birth attracted clearly had to do with the fact that she was the oldest American woman to have used the technology rather than with the procedure itself. Mary and Don had not intended to bring their decision to the attention of the public, but while watching television, they heard a prominent author criticize menopausal women for becoming pregnant. They were so disturbed by the television program's one-sided view of the procedure that they arranged to tell their own story to the press. "I went public to show that it is not a negative procedure. It is extremely positive," Mary says. Although she is very serious about delivering her message of hope to older mothers, she often uses her natural sense of humor to convey that message. In response to the author's prediction that teenagers born to older women will have trouble relating to mothers in their sixties or seventies, Mary jokes, "My daughters will probably relate to me about as well as any teenager relates to their mom—they won't!"

Mary knows the challenges of being a parent. She and her first husband had three babies by the time Mary was twenty-three. Mary recalls breaking the news of her decision to become a postmenopausal mother to her grown children: "My son—the oldest—and one daughter were immediately very happy. My middle daughter flipped. She said, 'Oh my God, Mom. What are you doing? You're crazy!' But as soon as she settled down she was tickled for me." Ironically, this daughter was pregnant at the same time Mary was, and their babies were born just ten weeks apart. "Now we are sharing baby clothes and it is really kind of funny," Mary admits.

Concerns about her own longevity seem not to have oc-curred to Mary. "I've got a great-aunt who is one hundred and two or three, and my dad is eighty-five and extremely active. I expect to live a good number of years." She acknowledges that her husband's age did play a part in their decision, however. "All our friends are in their thirties and have babies. His sisters have children. Our lifestyle is surrounded by babies. It is hard to say whether I would have done this if my husband had been in his fifties, but probably not because our lifestyle would have been different."

Mary and Don are delighted with their selection of a donor. "We have one child that looks like my husband. She's a real clone. And the other one looks like me. I just don't see how we could have chosen any better." Their good fortune in the genetic inheritance of their daughters was a matter of careful selection, however, and not mere luck.

Although Mary carried the twins from the time they were embryos of only a few cells, she has no genetic link with her daughters. Don has the genetic link because his sperm was used. They thought briefly about asking a member of Mary's family to be the egg donor so that Mary would also have a genetic connection. But Mary worried about the emotional entanglements that would result if someone in her own family were involved. "It would always be in the back of my mind, and it would probably always be in the back of the donor's mind, that this is her genetic child, especially being around each other and all. . . . I know this may sound stupid, but this way the babies are more mine."

Even after Don and Mary decided not to use a relative as the donor, they wanted to find someone who, as Mary says, "not only closely resembles me in physical appearance but in mental outlook and physical activity." Although they do not know their donor's name, they were allowed to see pictures of her and her children to help them in making their selection. Mary doubts that her memory of the pictures would enable her to recognize the donor if they were to meet on the street. The donor was not told the identity of the couple using her eggs. As for telling the twins about their conception, Don and Mary have kept scrapbooks of the publicity, and they plan to tell their daughters at some point. "If they wish to know information about their biological mother, we will tell them. If they don't want to know it, I'm not going to make an issue of it."

Before learning about the possibility of using a donor's eggs, Don and Mary had considered using a surrogate, but two things discouraged them. Through a common acquaintance, they were particularly familiar with the case of another California couple whose surrogate had attempted to revoke their agreement and claim custody for herself, even though the embryo she carried for the couple had been created from the couple's own egg and sperm. That made Mary very nervous about a surrogacy. In addition, Mary says, "We're not wealthy enough for surrogacy. Our procedure cost about $10,000, and surrogacy would have cost closer to $40,000."

Having decided to carry the fetuses herself, Mary discovered another advantage. "I bonded with these babies so much better than if they had been carried by somebody else. Because they were carried by me, I felt them move, I nurtured them, I supplied them with their blood. I even produced their milk. It was a very personal experience for me. It was a level of participation that I would not have enjoyed having gone through a surrogacy."

Mary approves allowing her doctor to determine whether she was physically capable of carrying a baby to term without damaging her own health in the process. She warns other women considering doing what she did, "Make sure you are in good physical condition. The bottom line is, if you are not, it could ruin your health. Pregnancy at any age is not all that easy."

However, the appropriateness of the couple's decision to have a child is not, in Mary's opinion, something that the doctor or the government should second-guess. "I think if the government were to step in, I would get real upset about that. They overregulate too much as it is. I wear seat belts, but I don't really need the government to tell me I have to. I think it is very smart to wear a helmet on a motorcycle, but I don't think the government should be telling us that we need to do it. So, I don't think any regulatory body should come in and pass judgment on the couple's decision to have a baby. The doctor knows the patient. The doctor can tell if the woman is in good physical condition and a good candidate." Beyond that, Mary believes the decision must be left to the couple.

Mary and Don have no doubts about the decision they made. When two-pound two-ounce Amy Leigh and two-pound twelve-and-a-half-ounce Kelly Ann were born prematurely on November 10, 1992, their daddy thought they were "beautiful, absolutely fantastic," and he still does. Don is, as Mary says, "very participating," doing his share of the feeding and diaper changing.

As for Mary, being a new mother at fifty-three has its advantages. "When I had my first three babies, I was much too young, much too immature. Today I am less self-involved, more mature, and more focused on these babies." Then the mischief slips back into her voice and she adds, "But I'll let you know for sure in a couple of years!"

CHAPTER 2

DO WE HAVE AN ABSOLUTE RIGHT
TO HAVE A CHILD?

Ask Americans whether they think the right to have a child should be absolute, and at least half of them will say "no." Press them further for a good reason why someone's right to have children should be restricted, and most will identify financial or mental inability to care for a child as appropriate reasons. But ask Americans the best reason for having a child, and nearly all of them will say, "For love." Our desire to love a child and be loved in return seems to be all the reason we need for conceiving our own children, but not reason enough for someone else whom we judge economically, mentally, or socially unfit.[1]

When Mary Shearing decided to have a baby at the age of fifty-three, many Americans questioned her decision, but the national debate concerning postmenopausal conceptions did not stir congressional action. In France, however, national concern over the propriety of technologically assisted birth by postmenopausal women led the National Assembly to pass a bill prohibiting it. The French Senate had still not approved the bill a year later, when news was released of the postmenopausal birth of twins to a fifty-nine-year-old English woman who had received an embryo implant at an Italian clinic and of the pregnancy of a sixty-two-year-old Italian woman treated at the same clinic. The conservative French government reacted to the announcement with renewed efforts to impose strict controls on all artificial impregnations, and proposed a requirement that infertile couples would have to obtain the consent of the donor and the permission of a judge before receiving an embryo implant.

As the Shearing twins celebrated their first birthday amid news of the birth of the English twins, the American media resumed the debate over older women having babies. Arguments seemed to focus on the potentially greater risks to the mother and the irresponsibility of giving birth at an age which makes it less likely that the mother can rear her child to adulthood.

It is not only postmenopausal pregnancies that have raised concerns, however. Many other unorthodox reproductive choices made by couples and single mothers have also been controversial. Some, like Mary Shearing's pregnancy, involve the use of complicated technology, but others are more a matter of ignoring traditional taboos. Could American legislators ever enact laws limiting our rights to have a baby? You may be surprised to learn that they have already tried.

In 1935 a chicken thief named Skinner ran up against an Oklahoma law requiring anyone convicted three times of a felony to be sterilized. Since stealing chickens was Skinner's third felony conviction, the court ordered him to have a vasectomy, and Skinner appealed that judgment all the way to the United States Supreme Court.

Nowhere in the United States Constitution does it say anything about the right to procreate, but in 1943 the Court ruled that the Oklahoma law was unconstitutional. According to the Court, "Marriage and procreation are fundamental to the very existence and survival of the [human] race." The decision in *Skinner v. Oklahoma*[2] became the Supreme Court precedent for our belief that the right to procreate is so basic, so fundamental, that government should not interfere with its exercise.

Skinner was an ordinary man who convinced the United States Supreme Court that he knew more about fundamental rights than the Oklahoma legislature did. The legal concept of fundamental rights remains the basis for protecting Mary Shearing and all the other reproductive pioneers who are expanding the social and medical definitions of who can have babies.[3]

Fundamental rights have been the subject of great legal debate since the Constitution was ratified. The Founding Fathers debated fiercely whether all those rights retained by the people and over which the government was being given no power should be listed in the Constitution. Some argued that listing all retained rights would protect against any infringement by the government, while others warned that some rights would certainly be forgotten and the incomplete listing would be more confusing than no list at all.

Among those opposing a listing of retained rights were James Wilson of Pennsylvania, who warned that "an imperfect enumeration would throw all implied power into the scale of the government," and James Iredell of North Carolina, who agreed: "It would be not only useless, but dangerous, to enumerate a number of rights which are not intended to be given up; because it would be implying, in the strongest manner, that every right not included in the exception might be impaired by the government without usurpation; and it would be impossible to enumerate every one." The representative from Massachusetts Theodore Sedgwick put it more plainly when he argued that if you tried to list every right that a man has, you would have to declare "that a man should have a right to wear his hat if he pleased; that he might get up when he pleased, and go to bed when he thought proper."[4]

Despite the fears these men expressed, the Bill of Rights that was added to the Constitution enumerates certain fundamental rights. Modern Americans tend to see these enumerated rights, such as freedom of speech and freedom of the press, as those most obviously reserved by the people because they are expressly stated in writing. The Founding Fathers may have felt, however, that there was no need to enumerate other rights precisely because they were too obvious to require enumeration. Clearly, the Founding Fathers intended to recognize protection of unenumerated rights, because the Ninth Amendment provides, "the enumeration in the Constitution, of certain rights, shall not be construed to deny or disparage others retained by the people."

Skinner may not have understood the legal theories of his appeal, but he believed that his right to have children was greater than the power of the state of Oklahoma to take that right away from him. Six decades later, Mary Shearing may never have heard of fundamental rights, either, but legal support for her opposition to government regulation of menopausal pregnancies comes from the Supreme Court precedent established by a chicken thief.

Fundamental rights, under our system of laws, are given the highest protection because we believe individuals withheld these rights to themselves when they consented to be governed. In other words, when our forefathers came together to form the government we now take for granted, they did not give away complete power over their lives. Today we are so accustomed to the constant presence of the government in our daily lives that the notion of power having come from the people in the first place sounds almost as revolutionary to us as it did to the rulers whose power our forefathers challenged over two hundred years ago.

Americans have lost their historical awareness that fundamental rights come from the people themselves and are not privileges to be granted or withheld at the whim of the government. At the same time, Americans must be reminded that the companion to retained rights is retained individual responsibility as well. When we examine the fundamental right to procreate, we must also remember the individual responsibility that goes with it.

Mary Shearing exercised her fundamental right to procreate, and the corresponding issue is whether she acted responsibly in making her decision. Does a woman at age fifty-three have the energy, the health, and the longevity to see her children into adulthood? Mary says she does, but should Congress follow France's lead and consider second-guessing her judgment or regulating other menopausal women who may not be so careful before they use the procedure?

Since the birth of Mary's twins, much older women have given birth. In Israel, a sixty-year-old woman, married to a sixty-eight-year-old man, lied to her doctor about her age in order to be accepted for the procedure. In Italy, Rosanna Della Corte gave birth at the age of sixty-two because she and her husband decided to have a baby after the death of their nineteen-year-old son in an accident. Since then she has expressed her desire to give birth once more so that their son will not be left without a family when she and her husband die. Some doctors see no reason to set age limits restricting the women who may be accepted into their programs. Doctors who attempt to limit candidates on the basis of age report that some women lie and falsify documents to gain admission. An American woman gave birth at the age of sixty-three years and nine months after telling her doctor she was fifty. The baby girl born in November of 1996 was the first child for her and her sixty-year-old husband, after many years of trying. Unlike Mary, these women have no young husbands to assume the parental responsibilities should they fail to survive long enough to raise their children to adulthood. The very real possibility of creating orphans in cases such as these makes the private decision between a woman and her doctor of even greater concern to society at large.

The majority of people responding to the Private Choices Survey were willing to relinquish the power to make reproductive decisions in certain instances. Before we implement any law that would touch an individual's fundamental right of procreation, however, we must proceed with great caution. If we are too ready to compromise our fundamental rights, we jeopardize the system envisioned by the Founding Fathers and enjoyed by Americans for the past two centuries. The fact is, so few Americans understand the concept that most people might consider giving something so valuable away without even recognizing what they had done.

While the Supreme Court has identified the right to beget

and bear children as fundamental, the recognition of other unenumerated rights that may also be involved in reproductive choices is not so clear. For example, the right of privacy may also be important in relation to some reproductive issues. Although a right of privacy has been recognized by the Supreme Court, the parameters of that right are still being defined by the courts. That is why it is so important to understand that if the right is fundamental, a definition that is too narrow takes from you something that you already have. If the right is truly fundamental, no permission is necessary, and it is recognition and not permission that the court is granting.

The problem is, of course, deciding what rights the people retained, since they are not described in the Constitution. Some judges are very reluctant to recognize a right that was not clearly retained and for them the Ninth Amendment has little practical meaning. During the confirmation hearings that ultimately led to his rejection from serving on the Supreme Court, respected jurist Robert Bork testified, "I do not think you can use the Ninth Amendment unless you know something of what it means. For example, if you had an amendment that says 'Congress shall make no . . .' and then there is an inkblot, and you cannot read the rest of it, and that is the only copy you have, I do not think the court can make up what might be under the inkblot."[5] Bork's interpretation of the Constitution is exactly what the forefathers who warned of the dangers of an incomplete enumeration feared.

Applying the concept of fundamental rights to reproductive technologies that could not have been imagined by our forefathers may make us feel as if a bucketful of ink has spilled across the Constitution. But since the Constitution describes what our ancestors relinquished to the government rather than enumerating everything they retained for themselves and their descendants, if something is hidden by an inkblot, it must be construed as a limit to the powers given government and not a sacrifice of a power retained by the people. To presume that we can only recognize enumerated rights leads to exactly the danger our forefathers warned against when they opposed a partial listing, and it is exactly that interpretation that the Ninth Amendment was intended to avoid.

Although fundamental rights are given the highest legal protection, they are not absolute. Sometimes the rights of the individual must yield to the greater needs of society. Once the retention of fundamental rights is understood, however, it is easier to appreciate that limits on those precious rights must be as minimal as possible.

There is an enormous difference between the voluntary relinquishment of individual rights for a particular purpose and an obligatory relinquishment mandated by the government. Mary Shearing voluntarily entrusted her doctor with the authority to determine her physical ability to experience a menopausal pregnancy because she felt he was better able than she to make that determination. "I think that a doctor's primary concern should be the woman's physical condition and her physical ability to carry a child. Whether he thinks a fifty-three-year-old woman *should* have children or not, I don't think that he should make that kind of decision," Mary explains, making it clear that she sought only his medical opinion.

If the majority believe that a person is exercising a fundamental right irresponsibly, can government take that right away from them? Most of the time, the answer is "no," but there are exceptions. If the need in society to regulate individual behavior is so overwhelming, the rights of the individual may be reduced to the extent required by the circumstances.

In the 1970s a mail-order business in North Carolina advertised nonprescription contraceptives in college newspapers around the country. Customers could clip the order form and send it to the company, and their order would be returned by mail. Today we might wonder why a college student would go to so much trouble to buy a condom, but in New York State at that time, the law prohibited the distribution of contraceptives to anyone under age sixteen. Even sales to older customers could only be made by pharmacists, who could not advertise or display contraceptives for sale.

Advertising in college newspapers and filling orders through the mail without any proof of age clearly violated the law, and New York officials warned the company to stop. The company, in turn, asked the United States Supreme Court to decide whether the New York law was constitutional.

In that case, two fundamental rights were involved: procreation and privacy. Finding that the New York customers buying contraceptives through the mail were exercising fundamental rights did not mean that New York was absolutely prohibited by the Constitution from regulating the sales. The Court indicated that certain state interests, such as safeguarding health and maintaining medical standards, might justify regulating the mail-order sales. The Court then explained the test for evaluating both the need for and the extent of the regulation. " 'Compelling' is of course the key word," the Court said. "Where a decision as fundamental as that whether to bear or beget a child is involved, regulations imposing a burden on it may be justified only by compelling state interests, and must be narrowly drawn to express only those interests."[6]

There you have the three-part legal test for considering government regulation of reproductive issues. First, is a fundamental right involved? Because rights of procreation and privacy will almost certainly be involved and the Supreme Court has already recognized those rights as fundamental, we can move quickly to the next part of the test. Second, is there a compelling need in the society at large which requires regulation of the rights of the individual to meet the overwhelming need of society? An affirmative response to this question requires more than proving that the individual's behavior is irresponsible or unwise; our Constitution protects our right to make fools of ourselves. The question also requires proof of more than general social disapproval or inconvenience. Rather, the government must establish a "compelling" social need for the regulation and not merely a desirable result from it. Even if a compelling need is shown, the government is not then free to strip the individual of all choice. A third part of the legal test must be met. Specifically, the regulation must be as narrow and limited as possible so that society's need is satisfied with as little infringement on the rights of the individual as there can be.

Mothers and fathers today are exercising their fundamental rights of procreation and privacy in unorthodox ways, and often they are assisted by donors, surrogates, and medical professionals. In some instances, you may believe that their actions are irresponsible and that strategies to combat such irresponsibility are desperately needed. In other instances, you may feel that their reproductive behavior has gone beyond irresponsibility and that a compelling social need exists to regulate their actions. Even then, however, you must consider what regulation could be devised to cause the least infringement on individual rights to meet the social need. Finally, you may discover that as unorthodox as some conceptions and births are today, it is society's acceptance of a new reproductive option that is called for rather than condemnation of the practice.

What makes all of this so difficult, of course, are the babies. While we instinctively guard against any limitation of our own reproductive rights, our protective instinct shifts to the babies when we consider the reproductive choices of others. Procreation is by its nature unique among all other fundamental rights, for its exercise by one individual creates another individual whose birthrights will be forever blessed or cursed by the actions of its parents at that conception. The struggle to balance those overlapping rights has grown more complex in the past decade as assisted conceptions have involved more participants in the process. There is also growing public resentment of the costs we perceive as having been caused by the irresponsible actions of others. We have begun to lose confidence in the ability of individuals to take responsibility for their actions, and have become angry that we are too often asked to pay for the problems others create. Technology has magnified the potential for irresponsible choices to extract unprecedented costs from the babies and from the rest of us.

Our ancestors were guided in making moral choices about reproduction by social values and taboos that had evolved over countless generations. The exploding technological changes during the past two decades have left us with a moral code that no longer seems adequate, and with no general consensus as to what society's ethical response should be. Legality has replaced morality as the guiding force in reproductive choice. As a consequence, people are calling for laws rather than trusting individual responsibility to control not only the risks to the babies being created but also the costs to society caused by the new technology and attendant loss of traditional taboos.

Have Americans lost their sense of moral direction so hopelessly that government regulation is necessary to get us back on course? Does the unique overlapping of rights between parent and child in the exercise of procreation necessitate intervention by courts and ethics committees? Let's take a closer look.

Which of the following are important and appropriate reasons for choosing to have a child?

- Having a child is the reason people marry.
- Spouse wants a child.
- To carry on the family name and inheritance.
- A child is important for a happy marriage.
- To prove you are able to have a child.
- Life is not complete unless you have a child.
- Pressure from your parents.
- Pressure from your friends.
- You think you would be a good parent.
- Your friends have children.
- You feel selfish without a child.
- You feel useless without a child.
- All women should experience pregnancy and birth.
- All men should experience fatherhood.
- You have a strong emotional desire to have a child.
- Your religion encourages you to have children.
- You want to share the things you know with a child.
- You want to love and be loved by a child.
- You want grandchildren.
- You want someone to take care of you when you are old.
- You want to pass along your genetic history.
- It is important to society.
- It is important to some group of which you are a part.

Should everyone have the right to have a child?

If you think there should be any limits on a person's right to have a child, what reasons are appropriate?

Do you think the number of children a person could have should ever be limited?

If you think there should be limits on the number of children a person should have, what number is appropriate?

What reasons are proper justifications for limiting the number of children a person could have?

CHAPTER 3

THE STORY OF LAURA CAMPO AND BABY THERESA ANN

During March 1992, all across America people gave their hearts to the tiny baby girl born without a brain. As Baby Theresa fought her impossible battle to survive, her family battled the legal obstacles to their plans for donating Theresa's organs to help other babies. Parents everywhere could not help wondering, as they read the daily news reports, what they would do if faced with such a tragic choice.

Throughout the week in which the media spotlight focused on her dying daughter, Laura Campo stayed in the background. Today she has returned to her job at a restaurant and has recently begun taking classes toward becoming a registered nurse, all of which she fits into her busy life mothering three children. The unexpected kindnesses of strangers since Theresa's death have helped her overcome her lifelong shyness as she relates the difficult weeks surrounding Theresa's birth.[1]

"You know how babies will settle down into your pelvis when you are on your feet, and wait until you sit down and relax to begin kicking?" she asks. "Well, Theresa kicked all the time. I had continued to work with my other babies, but this time I was worn out." In her thirty-third week of pregnancy, the cramping and pain became so serious that Laura Campo and Justin Pearson went to the emergency room to make sure their baby was all right. That is when they were told that Theresa was anencephalic.

Although Laura had been given a sonogram two weeks earlier, she had not been told of Theresa's condition. Now

Laura recalls her doctor's reaction to the first sonogram and believes that he knew or suspected anencephaly. She remembers, "When he saw the report, he said, 'Let's see what's wrong with your baby's head,' and he gave me another sonogram in his office. I thought he meant maybe something was wrong with the soft spot." She was told to schedule an appointment at the high-risk clinic, but the trip to the emergency room intervened, and she and Justin learned the shocking news of their baby's condition from the emergency room physician. "We stayed up all night talking," Laura remembers, trying to decide what was best for their unborn little girl whose name they had already chosen.

Parents like Laura and Justin, in the approximately five in every one thousand pregnancies involving anencephaly, have very few options. Most anencephalic babies are stillborn or survive only a few hours because the abnormal development of fetal nerve tissue causes missing brains, skulls, or spinal cords. Couples who learn early of the fetal condition often decide to terminate the pregnancy, but Laura was well into her third trimester when they were told of the anencephaly.

As they struggled all night to find some acceptable choice, Laura remembered a television news program about organ donation, and together she and Justin decided that donating Theresa's organs to help other sick infants was a way to make something good come out of their own tragedy. An unusual coincidence seemed to confirm that decision. "The next morning when we picked up our newspaper, there was an entire article in the lifestyle section about organ donation. It just seemed like we were supposed to do it," Laura recalls.

The newspaper contained the name of the director of the local organ-procurement center, and Laura called him. "He told us that because anencephalic babies have no skulls, often they do not survive normal birth. That is when I decided to have a C-section."

The cesarean delivery of Theresa Ann was scheduled two weeks before the due date, because Laura had a history of delivering her three older children early, and while the remainder of her pregnancy was brief, it was an extremely difficult time for Laura. "I would feel her kick, and I would think, 'Oh, you poor little thing.' I wanted to protect her, and there wasn't one thing that I could do."

Many people did not understand the love Laura and Justin felt for Theresa, regardless of the certainty of her death. Long before they were told she was anencephalic, Justin had chosen their baby's first name, and together they had decided she would share her mother's middle name. In their hearts, Theresa Ann was already their beloved baby daughter when they learned of her anencephaly, and not just some abstract medical condition or a source of donated organs. Even the first obstetrician Laura saw after the diagnosis failed to appreciate her feelings when he advised Laura against seeing Theresa after she was born, and Laura still resents the doctor's attitude. "He said my baby would look like a toad. Well, she didn't. She was beautiful. She looked just like my daughter, Ashley. I told the nurse not to schedule me to see that doctor again."

At last, the delivery day arrived. Everyone had been alerted to Laura and Justin's plans to donate Theresa's organs, and her medical team had discussed procedures with the organ-procurement center. Laura praises the doctor who delivered Theresa. "He was out of this world. He was so supportive. He said, 'Whatever you do, I'm with you.'"

Despite the advance preparations, Laura and Justin's legal complications quickly occurred. Theresa was immediately placed on a mechanical ventilator to assist the spontaneous breathing and heartbeat the brain stem produced. Some anencephalic babies are born with other defects that make organ donation inappropriate, but Theresa's organs were, at birth, apparently perfect. Even with the ventilator assisting her breathing, her life and the organs within her tiny body soon began to deteriorate.

With her brain stem generating sporadic breathing and heartbeat, Theresa could not be considered dead according to a cardiopulmonary definition of death. The alternative—

declaring Theresa dead because of the irreversible cessation of brain function—was complicated by the minimal functioning of the brain stem. The medical team trying to carry out Laura and Justin's wishes was faced with a legal dilemma: Although Baby Theresa was born without a brain, was she brain-dead?

The common procedure for determining the existence of brain activity in other patients could not be used with Theresa. As Laura explains, "How can you find out what kind of brain waves are going through? She didn't have a brain. There was nothing to hook those electrodes up to."

Laura and Justin were told by the doctors that with or without the ventilator Theresa would die, and unless some legal means could be found to permit them to declare her "brain-dead," the organs would gradually deteriorate beyond any usefulness for transplantation. As parents, Laura and Justin had been forced to accept the heartbreaking medical reality that their daughter could not be saved. Now they were also being asked to accept the disappointing legal reality that unless the court declared Theresa brain-dead, the other babies they had hoped to save through the donation of Theresa's organs would also be doomed.

In frustration, Laura's own mother contacted the media with her granddaughter's story, and the private decision Laura and Justin had made to donate Theresa's organs became the subject of public scrutiny nationwide. Laura tries not to be critical of her mother's action in exposing the family to such publicity, but she admits that the media attention at such an emotional time was difficult. "Even though the media was very nice to us, I didn't like the phone ringing every ten minutes from somebody wanting to get a story from us. I know they were trying to help, but it is hard to do when you don't feel good." The publicity did produce an offer of legal assistance, however, and a petition was filed asking for a judicial determination that Theresa Ann was brain-dead.

The public response to Laura and Justin's private decision was generally sympathetic, but the publicity also generated some criticism, and a small group of demonstrators protested outside the hospital where Theresa was clinging to life. Laura was particularly upset by one protestor's televised offer to adopt Baby Theresa. "Who ever said I didn't want my baby?" Laura asks indignantly. "I loved my baby."

After a hearing, the trial court denied their petition, and the appeals court affirmed the lower court's decision. Laura and Justin were left to watch their daughter's inevitable decline, knowing that by the time her tiny heart stopped, the organs that had been perfect when she was born would no longer be usable. The sadness, not only for her own family but also for the families of those other babies who might have been helped, can be heard in Laura's voice even today as she quietly speaks of the frustrations she and Justin faced. "I don't think that the courts or anyone has a right to tell you what you can do and what you can't do in that situation. You have a baby. Death is certain. Who are these people to tell you that you can't do this or you can't do that? I told them, 'I love my daughter. If I could take her home, I would take her home. With any handicap whatever, I would take her home and love her.' But I couldn't take her home because she was going to die."

Baby Theresa Ann Campo Pearson died on March 30, 1992, but in the single week that she lived she touched a million hearts. Laura speaks proudly of how Theresa's story made the public more aware of organ donation. "The center got so many calls from people wanting to find out how they could become organ donors."

Laura takes a plaque from her living room wall and begins reading from it. "It says," she reads, " 'And a little child will lead them. In loving memory of Theresa Campo Pearson. For grateful acknowledgment of her parents, who loved enough to make a difference.' " The plaque, given to them by the transplant center, is a constant presence in their home just as Theresa is a constant presence in the lives of the family.

Laura and Justin's other two children are too young to fully understand what happened to their baby sister, and Laura did not want them to attend Theresa's funeral because of the media presence. Instead, when the city planted a tree in Theresa's honor in Fernglen Park [Coral Springs, Florida], all of the children in the family were involved. "We had a little ceremony with a plaque in front of the tree with my nieces' and nephews' names on it, too. Everybody made their own special card for her, and we let balloons fly up in the air and dedicated the tree to her. Now the kids go there and pick up the leaves around the tree."

In November 1992, nearly eight months after Theresa's death, the Florida State Supreme Court agreed with the trial court that because Theresa's breathing and heartbeat continued, however irregularly, she was not dead under state law, and therefore no donation of her organs would have been legal. In reaching its decision, the court commented on both the unquestioned need for transplantable infant organs and the altruistic motives of Laura and Justin in seeking to donate Theresa's organs. The court's opinion also repeated the concern expressed by some that broadening the definition of death might lead physicians and parents to propose transplants from infants with defects less severe than anencephaly.[2]

Laura makes it clear that she and her attorney never sought such a broad redefinition. "I have heard people say that parents might use the law to bring about the death of their disabled but not terminal babies, but I think that is crazy. We were only asking that the law include anencephalic children, and in those cases the condition is clear. You can tell just by looking—if the child has no skull and no brain, there is no brain tissue there to keep the brain going." She continues, "The doctors described it to me in this way. They said the brain stem is like a battery that runs out. It wears out without the upper portion of the brain to keep it going." As to expanding the definition of brain death to include other disabilities or genetic conditions, however, Laura is emphatic that she never intended to change the law to that extent.[3]

Baby Theresa taught her family many things during the

week they shared together, and Laura is certain that her daughter changed her life. "I have learned that life is short, and you have to appreciate what you have. I watch my kids now, and I am more appreciative. And I also learned that you should try to help others—even if you don't really have the means to help. So many people supported us. We didn't even know these people, and they were so nice, so concerned."

But Laura finds no contradiction in celebrating the worth of her daughter's short life and in having sought a judicial determination of brain death so that Theresa's organs could have been taken to benefit other babies. "I can't tell anybody else what to do. I can only go by my own personal feelings, and I would do it all over again. When you know what you truly believe in, you must stick with it."

CHAPTER 4

PARENTS' RIGHTS, PUBLIC CONCERNS

With her tiny head covered to conceal the disfiguring void where her brain should have been, the news service photographs of Baby Theresa became a symbol for many Americans of the complicated choices with which medical technology presents us. Her brief life focused the public's attention on the intrusion by the courts into one couple's private decision concerning their daughter. In cases like this, the will of the family is often sacrificed to the legislative will of strangers who might have voted differently at the time the law was enacted had they imagined such a situation. Even the courts charged with interpreting the laws must sometimes acknowledge the emotional hardship imposed on parents who, believing they have made the appropriate moral choice for their child, are denied their choice by the law. The Florida Supreme Court said of Laura Campo and Justin Pearson, "We have been deeply touched by the altruism and unquestioned motives of the parents of Theresa. The parents have shown great humanity, compassion, and concern for others."[1] Despite that recognition by the court, however, it was the will of the Florida legislature that decided the fate of Baby Theresa and all the infants who were denied her organs by the courts' decisions, rather than the moral choices of the respective parents.

The choices available to Baby Theresa's parents were narrowed by the inevitability of Theresa's death. No treatment exists to save an anencephalic baby, and thus, her parents did not have to consider economic hardship or a diminished quality of life for their daughter.[2] Since they could not save Theresa, they were left with making the most of her abbreviated life. While other parents might have decided differently for their own children, few found the private choice Theresa's parents made to be immoral. Yet, even with the support of their medical team, Laura and Justin's decision to donate Theresa's organs was blocked by a state law that lacked any provision to declare an anencephalic newborn brain-dead, even though she had no brain.

The issue becomes more complex when treatment of the infant is possible. The medical community acknowledges that sometimes severely handicapped infants have been allowed to die, even in cases where medical technology could have been utilized aggressively to keep them alive. When the Private Choices Survey asked people their opinions regarding the morality of withholding treatment from a severely handicapped infant, a surprisingly strong 55 percent stated their belief that it is sometimes morally acceptable to withhold treatment from a severely handicapped infant. While 20.6 percent were uncertain of their feelings, only 22.5 percent of those participating in the survey believed that withholding treatment was never acceptable.[3] Those who advocate sustaining the lives of newborns at all costs seem to discount both the economic burdens and the personal toll on the lives of others when such single-mindedness prevails. If it ever were such a simple choice, it is no longer, and the survey responses reflect that public recognition.

In recent years Americans have been forced to admit that financial limits—not only on individual family budgets but also on the public purse—require us to make life-and-death decisions about medical treatments. In one particularly poignant example, the Missouri legislature attempted to allocate funds for a sixteen-year-old girl who needed a lifesaving liver transplant. When the public learned of the legislative allocation, six other families, desperate for the financial means to provide similar treatments for their own children, contacted the legislature for help. Fearful that by helping one child they would obligate the state to provide assistance to others in similar need, the legislators withdrew their allocation to the teenaged girl, leaving her family with no other way to pay for the operation their daughter required.[4]

Today's headlines detailing the crisis in America's health care system inevitably include references to the medical costs of saving drug-addicted newborns, as well as the ongoing costs of boarding these babies in hospitals because their mothers are unwilling or unable to provide the special care they need. Expenses for these babies can exceed $1,500 a day, with hospital stays of several months or even years, and the families pay only a tiny fraction of the cost. Medicaid pays most of it, and a significant portion is shifted, through increased hospital costs, to patients who can afford to pay—whether individually, through insurance, or with government assistance. Obviously the financial consequences of these parents' private reproductive choices are being borne by the public through higher taxes, increased insurance premiums, and inclusion in the costs of other government programs.

The cribs in neonatal intensive care units are not filled exclusively with drug-addicted babies, however. Other low-birth-weight babies and genetically disabled infants benefit from the aggressive lifesaving technologies. The Private Choices Survey asked who should bear the enormous expense of saving low-birth-weight infants, whether they have been disabled for unknown reasons or as a result of their mothers' substance abuse or AIDS, and most participants in the survey said the families of the children should bear the costs. In many cases, however, families are unable or unwilling to assume the expenses, and survey participants were less certain as to whom the unpaid costs should be shifted if families did not pay. Most frequently they said charitable organizations or state and federal government funds from existing social programs should pay if families did not. They were clearly opposed to raising taxes, increasing insurance premiums, or allowing hospitals to pass these costs on to other patients.[5] Even if the delivery of health care changes radically in future years, the costs of expensive technologies must be borne by someone.

The days of assuming we can have it all have passed, and Americans realize that the money to sustain these tiny lives must come from somewhere, which may mean eliminating medical care for someone else. Medical rationing is already occurring simply because there is not enough money to go around, but the idea of formalizing such rationing in an effort to utilize our resources more effectively has not gained universal acceptance. The hard fact is that the daily expenses of one premature infant could fund many prenatal programs that would reduce the risk of the birth of other low-birth-weight babies or could pay for treatments intended to correct or cure rather than merely maintain.

In 1991 the debate over rationing neonatal care to severely disabled babies raged in the editorial pages of the Atlanta daily newspaper. The paper had reported the technological miracle occurring in the neonatal intensive care unit of Grady Hospital. A tiny baby, found cold and unbreathing on the floor of the bathroom where her crack-addicted mother had given birth, amazed everyone by clinging to life following resuscitation by an emergency medical team. Pumpkin, as she was called by the hospital staff, required expensive technology, imposing yet another financial burden on a publicly funded hospital already begging for operating funds. The news that Pumpkin's care was costing $2,000 a day had an immediate impact on a financially imperiled community in which many county services were being slashed. One letter to the editor criticized hospital personnel for intervening so aggressively to save Pumpkin's life. "This poor little creature is being treated like a laboratory animal, just to prove that it is technically possible to make her survive. Will whoever decided to resuscitate this child repeatedly when she could have died in peace take her home or send her to an institution when he's through with her?" The writer concluded her letter by saying, "While sick babies may tug at the heart, decisions made with the head may do more for all babies now and in the future. It's time social programs were based on rational planning and not emotional appeal."[6]

A registered nurse with sixteen years' experience in the field of neonatal special care wrote a response to the letter. She described her joy in seeing the children for whom she had cared return for the hospital's annual "Preemie Reunion Party." "These children and their parents are forever connected to our hearts," she began her letter. "Some of these children are defined as perfect and some, to the eyes of the world, may suffer imperfections, yet for us their lives began very much the same. They arrived struggling for the one thing that we all have need of, the breath of life. What person with the ability to assist in giving it, not knowing the outcome could with clear conscience withhold it?"[7]

In the early 1980s, the question of who should have the right to decide whether to treat severely disabled babies focused for a time on a baby known only as Baby Doe. In Bloomington, Illinois, on April 9, 1982, a baby with Down syndrome and other disabilities was born. Among the baby's problems was an esophageal obstruction that precluded normal feeding. When the parents withheld their consent for surgery to correct the blockage, the hospital sought judicial authority to override the parents' refusal. The court denied the hospital's request but appointed the county Department of Public Welfare as the baby's guardian so that an independent evaluation could be made to determine whether the denial should be appealed. When the county welfare officials decided not to appeal, the county prosecutor's office took up the cause of Baby Doe. After failing to obtain any relief in state courts, the deputy prosecutor was carrying the appeal for emergency relief to the Supreme Court in Washington, D.C., when Baby Doe died at the age of six days.

This was not a case of euthanasia or mercy killing, but rather a case of withholding medical treatment that almost certainly would have been utilized if the baby had been less disabled. Although reports of medical practices at that time indicate that Baby Doe's death was not unique,[8] it attracted public attention and became the rallying cry for legislation to prohibit the withholding of medical treatment solely because of an infant's disability. Only one month after Baby Doe's death, President Ronald Reagan had begun the administrative procedures that led to rules prohibiting health care providers that receive federal financial assistance from discriminating against handicapped infants in decisions regarding treatment. In other words, if medical treatment would be given to a nonhandicapped infant, it must also be given to a handicapped infant. Since virtually all hospitals receive some form of federal financial aid, the law applies in nearly all cases.

The Private Choices Survey found widespread participant agreement on very few issues, but when participants were asked who should make life-and-death decisions concerning the treatment of severely disabled infants 86 percent said that parents, with the advice of the treating physicians, should be left with that choice. A small 5 percent preferred a hospital committee consisting of medical professionals, and even fewer, 2.6 percent, preferred entrusting a committee of medical, legal, and religious professionals, but almost no one thought it was a good idea to place that awesome decision within the jurisdiction of the courts (0.6 percent) or some government entity (2.3 percent). Yet the Baby Doe law was specifically intended to inject government into the process.[9]

Initially, the Baby Doe regulations sought to impose a statutory duty on hospitals to treat handicapped infants regardless of parental consent. Eventually, the regulations were modified to expressly acknowledge that hospitals are not expected to overrule parents who withhold consent for sound medical reasons, whether or not those reasons involve parental discrimination against their child's disability. However, the law has continued to have a chilling effect in subtle ways. Medical professionals, aware of the law's prohibitions against discrimination, may be reluctant to speak candidly with parents for fear that they will be accused of participating in discriminatory practices should the parents decide to withhold consent for treatment. Obviously, the safest course for doctors and hospitals is to recommend whatever treatment options there may be.

Efforts to protect handicapped infants by shifting more influence or control to medical professionals may actually reverse the intended effect in some cases. The mother of a fetus diagnosed prenatally with a severely deformed heart appeared on a talk show to explain why she was motivated, at least in part, to have a third-trimester abortion: she feared that by delaying a decision until after birth she might be relinquishing control over her own baby's fate. "At twenty-five-and-a-half weeks I was told the left side of the heart had not formed, and the chance of the child living through a heart operation was one in four hundred. Basically it would be a life of pain and suffering before it would die anyhow. . . . If God intended this child to be born with this heart defect, and this child was born and it was left alone, it would probably die on its own in a very, very short time. And I was told, 'No, you are going to the best hospital with the best machinery and the best technology, and we've got to do this because we have to.' It wasn't my child anymore. It was their child. And the child would have all the suffering. It would have had everything and then it would have had a short life and it would have died anyhow."[10] Regardless of the law's express provision to the contrary, many doctors continue to see the Baby Doe regulations as a mandate to bring the full array of medical technology to bear on their tiny patients, no matter how sick or impaired they are, and medical personnel often pressure parents to acquiesce to heroic medical efforts.

The anguish of parents faced with treatment choices involving severely disabled children raises two questions that often divide caring and religious people. First, is it a more loving act to spare your child prolonged suffering or to preserve the child's life for however long at whatever quality despite the unavoidable pain and suffering the preservation of life causes? Second, is God's will honored more by allowing a natural death or by utilizing all the technology available to prolong life? How individuals answer these two questions is no measure of their caring or their faith, for devout and loving parents may decide differently, and valid moral arguments support both choices.

Because thoughtful people can disagree, sometimes Baby Doe laws and state laws intended to protect children from abuse and neglect are used by strangers who see themselves as defenders of infants whose parents' medical decisions are, in their eyes, misguided or immoral. However sincere the motives of these outsiders may be, the legal actions they bring force parents already suffering the heartbreak of a life-or-death medical choice to endure a legal challenge to their decision by a complete stranger to the family.

In the Baby Doe case, hospital personnel reported the tenderness the parents showed toward their baby. The father testified that his experiences as a teacher who had worked with Down syndrome children, as well as the couple's concern for their other two children, led them to the difficult choice they had made for their newborn. Despite the fact that their choice was supported by physicians, courts, and county welfare officials, outsiders continued to pursue legal means to thwart their decision, and the parents were made to suffer the further ordeal of the legal proceedings.

Another example of intrusion by strangers occurred in 1983, a year after Baby Doe's death. A little girl was born in Stony Brook, New York, with microcephaly, spina bifida, and other severe disabilities. Doctors told her parents that their daughter's life expectancy was two years. With various surgical procedures, however, their daughter might live to age twenty, the doctors said, but she would remain mentally retarded, incontinent, partially paralyzed, and probably epileptic. The parents decided not to have the surgery for their daughter.

The legal challenges that followed, including one brought by the Secretary of Health and Human Services (HHS) under the new Baby Doe regulations, eventually resulted in a stern reminder by the United States Supreme Court to the Secretary of HHS of the limitations of the federal statute that he had tried to impose: "Nothing in the statute authorizes the Secretary to dispense with the law's focus on discrimination and instead to employ federal resources to save the lives of handicapped newborns, without regard to whether they are victims of discrimination by recipients of federal funds or not. Section 504 does not authorize the Secretary to give unsolicited advice either to parents, to hospitals, or to state officials who are faced with difficult treatment decisions concerning handicapped children.[11] As a consequence of the limitations of the federal Baby Doe statute, today most legal challenges to parental decisions are brought on the basis of state laws, but hospitals and other strangers to the family continue to bring legal actions to overturn parental decisions with which they disagree.

Nancy Cruzan was certainly no infant. In fact, when she finally died, she was thirty-three years old, but the battle her parents waged in order to remove the feeding tube from her stomach had much in common with the decision Baby Doe's parents made not to surgically correct their baby's blocked esophagus. Both sets of parents suffered the public's criticism for allowing the starvation deaths of their children. And by personifying ethical issues that are difficult to consider in the abstract, both children became symbols of the moral and legal dilemmas raised by sustaining lives that can never be measured by normal standards. Although their children were years apart in age, both sets of parents faced the same challenge to their rights as parents to decide what was best for their children.

Nancy was a pretty twenty-five-year-old in 1983 when her car overturned on the way home from work. Although paramedics restarted her heart, she suffered irreversible brain damage during the fifteen minutes she lay facedown in a ditch before help arrived. Restarting her heart did not give Nancy back her life. For eight years Joyce and Lester Cruzan watched over their daughter's rigid body, and while she sometimes opened her eyes, Nancy never showed signs that she recognized them. Her feet and hands were contracted and bent, and occasionally she suffered seizures and vomited. Her parents decided it was time to let Nancy go, but when they asked doctors to remove the feeding tube that had been implanted in her stomach to allow nourishment, the hospital refused.

In 1987 the Cruzans asked for judicial permission to remove the tube, but they were opposed by the state of Missouri. On appeal to the United States Supreme Court, which had never before considered a case involving the right to die, the 1990 ruling recognized the states' rights to set their own standards concerning the right to die. However, the Court also held that if there were "clear and convincing" evidence of a person's having expressed a right to die in certain circumstances, that preference could be judicially recognized as well.

Nancy's parents returned to Missouri state court to present testimony from three of her coworkers that Nancy had said to them before her accident that she would never want to live "like a vegetable." With that proof, the judge finally gave permission for the feeding tube to be removed. The case turned upon a determination of Nancy's own wishes, however, and not upon her parents' right to decide her fate.

Living wills, which are recognized in many states, and the Patient Self-Determination Act, which requires hospitals and nursing homes that receive Medicaid or Medicare funds to explain to their patients the right-to-die options under their state's laws, offer no legal support to parents faced with deciding whether to withhold or withdraw treatment from their newborns, since these right-to-die provisions rely on expressions of preference by the patients themselves. Although such laws do not directly concern severely disabled newborns, they do reflect the public's growing awareness that there are some conditions of living to which death may be preferable.[12]

Even before the passage of the Patient Self-Determination Act, the American Hospital Association estimated that 70 percent of all hospital deaths are negotiated in some way, through decisions regarding whether to start or to withdraw life-support technology or treatment. Withholding or withdrawal of treatment does not go so far as actual euthanasia or mercy killing, but some people consider euthanasia more appropriate than allowing a slow death from starvation, as in the case of Baby Doe or Nancy Cruzan. When the Private Choices Survey asked participants whether they thought it was ever appropriate to administer a lethal injection to shorten suffering as inevitable death neared for an infant whose parents had decided to withhold medical treatment, 42 percent said it was. Twenty-eight percent said they would never consider it appropriate and the same number were uncertain of their feelings.[13]

Other cultures, both past and present, have not only practiced euthanasia or the abandonment of severely disabled infants but also have sanctioned the deaths of healthy newborns in certain situations. For example, the Netsilik Eskimos depended on male hunters to provide food during the long arctic winters, and men were often killed during the hunts. To ensure sufficient men for hunting without excessive numbers of women and children dependent on the men for food, the Eskimos practiced infanticide. In another society, the absence of cereal or animal milk in the desert environment made adequate milk from the mother essential to their baby's survival. Mothers among the nomadic !Kung Bushmen sometimes allowed one of their babies to die to ensure that there would be sufficient milk to keep a nursing toddler or a twin well nourished. Anthropologists who have studied the historical practice of infanticide in societies such as these have found that although the killing of newborns was tolerated in certain circumstances, the value placed on human life outside those circumstances was not diminished. Their studies found that children were cherished and treated tenderly, but newborns that threatened the welfare of the existing family or the society at large were killed or allowed to die to preserve the well-being of the existing members of the group.[14]

We may see these practices as uncivilized, but their drastic choices allowed them to survive in harsh environments that might otherwise have obliterated the entire group. Our own society's inability to agree about the moral issues raised by early abortions, months before birth, illustrates the extreme social taboo against infanticide in our own culture. Without accepting the practice of infanticide adopted by other cultures, however, we may observe through them that there are other ways of valuing life than those we have traditionally practiced.

The new options medical technology allows force hard choices. In August 1993, conjoined twins Amy and Angela Lakeburg were born with a single, malformed heart. Doctors told the parents that the reconstructed heart might support the life of one of their daughters if the other twin were separated from her. When the twins were seven weeks old, their parents allowed doctors to decide during surgery on anatomical considerations alone which of their daughters would survive the procedure and be given a chance to live. Baby Angela received the shared heart, and Amy's brief life ended.

Mike and Patty Hensel's conjoined daughters Abigail and Brittany share an undivided torso and two legs, but each has a separate heart and a stomach. These two beautiful little girls can run and swim, and when they grow up they can have a baby, but only with the body they share. If they were separated neither twin's severed side would support functioning prosthetic limbs, and the surgery itself could be risky. Their parents chose not to separate their daughters because, as their father explains, "They'd be in surgery for years, suffering all the time, and then they'd have half a body each." Although Mike and Patty declined technological solutions for their daughters' condition, they are second-guessed by those who feel that the twins' mercilessly shared lives will cause them emotional suffering as they mature no less severe than the physical suffering surgery might have caused.

The availability of technology to prolong the lives of severely disabled newborns, to provide prenatal information, or to alter the physical condition of infants' lives has outpaced the evolution of moral codes and taboos, leaving new parents with little guidance in these situations. One scholar observes, "Quality of life is an expression that has crept into our collective vocabulary over the last several decades. . . . The need for such a concept arose when natural death became a thing of the past, and the moment of dying ceased to be outside of our control."[15] Increasingly, quality-of-life discussions may be heard in the nurseries of our hospitals as often as they are heard in the geriatric wards and emergency rooms.

Most Americans are appalled by news reports of parents in India who smother newborn girls because they are too poor to provide the dowry for another daughter, but we do not know how to solve the budgetary crisis in our own country caused by keeping low-birth-weight babies like Pumpkin alive in publicly funded hospitals while other children go untreated for lack of funds. We are sickened by the prospect of a nursing mother withholding milk from a healthy twin, yet we sympathize with the Lakeburg parents who acted to save one of their cojoined twin daughters rather than allowing both to die. Just as harsh environments forced those societies to face hard choices, medical technology is forcing us into an unfamiliar reproductive environment, and we must stop ignoring the difficult choices being imposed upon us.

The overwhelming emotional and physical responsibilities that parents of a disabled child must bear are clear from these words of a forty-year-old mother of a severely microcephalic daughter: "I feel like I've wasted my life . . . waiting for life to happen. . . . After eighteen years, I am tired and bitter, and my back hurts from lifting her sixty-five pounds all day and all night." Yet despite the burden of caring for an endlessly dependent child with an IQ of no more than 20 and emotional problems that cause screaming fits lasting entire days and nights, this mother admits her greatest fear: "that she will be put in some place untended and unloved and maybe abused. She cannot do anything for herself, cannot protect herself. I'll say one thing. If I ever find out I've got cancer or anything, I plan to take Lori in the car with me and let the gas run. I won't leave her care to be decided by some judge, and I will not have this imposed on my son."

We do not have adequate funding to provide assistance for this mother and others like her, yet we demand that politicians cut government spending, not expand it. So before we endorse laws that increase the authority of medical professionals or judges to make life-or-death decisions about the treatment of severely disabled infants, we must remember that parents of children like Lori will be asked to make heroic sacrifices in carrying out their decisions. Lori's mother puts it more bluntly: "I think the judge who says 'This child will be taken away from these parents and treated' . . . should have to change the diapers when the child is a teenager, and the judge ought to have to walk the kid all night long while she's screaming."[16]

There is a requirement in the law called "standing." Put simply, it means that before a person can bring a matter before the court, he must have a personal stake or interest in the outcome, and that interest must be greater than some general concern as a member of society. If the law were to require a proof of "standing" from anyone who came forward to challenge the treatment decision made by parents of a severely disabled newborn—in the form of evidence satisfactory to the court that the challenger was ready, willing, and able to take full financial and emotional responsibility as a parent of the newborn for the remainder of its life (or to subsidize assistance to the parents if they prefer to retain custody)—there might be fewer legal challenges made in these tragic cases.

On the other hand, if society's solution is to provide assistance to the parents in meeting the increased emotional and financial demands of a severely disabled child, we must recognize that in addition to assuming the costs of caring for the numbers of disabled children currently in our population, the availability of assistance may encourage more parents to give birth or prolong lives of children needing assistance. We must also recognize that prenatal and neonatal technology will continue to expand the limits of sustaining tiny lives that could not survive without the technology.

Former President Ronald Reagan has been widely criticized for the inconsistency of his administration in sponsoring

Baby Doe regulations without also supporting funding for welfare programs to assist the disabled. Laws cannot be enacted without accounting for the full consequences of government interference. If government injects itself into parental decisions, it logically follows that people will expect government to assume more parenting responsibilities.

The parents who must live with the consequences of their decisions certainly have more "standing," in both the legal and the moral sense, to make life-and-death decisions concerning their newborn. We cannot always assume that they are best equipped to make those decisions, but before we invade their privacy, we must consider the alternatives. Medical ethicists, sociologists, and lawyers argue endlessly about the medical, moral, and legal issues raised by the new birth technology. Yet young couples, struggling with a tumult of emotions, must summon the wisdom to make the appropriate decision for their baby and themselves. What should amaze us is how ordinary people so often find the wisdom and courage to make the right decisions for their particular families rather than the fact that sometimes their choices seem terribly wrong. We must ask whether any committee of strangers would be likely to improve the overall quality of the choices made.

Sometimes there are individual cases that seem to call for the overriding judgment of an outsider. The same year Laura and Justin fought their legal battle to have Baby Theresa declared brain-dead so that her organs might be used to help other sick babies, the mother of another anencephalic infant waged a very different legal battle. Her newborn, known as Baby K, was placed on a mechanical ventilator to allow doctors an opportunity to evaluate her condition. Once they determined that Baby K would never be able to see, hear, or otherwise interact with her environment, doctors recommended to her mother that the baby be given nutrition, hydration, and warmth but that no lifesaving measures be employed.

Ms. H, the mother, insisted that her daughter receive mechanical assistance whenever she had difficulty breathing, treatment that Baby K's doctors felt was inappropriate. Ignoring the doctor's advice, Ms. H adhered to her Christian belief that all life should be protected. Although Baby K is permanently unconscious, she has survived longer than most anencephalic children and has been transferred from the hospital to a nearby nursing home. Occasionally she has difficulty breathing and is brought back to the hospital for respiratory assistance. These episodes led the hospital, joined by both Baby K's father and the baby's guardian ad litem, to request a declaration from the court relieving the hospital from providing respiratory support or other aggressive treatments.

Baby K's mother opposed the hospital by urging the application of a law enacted by Congress for the purpose of prohibiting hospitals from "dumping" patients who are unable to pay. The Emergency Medical Treatment and Active Labor Act (EMTALA) has had the effect of requiring the hospital to provide respiratory support to Baby K when she arrives at the emergency department in respiratory distress and her mother requests the treatment.

In ruling against the hospital, the court said, "We recognize the dilemma facing physicians who are requested to provide treatment they consider morally and ethically inappropriate, but we cannot ignore the plain meaning of the statute."[17] Standard medical care withholds aggressive intervention for anencephalic babies, Virginia state law allows a physician to refuse treatment he considers medically or ethically inappropriate, and both the baby's father and the guardian ad litem appointed to protect the best interests of the baby agree with the doctors that a ventilator should not be used to maintain this unconscious child. But because of the language contained in a law Congress enacted for another purpose, the hospital has been compelled to follow the mother's wishes.

Baby K's hospital care was originally paid by the mother's HMO, at a cost of about $1,400 a day. Her care is now paid by Medicaid.[18]

Baby Theresa and Baby K's cases, involving newborns with the least reason for life-prolonging treatment by any quality-of-life analysis, strip away the arguments about discrimination against the disabled and force a narrow consideration of who should make the wrenching medical decisions involving treatment of severely disabled newborns. Undoubtedly critics of both mothers may be found, but perhaps more revealing in both cases is how unsatisfactory the intervention of social institutions—in the form of medical professionals, ethics committees, and judges—proved to be in resolving the medical, moral, and economic issues.

The greatest weakness in trusting parents to make the right decisions about their newborns is asking them to do so at such an emotional time with too little opportunity to reflect, and sometimes, with too little medical information available to them. Rather than imposing postbirth review procedures by hospital ethics committees or legal bodies—in situations unavoidably complicated by emotion and the need for haste—medical professionals should direct their efforts toward prenatal counseling or, ideally, preconception counseling. Without an actual medical crisis, pregnant women and couples could be educated and encouraged to consider what they might do if faced with various decisions concerning their newborns. Laws, if they are enacted, should encourage the candid and confidential relationship between patients and their doctors so that life-or-death decisions can be made with the full benefit of the doctors' experience and knowledge. Laws like the Baby Doe statute are counterproductive if they instill in doctors a fear that they may be accused of discrimination or malpractice if they are too candid with their patients.

Too many of the programs we implement or propose fail to integrate the full consequences beyond the immediate problem they intend to solve, as in the case of the Baby Doe regulations, which separated the decision whether to treat from the ongoing care. The argument that it is immoral to consider the economic costs of prolonging life ignores the very real economic sacrifice of the medical needs of others which the heroic expenditures

cause. The neglect of their needs when the money is spent prolonging lives instead is a real financial and moral consequence.
We cannot resolve the reproductive and neonatal issues presented by the new technologies until we are willing to consider
all the implications of the isolated decision directly in front of us.

Those who criticize families and their physicians in certain
cases often accuse them of "playing God," but if making life-or-
death decisions is equivalent to "playing God," then doctors
assume that role whether they intervene to save a baby who
would otherwise die or whether they decline to use medical
assistance to prolong the life of a dying infant or save it at some
diminished level. Whether they act or fail to act, the choice they
make alters the life of that baby in a way that is godlike, and
criticizing either choice as "playing God" makes no sense when
the alternative is equally godlike. Valid moral arguments can be
made either way.

It is easier to define the economic costs and the medical limitations of the technology. We can save tiny lives, but scarce financial resources are expended in the process. We can save premature
and low-birth-weight babies, but they are far more likely than
other babies to suffer long-term physical and mental disabilities.

An Ohio team of researchers measured the extent of those
limitations by studying sixty-eight surviving very low-birth-weight
(under 750 grams) babies as they entered the early years of
school. Most of these children would have died soon after birth
without having received neonatal intensive care that cost hundreds of thousands of dollars. Their outcomes were compared
to those of two control groups, one of low (but more than 750
grams) birth weight and the other carried to term. The results
were discouraging, to say the least. In the researchers' words,
"These children are at serious disadvantage in every skill required for adequate performance in school." The researchers
noted that in spite of the enormous expenditure of neonatal
resources on each child and the educational programs intended
to help the children compensate for developmental difficulties, they were "inferior to both comparison groups in cognitive

ability, psychomotor skills and academic achievement. They had poorer social skills and adaptive behavior and more behavioral and attention problems." It should be noted that the children in the study were born before certain innovations in neonatal care, but the researchers discounted significant improvements in the long-term outlook for very low-birth-weight babies treated today.[19] In short, technology has made possible the survival of extremely small and immature infants, but it has not succeeded in giving them the lives they would have had if they could have been carried to term.

In 1949 the *New England Journal of Medicine* published the words of Dr. Leo Alexander concerning the euthanasia program ordered by Hitler. Dr. Alexander was a psychiatrist who had worked with the U.S. Counsel for War Crimes in Nuremberg, and he wrote, "It started with the acceptance of the attitude, basic in the euthanasia movement, that there is such a thing as a life not worthy to be lived. This attitude in its early stages concerned itself merely with the severely and chronically sick. Gradually the sphere of those to be included in this category was enlarged to encompass the socially unproductive, the ideologically unwanted, the racially unwanted, and finally all non-Germans. But it is important to realize that the infinitely small, wedged-in lever from which this entire trend of mind received its impetus was the attitude toward the nonrehabilitatable sick." Dr. Alexander's warning must not be forgotten or ignored, but neither should it be distorted to stifle thoughtful attempts to determine when the use of new medical technologies is appropriate. If our society has determined that it is moral to use technology, we have an equal responsibility to determine when it is moral not to use technology, and at no time is the decision more complex than when an innocent newborn baby forces the choice to be made.

Is it ever morally acceptable to withhold treatment from a severely handicapped infant?

Who should bear the expenses of caring for low-birth-weight babies, born with such severe disabilities that many will not survive and those who do will never achieve minimal levels of physical and/or mental normalcy?

- The federal government out of existing social programs
- The federal government out of new tax revenues
- State governments out of existing social programs
- State governments out of new tax revenues
- Hospitals by passing costs on to other patients
- Health insurance plans through higher premiums
- Charities and churches through greater member contributions
- Families of the children
- Other

Who should make life-and-death decisions concerning the treatment of severely disabled infants?

- The parents with the advice of the treating physicians
- A hospital committee consisting of medical professionals
- A committee of medical, legal, and religious professionals
- The courts of law
- The government
- Other

Should the government influence the choices of parents and physicians in favor of employing heroic medical treatments for severely disabled babies?

If a determination to withhold medical treatment from a severely disabled infant with a life-threatening condition has been made, is it ever appropriate to administer a lethal injection to shorten suffering as inevitable death nears?

CHAPTER 5

THE STORY OF LISA LANDRY CHILDRESS

During the years he coached the Dallas Cowboys, Tom Landry faced some tough opponents, but none as ominous as the one his daughter Lisa faced. Lisa Childress and her husband, Gary, had wanted a baby for several years, and in January 1991 they began the new year with the exciting news that Lisa was finally pregnant.[1]

Just before Christmas Lisa felt a lump, but she delayed seeing a doctor. The news of her pregnancy and the discovery of a tumor in her liver came almost simultaneously, and since her pregnancy limited the diagnostic options, she chose to wait until her second trimester before having a biopsy done. In March she learned the dreaded result—cancer.

"I told them at the very beginning that I wanted to have the baby and that I wouldn't have chemo or anything," Lisa remembers. Her prenatal specialist, Dr. Whitney Gonsoulin, agrees. "I think she had to decide early in the pregnancy whether she was going to choose her desire for the child vs her desire for her own longevity. Once she made the decision that she was going to do everything to deliver the baby, she had to disregard most of the recommendations that she received from her physicians about what they thought was best for her."[2]

Lisa was then given the option of a liver transplant. "Because of the type of tumor it was, they really thought that a transplant was my only chance. They usually do chemo at the time of surgery, but they decided they could proceed without it.

I think they gave me a 75 percent chance of getting through it fine."

Lisa agreed to the transplant and was placed on a donor list. For five days she carried a beeper, waiting to be called if a liver became available. Then tests showed other signs of cancer, first in the lungs and then, after those shadows were discounted, on her spine. "Immediately I came off the donor list, because they won't do a liver transplant if you have cancer elsewhere in your body."

Dr. Gonsoulin describes the mixed medical advice Lisa received. "There was a lot of controversy. A majority of physicians, especially the oncology people, thought the best thing for her would have been either a termination followed by treatment or at least treatment during the pregnancy. At the original evaluation they were only giving her six months to live." His own evaluation differed. "I felt that her chances were good for a normal outcome as long as we could get the baby to a survival stage and deliver it, and then deal with her medical problems after the pregnancy."

Faced with conflicting advice from her doctors, Lisa relied upon her religious beliefs. "I have a lot of faith, and I was just trusting God for both our lives. I had prayed for her for five years. To me she was a gift and an answer to prayer, and I knew that somehow she'd be OK. We both would."

The medical profession recognizes the vulnerability of patients at such times, and Dr. Gonsoulin was aware of Lisa's reliance upon his opinion in rejecting the prognosis of the oncologists. "Patients interpret the information they receive—if they have a feeling that the information that they are getting is wrong, then they don't really put that information into their decision making." In her heart Lisa could not believe what the cancer specialists were telling her, and so, relying upon her religious faith and Dr. Gonsoulin's evaluation, she focused on her baby's health rather than her own.

Although her family respected Lisa's wishes, it was very difficult for them not to want her medical needs to come first. Her husband, Gary, spent hours talking with Dr. Gonsoulin about what was being done and seeking reassurance that the doctor really differed in his diagnosis from the other physicians. While Gary was supportive, Lisa knew that he could not put their baby ahead of his feelings for her. "He didn't want to lose me and he even told me that. He said I was the most important thing, but he understood my decision."

Amazingly, the tumors did not grow as expected. "I went through my whole pregnancy with very little change in them. The doctors couldn't believe it. They didn't think I'd make it through my pregnancy."

During the last eight weeks of her pregnancy, Lisa was given steroid shots to enhance the baby's lung development. Five and a half weeks early and weighing a surprising five pounds six ounces, Christina Childress was born by cesarean section. Lisa's faith had paid off for Christina. Now it was time to turn her attention to herself.

Immediately after Christina's birth, exploratory surgery revealed that the tumors had begun to grow rapidly, spreading outside the liver and attaching to Lisa's intestines, but cancer had not appeared elsewhere in her body, making her an appropriate candidate for a transplant. Ten days later, Lisa finally had the liver she needed. With Gary at her side day and night, Lisa remained in the hospital for five weeks, battling her body's rejection of the new liver and the infections to which she was exposed by the antirejection drugs she had been given. Baby Christina was able to leave the hospital in the care of Lisa's parents and sister long before Lisa could, but nearly every day she came back to the hospital to visit. "She would sleep on my chest, just sleep there with me," Lisa remembers.

The balancing of medical risks to herself and the fetus seemed simple to Lisa. "As for Christina, it wasn't anything I had to think about. As for the liver transplant, I didn't want to do it, but I didn't really have any choice if I wanted to be around to be Christina's mother." As simple as she makes it sound, Lisa does understand the complex position of her doctors when appropriate medical treatments for her posed risks for the fetus. "They respected the idea that I wanted to have the baby, but if it would have come down to me not having a chance to make it, I think they would have tried to convince me to change my mind and not have the baby," Lisa believes.

While Lisa is confident of the decision she made about her own medical treatment during the pregnancy, she does not suggest that everyone should make the same decision. "I did what was right for me, but I don't want my experience to turn into some kind of example. Everyone must make their choice. Sometimes you just have to take a risk in what you believe."

Epilogue

Lisa and Gary had been told so often that Lisa's time was short, and then she would get better. Gary smiles as he remembers. "Her doctors could not believe it. They said that whatever we were doing we should go home and keep doing it, because it was working!"

After the liver transplant, Lisa continued treatments and tests, but what she hated most was going to the doctors to hear test results. "It was hard for her to keep a positive attitude when she had to listen to all the bad news they were telling her, so she would send me instead," Gary explains. Living positively included traveling, scuba diving (even after having had lung surgery), and enjoying family. "We knew that Lisa's condition was very serious, but she had battled her way through so much that it seemed as if she could fight off anything. I know it may sound funny, but that was really one of the happiest times in our lives," he recalls.

On May 28, 1995, the cancer that Lisa had so stubbornly kept at bay finally was too much to overcome, but Gary insists that the time she won for herself and her family was a victory. "She never doubted her decision to put Christina first. The only fear she ever had was that she might not live long enough for Christina to have a clear memory of her, and Christina definitely remembers her mother. We took lots of video that Christina and I watch together so that she won't forget." Doctors told them that the normal life expectancy for Lisa's type of cancer is four months, but she lived four years beyond her diagnosis date. "Lisa really believed that it was her faith and her desire to be with Christina and me that kept her alive so much longer than the doctors predicted," Gary says.

Today, raising their daughter alone, Gary looks back on the years he and Lisa were together, from the time they began dating as kids. "I never thought much about being married to Coach Landry's daughter until Lisa got sick," he admits, "but the high regard people have for him gave us special access. We were able to talk with many experts, and their advice helped us with the medical decisions we had to make," Gary explains. In the end, however, all the expert consultations could not make their choices any easier than those faced by many other families needing donor organs.

Lisa's death was not the happy ending her friends and family had hoped for, but her doctors would probably say that the time she had with Christina really was a miraculous ending for her too short life. Now that Lisa is gone, Gary and the Landry family have not forgotten the other families they met while awaiting the liver that gave Lisa her miracle. In Lisa's memory, Gary and her parents have formed a foundation dedicated to educating young people of the need for donor organs.[3] They know how grateful Lisa was for the organ donation that gave her a chance to live, and they hope that through education they can help others share the miracle.

CHAPTER 6

WHO IS THE PATIENT?
BALANCING MATERNAL
AND FETAL RIGHTS

When a woman goes to the doctor for prenatal care, who is the doctor's patient—the woman or the fetus she is carrying? She is pregnant, not sick, and her visit is probably motivated by her desire to have a healthy baby. It is doubtful that she even considers whether she or her baby is the patient, and most of the time, what is good for her is good for her fetus, too.

Sometimes, however, what is good for one is not good for the other. If the woman is ill, the treatment she needs may be harmful to her fetus, and she will have to decide whether to do without treatment for herself in order to protect her baby. Carried to the extreme, it may be the pregnancy itself that is dangerous to the woman, and she will be faced with the hardest choice of all.

As technology has allowed doctors greater access to the fetus, they have learned how to treat certain defects even before the baby is born. Increasingly, therefore, treatments may be beneficial to the fetus which are harmful, or at least risky, to the mother. As the technology expands in this area, mothers may be asked more often to jeopardize their own well-being to allow access to the fetus. We must address the maternal-fetal conflict with which technology presents us and decide whether the mother and her doctor should resolve the dilemma, or whether the courts or some new ethical advisory institution should intervene.

When Lisa Childress faced the conflict between treatment for herself and risk to the fetus she carried, she followed her heart and the advice of one doctor, and she never doubted that she had made the right decision. But Lisa also believed that each woman must make her own choice. As George Hughes, who faced a similar crisis with his wife, says, "You don't know what decisions you are going to make until you face something like that. It is very difficult for somebody to tell you what you should have done or what you should not have done if they have not experienced what you went through."

George and Mary Ann Hughes were expecting twins when she was diagnosed with lymphoma, and her health quickly deteriorated. As George says, "We decided that the pregnancy had to take a backseat to Mary Ann's condition." Like Lisa, George does not presume to judge the decisions others have made when faced with such circumstances. "I don't know what other people's emotions are. I just know that I had loved Mary Ann very much throughout our lives, that we had already been blessed with a beautiful daughter, and that at that time my priority was Mary Ann."[1]

Even though technology has opened up the world of the fetus to view in ways unimaginable a generation ago, doctors still lack the ability to see in advance just how the fetus will react to treatments the pregnant woman receives. In Mary Ann's case, doctors warned that her treatments were likely to cause harm or the loss of the twins. But because she was in a Catholic hospital, an abortion could not be performed without transferring her to another facility. Before that decision could be made, her own health required emergency treatments that left her without the strength for such a transfer. The best medical advice was that the twins would never survive the chemotherapy Mary Ann required, and abortions would occur spontaneously. George remembers, "There was concern for the fetuses, but Mary Ann was the patient. They were treating Mary Ann. They took precautions because of the babies, but the treatment was geared for Mary Ann." There were, however, certain things the doctors would not use which would otherwise have been available, such as the use of a CAT scan to evaluate the progress of the disease.

George knows that he and his wife may have been criticized by some for putting her survival ahead of the survival of the fetuses or for having considered an abortion. "There are people that would tell me that we had no right to have an abortion, but at that particular time I would not have listened to them. It was none of their business as far as I was concerned. That was between Mary Ann and myself, and we made the decision that was the right decision at the time. I knew that I wanted Mary Ann to live, and if it meant termination of the pregnancy would give her a better chance for that, then that was the decision that was made without a second thought."

Despite all the predictions the doctors had made, the twins did not abort, nor did they suffer the expected ill effects. On May 11, 1984, a boy and a girl, each weighing almost five pounds, were born by cesarean section. Today George says, "Mary Ann and I both looked back after the babies were born and we thought to ourselves, this almost didn't happen because of the decision we made, but we never felt that our decision was wrong. When I watch my son play basketball or my daughter take piano lessons, or we take their science projects to school, I thank God we didn't lose them. But there's no way anybody ever will convince me that, had we gone through with an abortion, that we didn't do the right thing."

On April 10, 1985, when the twins were eleven months old, Mary Ann Hughes lost her battle with cancer, and George says, "Now, I have two more beautiful children that I love dearly. They are her legacy." Knowing now how precious his children are to him and how the treatment decisions he made with his wife might have cost the lives of the twins in utero, he does not second-guess his feelings, because he is convinced that decisions must be evaluated within the context of the times in which they are made. Neither is he willing to tell others how they should decide. "The only thing that I am able to tell somebody facing something like this is, they would know what to do."

If society no longer trusts the judgment of individuals facing these wrenching circumstances to decide what is best for themselves, this question remains: Who could possibly be in a better position to decide than the person who will suffer the consequences? In medicine, the ethical principle of autonomy, or an individual's right to choose treatment for herself, guides doctors. Doctors may urge the treatment they think is best for the patient, but ultimately they must respect the patient's choice. Doctors are also guided by the ethical principle of beneficence, or the obligation to promote the well-being of others. In the treatment of a patient, a doctor must balance these two principles, but in the treatment of a pregnant woman, the doctor is faced with the unique circumstance of having an obligation to respect the woman's autonomy while also assuming an obligation of beneficence toward the fetus she carries.[2] Historically, both medicine and the law have agreed that the woman herself must be allowed to make the decisions affecting her fetus, and her autonomy should not be sacrificed because others disagree with her choices.

There have been exceptions, however. Courts in some states have ordered women to undergo medical treatments they had refused—a blood transfusion or a cesarean section—because doctors testified that the treatments were necessary for their babies' survival. The American College of Obstetricians and Gynecologists advises its members that resorting to the courts is almost never justified because of the destructive effect of court orders on both the autonomy of the patient and her relationship with the doctor.[3]

In 1987 doctors in Washington, D.C., asked a court for a declaratory judgment to allow them to perform a cesarean section on a twenty-seven-year-old woman dying of cancer. The woman's feelings were somewhat unclear, and by the time the doctors sought the advice of the court, the woman was heavily sedated. She and her doctors had previously discussed taking the baby by C-section when it reached the gestational age of twenty-eight weeks, and she had indicated her willingness to relinquish her own life at that time if necessary. The rapid decline of her condition led the doctors to believe that the baby should be taken sooner, a possibility they had not discussed with her prior to her sedation. Getting her consent for doing the cesarean at only the twenty-sixth week of pregnancy, when the baby's chances of survival were lower, was obscured not only by her sedation but also because she agreed to the surgery when speaking to one doctor during a period of lucidity but mouthed the words "I don't want it done" to a second doctor who was trying to verify her consent. The trial court determined that the cesarean section should be performed, and although the panel to which the trial court's decision was appealed was reluctant to intrude in an area it believed should be left to ethical groups within the health care system, it sustained the order permitting the surgery. On June 16, 1987, the operation was performed, but both the child and mother died soon afterward.

Because of the legal precedent the decision set for future cases, the American Civil Liberties Union, the American Medical Association, and thirty-eight other organizations asked the full appellate court to reconsider the decision of its three-judge panel, even though it was too late to make any difference in the life of the young mother. The groups were particularly disturbed by the panel's apparent determination that a dying person's wishes had less legal significance than the wishes of a healthy person. With the benefit of time for research and reflection—which had been unavailable earlier because of the urgency of the medical situation—the full, eight-member court reversed the panel's earlier decision and held that a pregnant woman, even if she is near death, should not be compelled to undergo a cesarean delivery against her will, and that if she is incompetent to decide, the only power of the court should be to determine her wishes and follow them, unless there are "extraordinary or compelling" reasons otherwise.[4]

In the fall of 1992, the world was again troubled by news of a dying young woman subjected to medical procedures for the benefit of her fetus and not herself. An eighteen-year-old

German woman named Marion was declared brain-dead following an automobile accident, but she was placed on life-support
equipment and physical therapists manipulated her body in an
attempt to bring her thirteen-week-old fetus to term. Since the
head injury she suffered had made it impossible for her to either
consent to or refuse the procedures, the doctors themselves had
decided to attempt to keep her and her fetus alive until the baby
could be delivered by cesarean section. Newspapers learned of
the woman's case when her distressed parents contacted the press
to express their opposition to what was being done to their
daughter, but later they appeared on television to tearfully pro-
claim their change of heart. A court named them guardians of
the baby, if it were to survive, and they said they looked forward
to its birth. The identity of the baby's father was locked forever
inside the brain of the unmarried, dying woman as she was
nourished artificially, given hormones, and had recorded music
played for her by doctors, nurses, and therapists intent upon
doing whatever they could to achieve a healthy birth.

While the world argued fiercely whether her treatment represented a medical miracle for her fetus or a violation of her
own right to a dignified death, nature intervened. On November 16, 1992, Marion miscarried her nineteen-week-old fetus,
and the equipment that had kept her body functioning for six
weeks was at last turned off.

This German drama is not unique. On April 19, 1993, a
twenty-eight-year-old woman was admitted to Highland General Hospital in Oakland, California, with a bullet wound to
her head. Although she was legally brain-dead, the heart of the
tiny, seventeen-week-old fetus she was carrying continued to
beat, and relatives asked the hospital to keep her alive, if possible. Unlike the German health care givers, Highland General
personnel employed no special technologies beyond traditional
care to sustain the woman's life—essentially a ventilator and
IV tubes. One hundred and four days after the woman was declared legally brain-dead, she gave birth, four weeks prematurely,
to a baby boy by cesarean section.[5]

As medical technology has increased the likelihood that fatally injured patients may be subjected to life-prolonging treatments without any possibility of lifesaving benefits, Americans have been encouraged to execute living wills. These documents permit the patient's wishes to be carried out if there is a directive not to begin or to continue life-prolonging procedures when there is no hope of saving the patient's life. In the majority of states with living will laws, however, exceptions to the laws require that the express, written wishes of the patient be disregarded if she is pregnant. In effect, state legislators have decided that the state has a greater interest in protecting her unborn child than in carrying out her wishes regarding her own dignified death.

The newest area of conflict between maternal and fetal rights is the result of technologies that allow treatment of the fetus while it is still in the womb. Not only is a pregnant woman still expected to behave in ways that cause no harm to her fetus—at a time when the list of suspect behaviors is growing longer every day and already includes such seemingly innocent pleasures as drinking coffee and taking hot baths. Now she may also be asked to submit to diagnostic procedures, medical therapies, or surgical procedures directed toward the well-being of the fetus which pose significant risks to her own well-being.

In the spring of 1991, Mioko Shinn faced the choice of whether to submit to an experimental surgery that offered her twenty-two-week-old fetus its only chance to be born. Mioko was told that if fetal surgery were not performed to correct her fetus's condition, called congenital cystic adenomatoid malformation, it would not survive.[6] The condition was discovered at a very emotional time for Mioko. Her father in Japan was gravely ill, and Mioko had requested a sonogram to send to him because she feared he might not live until the birth of her child. Without that elective sonogram, doctors probably would not have discovered the problem in time for surgery. To save her fetus, Mioko had only a few weeks in which to decide whether to allow a team of surgeons to cut into her abdomen, open her womb, and operate on the fetus she carried while keeping its head submerged in amniotic fluid. Following the surgery she would have only a few more weeks to recover, assuming that the fetal surgery succeeded, before returning to the hospital to deliver her baby by cesarean section. For Mioko, the procedure would mean subjecting her to the surgical risks of a cesarean section twice within a five-week period.

Ironically, one of the major disappointments for Mioko as she faced the decision was giving up her dream of natural childbirth. "That really bothered me. I don't know why, but since I was small I wanted to have a natural birth and have my husband there."

Her husband David, a doctoral student in chemistry, encouraged Mioko to get past the emotion surrounding the decision by reading all the information on the procedure that he could find in the medical school library at the university he attended. She eagerly accepted his idea. Mioko also consulted her mother, who is a gynecologist in Japan, for medical advice and found that the procedure was so experimental that her mother knew nothing about it.

Finally, after all their research, Mioko admits that her decision probably came more from her heart than her head. "I'm a daddy's girl. I wanted to show my baby to my father, and he was ready to pass away."

Doctors had already tried draining the cyst and using drugs to deflate it, but it was apparent that the fetus needed surgery to survive. There was only one place in the United States where it could be done. On April 25, 1991, Dr. Michael Harrison and a team of surgeons at the University of California at San Francisco performed the surgery, and afterward David and Mioko flew back to their home in Georgia with orders for Mioko to await the baby's birth in bed. Sonograms indicated the need to deliver the baby four weeks early, and on June 19 their son Michael was born. Although Mioko thought she would be disappointed at not having experienced natural birth, today she says, "I just don't think about it, now that I'm quite happy about the C-section. It was so easy." Since his birth, Michael has faced medical problems unrelated to his fetal surgery, but today he is a healthy little boy who would never have been born without a pioneering team of physicians and a courageous mother.

Soon after Michael's birth, Mioko flew to Japan and shared pictures of her new son with her father before his death. Mioko may have been led to her decision by her heart while David followed his intellect, but together they reached the right decision for them.

Mioko and David's advice to other couples facing this sort of decision reveals the same individuality they showed in facing their own difficult choice. Ever the scientist, David says, "I'd suggest they read the articles on the procedure, and I would warn them that you've got to make your own decision. Don't let the optimism of the medical professionals make the decision for you. They're awfully convincing." Expressing her more emotional view, Mioko says, "I would tell them this is the great opportunity to save your baby. I won't say it's going to be successful or not successful, because there's no promise to it, and I would tell them all the things that I went through, of course. But since this is a successful case for us, I would tell them a positive answer." Even David admits that the best argument in support of the decision his wife made is "looking at this little, good-looking boy and seeing him smile."

David's advice highlights the medical dilemma, however. Should the optimism of the doctor be allowed to coerce a pregnant woman to assume significant risks for the benefit of her fetus? As Dr. Gonsoulin acknowledges, a woman is very vulnerable to persuasion when she faces choices between her own health and the health of her fetus, and she may tend to disregard medical advice she does not want to hear. As the technology for fetal therapy advances, doctors must be increasingly sensitive in obtaining consent for fetal treatments from their pregnant patients. Although the fetus is increasingly becoming a treatable patient, access to this tiny patient remains available only through the pregnant woman, and the American College of Obstetricians and Gynecologists has concluded: "Although it may be agreed that a pregnant woman has fundamental obligations toward her fetus, no other party, including the state, should override her autonomy in order to enforce those obligations."[7]

There is now a second option for fetal surgery. In March 1993 Dr. Ruben Quintero performed endoscopic fetal surgery on twenty-four-year-old Toya Graham, pregnant with twins. Although endoscopic surgery has a number of effective uses with adults, it had not been dependably successful in fetal surgeries until then. Toya was four months pregnant with twins—one a healthy fetus and one a malformed fetus with missing limbs, no brain, and no heartbeat. The heart of the healthy fetus was pumping blood for both twins, and without surgery to stop the blood flow through the malformed twin, the healthy twin's heart would almost certainly fail from the added effort. Dr. Graham performed surgery through needle-sized holes, guided by tiny cameras, and tied a knot in the malformed twin's umbilical cord. Four months later, Santerras Graham was born, thanks to an experimental procedure that made medical history.

If society begins to expect women to routinely consent to all fetal treatments, we may make legal adversaries of mother and child from the moment of conception until birth. In 1988 the State Supreme Court of Illinois was asked to decide whether a child could sue its mother for unintentional prenatal injuries. The court acknowledged that if someone else unintentionally injures a pregnant woman, both she and her fetus can sue for damages, but suits by both mother and child against a third person are intended to benefit both of them and do not place the interests of mother and child at odds.

In order to find that the mother had neglected the prenatal care of her fetus, the court would have had to define an appropriate standard of care. The judges' opinion summarized how difficult that would be. "The circumstances in which each individual woman brings forth life are as varied as the circumstances of each woman's life. Whether a standard of care to which a woman would be held while pregnant should vary according to whether a pregnancy was planned or unplanned, to whether a woman knew she was pregnant soon after conception or only knew after several months, to whether she had the financial resources with which to access the best possible medical care available or was unable to get any prenatal care are all questions which deserve much thought and reflection." The court denied the child's claim against its mother and commented that society should encourage the birth of healthy babies through education, not litigation.[8]

Some people disagree with that conclusion and believe that an appropriate standard of care should be established against which to judge the conduct of pregnant women. One member of the ethics committee of the American Fertility Society who is a law professor has suggested that for a sexually active woman whose period is late, "it does not seem unreasonable to require her either to have a pregnancy test or to refrain from activities that would be hazardous to the fetus if she were pregnant."[9] Of course, the frightening word in his suggestion is "require." Society may encourage responsible prenatal care by making available to women of childbearing age information that explains the risks of certain activities and the benefits of others, but requiring women to conform to behavior established by someone other than themselves merely because they *might* be pregnant presents both practical and moral problems. First of all, the list of hazards changes constantly, and experts disagree. Second, in order to enforce such a requirement, we would turn doctors into policemen, friends into snitches, and strangers into judges, and their suspicious eyes would have to be directed at every woman between puberty and menopause since no evidence of pregnancy would necessarily be detectable. Third, requirements could be effective only if some means of enforcement were imposed, so society would have to devise an appropriate punishment for women who disregarded the rule. And fourth, not all women have dependable menstrual cycles. For reasons such as these, as well as those given by the Illinois court, his proposal should never be implemented.

Surely this law professor meant only to suggest that more responsible behavior on the part of some women should be encouraged, and not that a new branch of law enforcement charged with the responsibility of checking a woman's pregnancy test results before she is served a drink, sold cigarettes, or permitted to change her cat's litter box should be created. Certainly he did not mean to suggest that all medication should be withheld from women for two weeks of every month. Women of childbearing age do have a unique responsibility not shared by others, but contrary to his suggestion, it is not reasonable to create a class of Americans whose lawful and normal activities should be restricted for half their lives.

Over the years doctors in several different cases have gone to court when they believed a cesarean delivery was urgently necessary and the mother refused to consent, often because of her religious beliefs. As 1993 drew to a close, such a case made national headlines. Tabita Bricci was told by doctors that her fetus was not getting enough oxygen and would probably die or be brain-damaged unless she agreed to allow doctors to perform a C-section. Tabita and her husband Mircea, as Pentecostal Christians, believe that it is wrong to terminate a pregnancy before term for any reason, including a cesarean delivery, and she declined to permit the procedure. Anxious to save the baby's life, doctors initiated legal proceedings that were expedited all the way to the U.S. Supreme Court, but the parents, rather than the doctors, were allowed to decide how the baby should be born. Callian Bricci was born vaginally on December 29, 1993. Patrick Murphy, the Cook County public guardian appointed by the court to represent the fetus, says he has no problem with the outcome of the case. "Illinois law was not clear at that time, and we were appointed to represent a person. We did the best we could, but now the appellate court has said it was not a person, it was a fetus." While Murphy accepts the court's decision, he reveals some lingering reservations when he adds, "Obviously, medicine has not reached the point where they can predict these things with certainty. If they could, it might be a different situation."[10]

The families in this chapter have faced a variety of maternal-fetal conflicts and reached differing conclusions, but the one common characteristic is their emphasis that each family must decide for themselves what is right for them, consistent with their circumstances, their moral beliefs, and their particular medical advice. As the fetus becomes more treatable apart from the pregnant woman who carries it, society will be tempted to strip away from the woman some of the autonomy that shields the bodily integrity of the rest of us, particularly in cases involving sedated or comatose patients for whom there is no hope of survival but whose dying bodies hold fetuses that might be saved. We must be reminded that most women, with their families, make responsible choices without the inflexible mandate of law. To gain the benefit of regulation in a few cases, we risk sacrificing the unique wisdom and courage women have voluntarily brought to their resolutions of maternal-fetal conflicts. Medical knowledge and judgment are limited and fallible, and if the decisions of pregnant women are sometimes imperfect, shifting the responsibility away from them is no guarantee of infallibility. What committee could consistently be expected to make the right decisions any more frequently than pregnant women, following their own hearts and consciences, already make about the fetuses they carry? Society must beware of imposing the artificial weight of courts and committees in the balancing of maternal and fetal rights.

Should a woman be punished for actions during pregnancy that damaged the fetus she carried, such as:

- Refusing medical treatment for herself that would have benefited the fetus?
- Exposing herself to X rays during pregnancy?
- Continuing to work in an environment unsafe to the fetus?
- Cleaning a cat's litter box during pregnancy?
- Failing to eat a well-balanced diet during pregnancy?
- Failing to get adequate rest during pregnancy?
- Drinking coffee during pregnancy?
- Failing to obtain prenatal care?

CHAPTER 7

THE STORY OF
BREE WALKER AND JIM LAMPLEY

Perhaps strangers felt as if they were personally acquainted with Jim and Bree because the couple had been in their homes so many evenings as coanchors of Los Angeles's KCBS nightly news. Perhaps it was because Jim had been their regular companion for so many great football games as a sportscaster for ABC Sports. For whatever reasons, when television broadcasters Bree Walker and Jim Lampley decided to have a baby, complete strangers discussed their decision with a familiarity normally reserved for family members.

On a July evening in 1991, a radio talk show hosted a two-hour public debate over whether Bree and Jim should have chosen to have a baby. As she invited callers to express their views, the host made it clear that she disapproved. "Is it fair to bring a child into the world that you're pretty sure has a very good chance of having a disfiguring disease? . . . Is this an appropriate thing to do? Is it fair to the kid to bring him into the world with one strike against him?" she asked her listeners. And, as if her tone left any room for doubt, she added, "I have to say, I don't think I could do it."[1]

As broadcasting professionals, Jim and Bree recognize the importance of public awareness of the moral issues raised by new reproductive technologies, but exposing their private decision to public debate by uninformed strangers seemed to them beyond appropriate journalistic inquiry. Jim thinks the problem was the way the radio station went about it. "It is good for these subjects to be discussed—in the right manner and at the right emotional and intellectual level."[2] He explains, "Radio talk shows depend for fairness on the presence of divergent points of view." Based on information learned since the show aired, Jim believes, "In this instance, callers who wanted to defend us were discouraged from doing so and, in fact, were summarily dismissed. Callers who wanted to criticize us, as the talk show host did, were encouraged to go into full flower and stay on the air for a long time."[3]

It angers Bree that the host "hadn't done her homework." Bree's condition, known as ectrodactyly, involves a partial fusion of bones in her fingers and toes. She has no objection to others describing her condition as a deformity or a disability, but she believes the host had a responsibility to be accurate. "She was mistaken, because she had not done her research well enough to understand that ectrodactyly is not a degenerative disease. She did not understand that it is pure and simple a shape deformity."

Andrea, Bree's daughter from an earlier marriage, has hands and feet like her mother. Bree and Jim knew there was a fifty-fifty chance that their baby would inherit ectrodactyly from Bree. But because Bree has never let her own condition limit her participation in whatever she found challenging, she saw no reason why her child should be less than a full participant in life, either, whether he did or did not inherit the condition. Jim agrees: "People have made a great deal about this issue ever since Bree became pregnant, but I will be perfectly honest with you. I think in a given week my wife spends less than ten minutes worrying about the shape of her hands and her feet. Our judgment is that our children will probably be pretty satisfied with the 167 hours and 50 minutes of relative peace of mind every week on the subject as well. It is not as if this is something that bedevils your every daily move. You get used to it, like anything else in life. I never want to belittle the depth of this experience for my wife or our children, but I think there is a tendency on the part of the media to make a little more out of it than is justified."

Bree certainly knows it isn't always easy, but not because

the condition is disabling for her. Rather, the difficulty comes from the reactions of others. She remembers the hurt of being called "Lobster Claws" when she was growing up and says adolescence was particularly tough. The condition itself is not painful, but Bree admits that her own attempts to conform her appearance caused not only emotional but also physical pain. "My feet were painful, because I forced them into shoes that were made for conventional feet. . . . I didn't feel like I was, quote unquote, normal if I wore shoes that were comfortable for my feet. They would be misshapen shoes, and that was not acceptable to me when I was extremely interested in being attractive."

Bree herself had benefited from the wisdom of her own parents when she was growing up with three other siblings, the oldest two of whom do not have ectrodactyly. Bree is the youngest, and she says she and her brother were expected to do exactly the same chores as the older brother and sister and were not treated differently. If there were any feelings of jealousy or guilt among the siblings, Bree was never aware of them. Her parents' skills in raising her have provided a road map for Jim and Bree as they plan for their own children, just as her mother, who also has ectrodactyly, has always been a role model for Bree.

Bree and Jim were confident they had made a responsible decision and were looking forward to the birth of their son. They had learned early in the pregnancy, through a test called chorionic villus sampling, or CVS, that the condition had been passed to the baby. An early abortion could have been performed at that time, but they had not requested the test in order to abort if ectrodactyly were found. "We knew that we wanted to have a child together. What we learned from the CVS was not going to make any difference, but Jim and I are both the kind of people who think it is good to have as much information as possible, and that is why we had the test done," explains Bree. In August, Aaron James Lampley was born, weighing seven pounds fourteen ounces.

Jim and Bree realize that their financial circumstances offer advantages that other couples may not have, and they acknowledge how lucky they are to be able to afford the orthopedic surgery, special shoes, and other expenses associated with their children's conditions. Bree remembers that financial concerns were a worry for her parents, and it has made her sensitive to the differing circumstances of other couples that may cause them to decide differently when faced with a similar situation.

They also recognize the vast differences among defects and diseases that may be passed on genetically and feel that these differences call for individual choices. During the publicity following the radio talk show, both pro-choice and pro-life groups approached Jim and Bree with requests for them to make certain public statements, but they declined, believing that this difficult decision is one each couple must make for themselves. Bree is quick to recommend counseling to assist couples, but Jim adds, "We don't think government should play a role in determining birth choice here. We think that would amount to an unwarranted abridgment of civil rights."

One of the things Bree finds infuriating about the viewpoint of the talk show host is the assumption that their baby, and others like him, will face limited options throughout their lives. "Jim and I both want all four of our children to be raised with an attitude that whatever work makes them happy is productive, important work. On that program one of the things the talk show host kept pursuing was the idea that I had been really lucky in television, and what if my own children didn't get that lucky? That infuriated me personally because it was such a narrow vision of a worthwhile life. We have to stop having a narrow view of what makes a life worthwhile, or we are going to continue to have values in this society that are absolutely not worth pursuing."

Although they are unwilling to allow themselves to become public spokespersons in the abortion debate, they are enthusiastic advocates for the disabled. "I have always called myself a disability-rights activist," Bree says, "and I felt I couldn't carry that torch with any honesty if I didn't do anything about this personal attack."[4] The method they chose for protesting the talk show was to join with national disability-advocacy groups and about one hundred other individuals in filing a complaint with the Federal Communications Commission against the radio station.

It was a difficult decision for two people whose careers are devoted to the idea of a free press, but for Bree the complaint they filed was not a freedom-of-speech issue. For her the issues were dignity, privacy, propriety. "It's about how far do you stretch for ratings? How far do you stretch in shock radio? Just to get people to tune in, even if it means exposing someone's most personal decisions."

It was also about bringing media attention to another viewpoint: that of the people with disabilities. At the press conference they called to announce the filing of the formal complaint against the station, Jim made a direct appeal to their friends and colleagues in the media: "Acknowledge your understanding on the air, that this is a larger story than just a story about Bree and Jim and their baby son, Aaron. This is a story about millions of other people."

They also wanted to educate the media about language. Bree speaks of doing all they can to make their children's lives as *conventional* as possible, and then she interrupts herself to explain why she has chosen that word. "We hate to use the word 'normal,' because in all civil rights movements, language becomes a very important, volatile issue. This is one of those last civil rights movements where so much of the media hasn't yet gotten on board with the right language. In our business, we still see words like 'a crippling condition' used all the time."

Correcting the language is only a means to reach the greater purpose for Bree, as she carefully tried to explain at the press conference: "Because I choose to remain hopeful that someday ours will be a society that values the differences among its people, and their unique contributions, I feel it necessary to fight the views that would stand in the way of this progress."

Their complaint against the station was ultimately rejected by the FCC, but Jim and Bree feel that the broader purposes they had for filing the complaint were served. However, they both feel society is paying too little attention to the effects that advancing technology may be having upon decisions surrounding birth. Jim believes, "Every institution, be it church, schools, hospitals, clinics, workplaces, insurers, etc.—every institution that concerns itself in any way with the moral, emotional, and medical well-being of the society—ought to be concerned with this issue in some way. Because this issue in the twenty-first century is going to affect all of us much more dramatically than we now envision."

When they were interviewed by Barbara Walters for a *20/20* television segment, she asked them about questions listeners had raised during the radio talk show: "Why bring a child into the world who's going to have so much personal, emotional, and perhaps physical pain? Why do this to a child?" Jim answered her first: "Because we're confident that we can provide the love and support necessary to offer our child the chance to have as worthwhile, as valuable, as meaningful a life on this planet as his mother has had." Bree's answer went beyond the subject of their own decision to address the impact of such questions upon all of us. "Here's the problem with saying that it's not right to bring a child into the world who may have that kind of difficulty to face. That is saying that there's only one set of standards that's acceptable for society. And that devalues all of us. If we have such a narrow-minded look at what's valuable in life, what kind of life is worth living, then how can we ever feel like we're in a society where everybody can feel great about trying to contribute?"

Jim and Bree do not oppose technology or want to urge everyone to decide as they did. Jim says, "The advancement of the technological curve brings up whole new complexes of moral choices that people haven't envisioned before. We tried to help prepare the landscape for people to make those choices." Bree worries that greater scientific knowledge may eclipse the personal wisdom of parents, and they agree that the couples themselves must be entrusted with the difficult decisions raised by the technology. As Jim says, "We're talking about individual choice and the privacy that ought to surround it."

While Baby Aaron was still in diapers, research moved forward with such unexpected speed that were Jim and Bree planning his birth today, different technologies might be available. Once the gene causing ectrodactyly can be isolated, it may be possible to use in vitro fertilization to select an embryo that does not carry the trait. The mother could be implanted with the selected embryo and avoid the risk of passing the condition on to her baby. Had that technology been available in 1991, they believe they would have used it. Bree does not regret having proceeded with her own pregnancies, but she sees the technology as a positive reproductive option for her children when they are ready to plan their families. "Andrea and Aaron's will be the last generation with ectrodactyly," she says. But then she corrects herself: "At least the technology will be there for them if they choose to use it."

In the summer of 1996, the Lampley family left Los Angeles, even though the move requires Jim and Bree to commute to their work with the television and film company they have formed. They believe their new community will foster the "conventional" life they hope to provide for their children, and they are already pleased with how well Andrea and Aaron have fit into their new public school classes. "In retrospect, I understand how stressful it was to be at the center of controversy while remaining on the air during my pregnancy," admits Bree. Although she plans to return to broadcasting when Andrea and Aaron are older, for now Bree says, "I am relieved to be out of the spotlight while raising my children."

CHAPTER 8

THE DILEMMAS OF GENETIC KNOWLEDGE

"I'm going to have redheaded grandbabies!"

News of the engagement had barely been announced before the young woman's mother had thought back three generations to a fiery-haired great-grandfather, had recalled each auburn-haired cousin born since, and had concluded that her daughter's marriage to a sandy-haired young man would surely produce red-haired offspring. This mother may never have heard of genetics, but she knew how to calculate the odds when it came to her own grandchildren!

Half the fun at family reunions has long been comparing unmistakable profiles or shoe sizes or blue eyes that everyone recognizes as sure signs of pedigree within that family. Countless children have been confused by accusations that they have a disposition just like uncle so-and-so or an artistic gift like cousin what's-her-name, even though the bewildered children have never met these absent kin to whom the comparisons are being made. A common ache described by adopted children is not knowing from whom they inherited their freckles or talents, and missing the sense of connection that comes with seeing siblings and extended relatives with common physical traits.

Genetics may have come to dominate scientific research rather recently, but people have predicted good and bad family characteristics for generations. The knowledge that somehow family traits of appearance, health, and even personality and talent passed from generation to generation has been around for centuries. Scientific research to explore just how this occurs can be traced back to 1860, when an Austrian monk began experimenting with garden peas, systematically crossbreeding and recording the results from which he formulated principles of heredity.[1] Experiments with plants and animals allowed scientists to control breeding choices and to observe many generations over a far shorter period than could be done with humans.

The basic unit of inheritance is called a gene, and more than fifty thousand separate human genes have been identified. Each gene carries coded instructions that make up the unique characteristics of every individual. This genetic code is contained within molecules of a long substance, often described as being like a chain or a twisted ladder, called deoxyribonucleic acid, or DNA. The DNA substance and some protein make up the chromosomes present in the nuclei of cells. It has been said that if the information encoded in one human DNA molecule could be translated into English, it would fill a thousand books with about a thousand pages in each book.

Scientists with federal funding are mapping the location of every human gene. The Human Genome Project is planned for completion in the year 2015. One of the most promising applications of that research is locating the genes that transmit inheritable diseases.

Locating genes does not mean, however, that treatments and cures for genetically transmitted diseases necessarily follow. During her tenure as president of the National Society of Genetic Counselors, Betsy Gettig supported the project but expressed reservations about whether the enormous expense justified the diversion of those dollars from other research. "The Human Genome Project is funded at a level greater than NASA was during the moon-exploration years," she says. "But I haven't exactly heard the public screaming for this information. I think the public is screaming for universal access to medical care, but I'm not sure they are as excited about this project as the government is. The carrot that has been placed before us is that by 2015 we will be able to identify the locations of all genes, but unless we also learn some type of treatment, that really is meaningless." She adds that the location of some genes has been known for a long time without any treatment or cure resulting.[2]

Dr. Paul Billings, a physician and bioethicist at California Pacific Medical Center in San Francisco, is more hopeful concerning the practical applications of mapping human genes. "Genetic analysis provides another avenue of hope. Insight into how we function, that we have never had before, may lead to the development of new treatments for a variety of troubling maladies of man."[3] One of the most troubling of those maladies is cancer.

When Lyndall Southern was only eighteen months old, she was already a cancer survivor. By the time she was fourteen, she had faced her second surgery for cancer, only a few months after her mother's death from cancer at age thirty-two. Her maternal grandfather had died of a brain tumor at the age of twenty-six, and although cancer had threaded its way through three generations, none of their cancers was the same.[4] Before genetic testing permitted doctors to identify the mutant gene for a rare syndrome, called Li-Fraumeni syndrome, that made the family extremely susceptible to cancers, Lyndall says the family suspected that the diseases might have somehow been inherited. "Even before my two brothers ended up having cancer, we suspected it, but the connection seemed a little far-fetched because of the differences in the cancers. But when three out of four of us were affected, we thought it had to be something." Her two brothers, both younger than she, died at ages twenty-four and twenty-seven, and at age thirty-five Lyndall has survived four separate cancers.[5] Only her sister, who is one year younger than Lyndall, has never been affected.

When researchers identified the mutant gene, p53, causing the family's susceptibility to cancer, the youngest of Lyndall's three daughters was two months old, and she has had no children since. Even if the mutant gene could have been identified earlier, Lyndall believes that she would have chosen to have children. "At the time I was pregnant with my oldest daughter, before we really knew anything, one of my concerns was, What if cancer is hereditary? When I asked what the chances of me having a child with cancer would be, I was told that even if it was inherited, there was still only a fifty percent chance that my child would have it, and even then there was no way to know if they would have it at a young age or not until they were eighty years old. I have always wanted kids, and I don't know how much difference knowing the test results would have made."

Lyndall admits that her feelings might change if one of her daughters actually had cancer. "It is a lot easier going through this myself than watching somebody else—watching my brothers, sitting outside in the waiting room for them to come out of surgery." Feelings of guilt for having caused suffering and death among offspring is not necessarily limited to the parent who passed the genetic trait for the disease. Lyndall recalls her grandmother's expressions of regret for having married and borne children with the man to whom the mutant family gene has been traced. "If I had never married Clarence, none of this would have happened," she remembers hearing her grandmother say at the funeral for Lyndall's eight-year-old cousin.[6]

Genetic counselor Gettig describes the complex emotions these parents face: "Parents of children with genetic diseases go through a stage of emotional development that I don't think has been very clearly defined. It is not just the grief process but the anguish, when it is an incurable, untreatable condition, of seeing their child die before their very eyes in a slow manner. Human beings are such control freaks. We don't want anything to go wrong. We feel we don't deserve it. When something does, there is a level of jealousy. You see someone walking down the street with six children, and they've got a beer in one hand and a cigarette in the other, and you think—look at that! We did everything right and they are the ones with six children. People are so hurt by these conditions, and then to know that the condition is inherited gives them a whole second level of guilt to go through."

For some people it is easier not to know. Since nearly all

of the adult members of the family have been tested by the researchers studying the mutant family gene, Lyndall's sister probably could learn whether she, too, carries the mutant gene that passed through her mother to all three of her siblings, but Lyndall does not believe that her sister has asked the researchers for that information. Genetic counselor Gettig understands. "Just to identify genes serves no great purpose for most people unless you also identify a treatment, cure, or some regime of alleviating the symptoms of that disease. Having to say, we have identified this gene but we can't do anything about it, is a tough situation."

For Lyndall, however, the knowledge is important, even if it would not have affected her reproductive decisions. "My own personal feeling is that it gives you a choice."

Lyndall intends to have her three daughters tested. "I want to know whether I need to pay more attention to a suspicious bump or anything like that," she explains. However, she does not necessarily intend to share the results with her daughters. "I want to let my children know that they could find out the information if they needed it, but I don't want to take away their choices, either." Her children are not about to miss out on the joys of childhood if Lyndall can help it! "My kids run and jump and play and fall down and ride their horse and jump on the trampoline. I don't see myself doing any different than any other mother."

She credits her positive attitude to the way she was raised. "Regardless of what I went through, I was never given the idea that I couldn't do anything that I wanted to do. I might look a little bit different than somebody else [because of the cancer surgery to her face and jaw], but I was never permitted to sit back and feel sorry for myself all the time, like, poor-pitiful-me." She describes herself as having "this terrible habit of making the best of what I have."

But she understands that not everyone is able to deal with knowing that they are genetically at risk for an inherited malady. "I am a strong believer in giving people the information to make informed choices, not necessarily to alter anything but so that they can know the likelihood or whatever. But finally, it ought to be left up to the individual—how much they want to know and what they want to know."

Lyndall admits it may be tempting to criticize another person's decision to have children in spite of the likelihood that a genetic disease or disability may be transmitted but says, "I don't think anybody should ever sit in judgment and tell somebody what is right or what is wrong with their lives, even if they think they have had the same circumstance." She has concerns but no regrets about her own decision to have children. "They have made such progress in treating cancer that even if my children do get it, their chances of survival are a lot better than they were when I had it."[7]

Both Lyndall Southern and Bree Walker faced the decision about whether to conceive a child, knowing that there was a 50 percent chance that their child would inherit the genetic trait with which each mother had lived all of her own life. Neither of them wished for their baby to inherit the disabling gene from them, but each of them felt it was a responsible reproductive choice to take that risk.

In the past, the mother's and father's genetic contributions were random, and the unique genetic characteristics of their offspring were capable of some predictions, based on knowledge of dominant and recessive genes and family medical histories, but incapable of control. Once the embryo was created, genetic character was fixed forever. The ability not only to predict but also to control or alter genetic characteristics is changing rapidly. Jim Lampley emphasizes the dramatic impact that genetic technology will have on all of us in the twenty-first century, and recognizes the difficulty of our relying on the moral values of the past for guidance. "There are old standards that probably aren't relevant to these situations because a lot of what used to be guesswork isn't going to be guesswork anymore," he says.[8] Technology offers the ability to modify the random fertilization of

egg by sperm and provides genetic information about the embryo or fetus long before birth. We must decide whether it is
immoral to use this technology or immoral not to.

Unfortunately, the use of genetic information in reproductive choices is too often complicated by abortion politics.
While organized groups would have you believe that the stance
advocated by their leadership is the only appropriate position
for those holding particular views about abortion, individuals
willing to think independently about the complex issues raised
by genetic technology often reach conclusions unrelated to their
feelings about abortion. A possible exception may be how they
feel about pregnancies achieved with the intention to abort if
prenatal testing reveals the presence of the disabling genetic trait
in the fetus, but even this practice is neither universally approved by pro-choice advocates nor condemned by pro-lifers.
The issues raised by our growing access to genetic information
deserve more than a knee-jerk response generated by tapping
into preexisting attitudes toward abortion.

Among participants in my survey, 64 percent identified
themselves as pro-choice, 25 percent as opposed to abortion,
and 10 percent as undecided.[9] When this group was asked if
they would take a test to screen for genetic diseases they might
pass to their children, nearly everyone said that they would.[10]
There was less unanimity about how they would use the information learned from genetic testing. Seventy-three percent said
that if the test revealed they were certain to have an abnormal
child, they would choose not to have children, but 19 percent
were undecided, and 6.5 percent said even the certainty would
not stop them.[11] When asked about a test result that revealed
only a high probability of having an abnormal child rather than
a certainty, fewer were willing to forgo having children, with
only 54.5 percent saying that they would, 9 percent saying
they would go ahead regardless of the high risk, and 34 percent
undecided.[12]

As for proceeding with conception, with the intention of
aborting if prenatal testing revealed the genetic abnormality in

the fetus, 24 percent said that was a choice they would be willing to make, 51 percent said they would not, and 22 percent were undecided.[13] These responses are in sharp contrast to those the participants gave when asked if they would terminate a pregnancy if prenatal testing revealed an abnormality (without the element of preplanning a possible abortion at the time of conception). In the unplanned situation, 42.6 percent said they would abort, 19 percent said they would not, and 38 percent were undecided. Obviously, participants saw the two situations very differently.[14]

With these survey results in mind, we can conclude with some confidence that individuals are willing to examine genetic issues apart from the rigid positions mapped by abortion advocates. In order to bring the collective common sense of everyday Americans to bear on these issues, however, most of us need a clearer understanding of how the expanding access to genetic possibilities may touch our lives.

We have always practiced genetic selection to some extent. When the beautiful homecoming queen marries the brainy debate team captain instead of the brawny football captain, their romantic selection of each other is based on the features or abilities they find desirable in a mate, and that selection process dictates what sort of offspring they will have. Social pressures against marrying outside an individual's racial or ethnic group preserve the genetic traits of that group, and when governments set immigration limits, or in the past prohibited interracial marriages, these laws affected the genetic selection process. However, genetic technology did not call forth some new urge to create perfect babies. Families usually hope that their babies inherit the best qualities of each parent and avoid the undesirable traits. Wishing for a perfect baby may have been a harmless fancy for parents in the past, but as the technology to fulfill such wishes begins to emerge, we must reevaluate the wisdom of such a goal.

The best place to start is not after conception but before the baby is conceived. Betsy Gettig does her genetic counseling at a Pennsylvania hospital, where counselors have about twenty-five hundred consults a year. "I would *love* to do preconceptual counseling, but the problem is the public," she says. "I could say during the course of a year we maybe have twelve patients that come in preconceptually to discuss risks in childbearing or inherited conditions in the family or unknown medical conditions that might be genetic. Most of the people that we see come in under the stress of an ongoing pregnancy, when issues they may have been thinking about for a couple of years now have to be resolved one way or the other. Most people just don't plan that far ahead." She acknowledges that part of the public neglect occurs because preconceptual counseling is not covered by most health insurance.

"I think women should consider pregnancy not as nine months but about a year and a half and spend a few months altering their lifestyle before becoming pregnant, but that assumes a planning phase and not all pregnancies are planned," she admits. Not only could women use this preconception period to alter their diets and exercise and their use of alcohol, tobacco, and both over-the-counter and recreational drugs, but they could also use the time to consider genetic factors without the pressure of an actual pregnancy. Gettig thinks that the best opportunity to increase public awareness of preconceptual genetic counseling is in connection with annual gynecological examinations, but it is apparent that a great deal of public education is needed for that to become a reality.

Some couples do plan their families based on known genetic factors, and that planning may include the decision not to bear children of their own. Other couples plan to have families with the assistance of donor gametes, relying on the genetic heritage of a stranger to replace the genetic material of the spouse carrying the defect.

Couples may also use gender preselection in their family planning, but only if the genetic condition they are seeking to avoid is linked to a specific gender. For example, those who suffer from hemophilia, an inherited bleeding disorder, are almost exclusively male, although females may be carriers of the disease. If a couple at risk for transmitting hemophilia to their offspring wanted to avoid conceiving a child that would suffer from the disease, they could use technology to enhance the likelihood of conceiving a girl. The technology for gender preselection enhances the odds but does not guarantee that the preferred gender will be conceived.

While other genetic options exist, the expense and the limited number of medical facilities doing these procedures exclude most couples. As procedures become more widely available and more affordable, more couples will be able to consider such technologies as in vitro fertilization, in which a cell is taken from the fertilized egg for DNA testing to determine whether the genetic condition was inherited. The embryo is transferred into the mother's body for gestation only if the condition is absent. Cam Knutson is a genetic counselor in Charlotte, North Carolina, and although she has counseled patients about that procedure, none has been willing to travel to the out-of-state medical facility offering the technology. "It is very expensive, and I haven't had anybody decide to go through with it." Since these procedures focus upon the particular trait the couple is seeking to avoid, Knutson worries that genetic testing may raise unrealistic expectations in some couples. "It is important for people to realize that just because you do these prenatal tests that you cannot guarantee that the baby is going to be perfect."[15]

The role of a genetic counselor is to provide information and support to couples in a nondirective manner, and Knutson strongly believes in trusting individual parents to decide "what they can deal with financially, emotionally, and timewise." Professionally, she tries to give her patients impartial information about the genetic condition they are facing, both positive and negative. She puts them in touch with families raising children with the condition and introduces them to physicians who treat the condition, so that when couples make their decision they will have as much firsthand knowledge as reasonably possible.

Privately, she worries that couples may be intolerant of children who are different.

Knutson believes that couples who have delayed child-bearing are more likely to want a perfect baby. "I think high expectations go along with people waiting later to have their families. They are more financially secure, and they want every-thing just so, including planning their children just so. It does concern me a little bit that some people have no room for a child that is a little bit different."

She is not alone in her concern. In fact, some Americans believe that employing genetic knowledge to eradicate disease and disability is wrong, because it treats people with diseases and disabilities as less worthy of life than other humans. As Nancy Becker Kennedy says, "I am very concerned about quan-tifying people's value by how many body parts work. What are we talking about? Humans are not interchangeable parts. We are not cars. We have souls." Kennedy lived the first half of her life without the disability that resulted from a spinal cord injury at age twenty. "If somebody would have told me a month before I broke my neck that I would be paralyzed from the neck down, I would have told them, 'Kill me.' What happened was that, after my injury, my world opened up tenfold into the richest experience. I think I was put on the planet to share the lesson that I learned from my disability, which is, your humanity is not based on how many parts move."

Kennedy disagrees with those who see no distinction be-tween utilizing medical technology in treating people, like her-self, who are already dealing with disabilities and utilizing the technology to avoid the birth of more disabled babies. "What are the implications for a culture that weeds out defectives?" she asks. "I believe it morally and philosophically ruins a civiliza-tion. I think perhaps these babies are our teachers, that they may mirror something really important back to us. Sometimes the things we think would be the worst things can turn out to be the best things."

Her strong feelings about the importance of each human

life have not led her to a pro-life position on abortion, however. "I would wish everybody could rise to the occasion of loving whatever child is born to them, but I would not mandate it," she explains. "I am pro-choice and believe that anybody who feels that they are not prepared to have a baby shouldn't have one. . . . If they really feel that they can't handle parenting, then I would prefer to see them give their baby up for adoption. And, I certainly don't think their decision should be dependent upon disability. I think that if you are ready to be a parent, you should be ready for any child. [But] if other people search their souls and believe that what they are doing is right, I don't want to shame them. God may be speaking to them differently than He speaks to me."[16]

Emily Perl Kingsley is also a forceful activist for people with disabilities. She was thirty-four years old when she gave birth to a son with Down syndrome. She and her husband Charles were told by their doctor that their son, Jason, would never walk, talk, or be able to distinguish them from other adults. Her obstetrician advised her to institutionalize Jason and tell her friends and family that he had died in childbirth. Today she says, "In a relatively short period of time we realized we had been given some really crazy advice. Not only was our child doing all those things he was not supposed to do, but he was quite bright. He was reading at four years old, and at seven he could count to ten in twelve foreign languages."

Instead of warehousing Jason in an institution, as so many parents of children with Down syndrome did then, the Kingsleys decided to encourage him to be the best that he could be. Jason not only has distinguished himself but also has influenced public attitudes. Beginning with his early appearances on "Sesame Street" through the recent publication of a book coauthored with a friend who also has Down syndrome, Jason has demolished many public misconceptions about the limitations of people with Down's.[17] In a voice containing equal parts anger and triumph, Emily says, "That is a far cry from what that doctor predicted!"

The Kingsleys have made an effort to share their own experiences with parents of babies with Down syndrome before and after birth. "We will drop anything we are doing to make sure other families aren't misled by receiving outdated, obsolete counseling as we were," Kingsley says. Although she feels strongly that each couple must decide for themselves whether they can raise a child with Down syndrome, she emphasizes the need for them to carefully examine what such parenting actually involves. "We encourage people to meet with other families, to see children, to go to a school, to do some reading before making these decisions. Couples need a tremendous amount of real, hard information about the facts and what children like this are capable of, what their potential is. The most important thing is that people do their homework and not make any decisions based on fear." She also believes that an important part of that information, should they feel unable to raise their child, must be the awareness that other couples are willing to adopt these babies.[18]

Emily Kingsley does not pretend that parenting a child with Down syndrome is easy. "It is a disability. It is not optimal. There are sad days and days that you wonder what your kid might have been like if he hadn't been born with the disability. There are hassles getting access to certain kinds of programs and arranging for appropriate socialization, although things are definitely improving." She is convinced that the outlook for these children is brighter than it has ever been, but her belief that parents must ultimately decide whether they should continue the pregnancy remains firm. "It is a matter of personal choice, and if somebody still decides to terminate the pregnancy after receiving the most current information, that is certainly up to them."

However, Kingsley does question the appropriateness of responding to the prenatal diagnosis of all genetic disabilities and diseases in the same manner. "I think that there are certain conditions, such as anencephaly or Tay-Sachs disease, that offer nothing but heartbreak for everyone. Although I am an advocate for individuals with disabilities, I confess that I have a hard time evaluating the quality of life of a person born with no brain." She points to diseases involving total physical and mental deterioration, culminating in the child's early death, and says, "That is a nightmare for all concerned! To me, these are conditions that make no sense, and if I faced that situation, I would probably terminate the pregnancy." She is quick to add, however, that she does not believe Down syndrome presents such heartbreaking circumstances.[19]

To some parents, even a brief and limited life for their child makes sense. Among the parents of disabled and genetically at-risk children, or even among the disabled themselves, little more consensus can be found than among the public at large. However, we can certainly no longer pretend that the birth of a child with a severe genetic disability is the same matter of blind chance, as it was a generation ago. It is simply false to suggest that the parents of an infant born with genetic disabilities have no more control over their child's condition than the parents of a child disabled by an accident. Making a distinction between the two circumstances does not resolve the question of society's responsibility to aid such families, but disability advocates must stop hiding behind the pretense that genetic disability strikes as randomly as a drunk driver careening into children waiting at a bus stop. Social strategies must take these differences of predictability and control into account.

Prospective parents today may have the benefit of preconceptual genetic information, especially where there is a family history of the trait to alert them to the possibility of genetic transmission. As genetic counselor Gettig urged, the least stressful time for facing reproductive choices is preconceptually, before arguments arise about when life begins. Unfortunately, until the technology exists to isolate the genetic material prior to fertilization of egg by sperm, and, equally important, until that technology is affordable, couples are left with only two options: choosing not to have their own genetic children by avoiding pregnancy altogether or facing the choice of whether to abort a fetus (or perhaps to destroy an embryo) if prenatal (or preimplant) testing reveals that the genetic trait has been passed.

Amniocentesis was the first type of prenatal genetic testing available, but because the test is associated with the risk of miscarriage, it was not generally used unless the woman's age or a family medical history suggested the need. The risk of miscarriage from prenatal testing remains difficult to quantify, since the women who are tested may already have a higher potential to miscarry. Amniocentesis is not performed until after the first three months of a pregnancy, delaying news of genetic inheritance further into the pregnancy, when abortion is both more medically dangerous and emotionally traumatic.

Today, other prenatal tests are also available. Chorionic villi sampling can diagnose chromosomal abnormalities in the fetus between the ninth and twelfth weeks of pregnancy, much earlier than amniocentesis test results can be learned. If the woman decides to terminate the pregnancy, the fetus is less fully developed, and the procedure is safer for the woman. The emotional stress may be lessened, since the woman will not have experienced the fetus moving within her and her pregnancy will not yet be publicly apparent. Blood tests can also detect certain genetic conditions, at less expense than more invasive procedures.

The purpose of prenatal genetic testing is not only to allow couples to terminate a pregnancy if their fetus has an unwanted genetic disorder. Betsy Gettig explains, "Genetic counselors have to spend their whole careers avoiding the stigma of being considered abortion brokers. We also help people who continue their pregnancies, aligning all the services and the physicians so that there is a plan for their delivery. Overall, about half of our patients diagnosed with a genetic problem continue their pregnancies and about half end them. It really depends on the diagnosis."

Cam Knutson agrees about the importance of using prenatal test results to prepare appropriately for the baby's birth, but she sees another role for the counselor. "Patients will come in and say, 'I am having the amniocentesis because my doctor told me to,' but really in their hearts they are not so sure that's right for them. Some people are relieved to find that they have a choice about having the test." She emphasizes, "Just because the technology is there doesn't mean that you have to use it."

Not everyone would agree. If you believe that every baby should have an opportunity to live, you may find the refusal to consider prenatal testing irresponsible because it reduces the potential to make appropriate preparations for a difficult delivery and might mean a delay in lifesaving treatment for the newborn. If you believe that abortion is a responsible choice in some circumstances, you may find the refusal to be tested a cowardly means of avoiding a difficult choice.

We have already seen that participants in my survey seemed willing to use genetic testing in their family planning, even though they were less certain of the choices they might make based on information they learned from the test. A majority were even willing to require genetic screening, for instance as a part of blood tests in connection with marriage licenses.[20] While the majority were willing to require genetic testing, only a small percentage of the participants were ready to allow the government to intervene in their decision about whether or not to have a child based on knowledge learned from the testing. If they were certain to have a genetically abnormal child, 13 percent thought the government should prohibit the conception, 69 percent thought the government should not, and 16 percent were undecided. If there were only a high likelihood, rather than a certainty of the abnormality, 10 percent thought the government should prohibit their having children, 72 percent thought the government should not, and 17 percent were undecided.[21]

Although he believes the public needs to be better informed about the benefits and the limitations of genetic testing, in the end, Dr. Paul Billings is confident about who must make the decisions surrounding testing and use of the information if testing is done. "I think that the preservation of individual

choice in the use of genetic information is of absolute importance," he says. Dr. Billings feels the public must recognize that
some people will not want to know all the genetic information
that is available to them. "That is also their right, and it, too,
should be preserved," he believes.

Most genetic professionals fear that as more genetic information becomes available to couples, outsiders will exert pressure to direct their reproductive choices. Dr. Billings was among
the earliest to collect case histories of genetic discrimination in
an effort to evaluate whether such fears of abuse were well
founded. He has concluded that there is a genuine danger that
insurance companies, employers, and governmental and educational institutions (among others) may create a new social under-
class of individuals who possess genetic variations from the
norm, even though these individuals exhibit no symptoms, or
only mild symptoms, of the disability. He and his fellow researchers found that "genetic conditions are regarded by many
social institutions as extremely serious, disabling, or even lethal
conditions without regard to the fact that many individuals
with 'abnormal' genotypes will either be perfectly healthy, have
medical conditions which can be controlled by treatment, or
experience only mild forms of a disease."[22]

A young lawyer in Ohio has experienced genetic discrimination firsthand. Theresa Morelli's story is especially troubling
because she has not even been tested for the genetic condition
that led to the discrimination. "I was doing personal-injury law
at the time, and I saw so many of my clients struggling to get
by on Social Security after they were injured," she explains.
Although she was only twenty-eight, Theresa decided to apply
for disability insurance so that she would never face such a
financial struggle if she were injured in an accident.[23] Even
without the confirmation of genetic testing, she was turned
down because her father has been diagnosed with Huntington's
disease.

Huntington's is a degenerative nerve disorder that usually
does not appear until between the ages of thirty-five to fifty.

Children have a 50 percent chance of inheriting the disease if their parent has it, and because the condition generally appears in middle age, many of those with Huntington's have already had children before they are aware they may pass the disease to their offspring.

Theresa describes the onset of her father's illness: "He was about fifty-five at the time, and I was sixteen when I started to notice things about my dad, like erratic behavior and getting extremely forgetful. He was a carpenter, and he started having near mishaps at work." Over the next few years, her father's condition progressively worsened. Finally, a doctor noticed from their family medical history that Theresa's paternal grandfather had died in a mental institution in 1960, having been diagnosed as schizophrenic. This suggested to the doctor that both Theresa's father and grandfather may have had Huntington's. However, neither the two men nor Theresa herself has ever been genetically tested to confirm the diagnosis. When her father was originally diagnosed, Theresa says, "The marker test was not yet widely available, and I wasn't sure whether I could handle the test anyway. During this period I was going to undergraduate and then law school, so I really didn't want anybody to know all this."

Theresa became a legal activist in the fight against genetic discrimination after the insurance company denied her coverage. She has lobbied for the enactment of federal civil rights legislation similar to the Civil Rights Act of 1964 and the Americans with Disabilities Act of 1990 to protect people with abnormal genetic inheritances from discrimination. "There are a lot more out there like me, and if I could get them to come forward, I would." Theresa is frustrated by the tendency of insurance lobbyists to depict her situation as isolated and unusual. "They have called me 'just an anecdote' and have said, 'That just involves rare, obscure diseases like Huntington's,'" she recalls. The unwillingness of those with asymptomatic genetic conditions to come forward has hindered advocates' efforts to

show how widespread the potential impact of genetic discrimination is. Many people whose genetic disorder is not apparent
fear they will lose their health insurance or their jobs if they
speak out. But Theresa says that coalitions of nonprofit organizations, representing not only relatively rare diseases like Huntington's but also more common genetic diseases such as diabetes
and sickle cell anemia, have successfully joined in efforts to make
lawmakers aware of the large number of people potentially affected by discrimination as access to genetic information expands. Then, she says, "the legislators can no longer call us rare
and obscure."

Huntington's disease is ultimately fatal, but in 1993 scientists finally located the gene that causes the disease and they are
hopeful that the discovery will offer clues for the development
of therapies. Theresa describes the dilemma of being tested for a
disease for which there is no cure. "I refuse to be tested until
there is legislative protection against discrimination, but even if
the state of Ohio enacted a law, I would have to be psychologically ready to handle bad results before I could be tested." She
pauses before adding, "If I were planning to have children, I
think I would want to know more. I'm not sure I would want
to take the test, but I think I would be much more likely to
do it."

Ironically, even couples who decide to adopt a child have
experienced genetic discrimination during the adoption process.
One thirty-one-year-old woman wrote to the research team of
which Dr. Billings was a member: "After many years of consideration, my husband and I decided not to bear our own children, but rather to adopt children, so as not to take the chance
of passing on the Huntington gene." Because she disclosed this
to the adoption agency, she and her husband were asked to
withdraw their application. She asks, "We understand the right
to choose the *best* fifty couples out of some five hundred appli-
cants per year for placement. Availability of children is incredibly limited. And yet, should I be judged by a disease that I am
only at risk for and that may not develop for some years to

come? Does this make me different than anyone with diabetes or cancer, for example, in their ancestry?"[24]

Obviously, we cannot expect to encourage couples to undergo preconceptual genetic testing in determining whether to have genetic children if these same couples are going to be broadly excluded from consideration as adoptive parents because of the information revealed by the testing. While society must develop strategies to encourage responsible reproductive choices, people who desire a family must not be left without options if the strategies are to succeed.

The potential for genetic discrimination is complicated in the case of some diseases by racial and ethnic factors. For example, sickle cell anemia is found primarily in the black population, and some have suggested that white doctors may intentionally mislead pregnant black women, advising them to abort or avoid future pregnancies for racial rather than genetic reasons. About 150 black children in every 100,000 have sickle cell anemia, but as many as 1 in every 12 has the sickle cell trait. Although those with the trait will not suffer the disease, if they marry someone who also has the trait, and they have four children, their family will (according to statistical averages) add to the black population only one offspring free of sickle cell. Two of their offspring will be carriers, continuing to pass the disease on to future generations, and one will have the disease. Among prior generations, few with sickle cell anemia survived long enough to have children of their own, but today, although the mortality rate remains high in early childhood, treatment allows more blacks with the disease to survive and bear or beget their own children.

One of the fears of treating those with genetic disorders, which allows them to reach the age to reproduce, is that the human population will gradually be weakened. We have successfully defeated Nature's elimination of the diseased and disabled, but the effect has been to increase the potential for passing genetic disorders to future generations. This is true of many genetically linked diseases in all races, but within the black population, the increasing numbers of babies born with sickle cell or the sickle cell trait is a real concern. The distrust between blacks and whites has led some people in the black community to see the threat as coming from doctors and genetic counselors rather than from the disease itself. If there truly were some racial conspiracy to use sickle cell to destroy the black population, the greater danger would be withholding genetic information and forcing couples to conceive children without the knowledge of whether both parents carry the trait rather than making genetic information available so couples could plan their families with the benefit of knowing the health risks they carry. So long as the black community distrusts the motives of the predominantly white medical community, genetic counseling is likely to be viewed as an attempt to reduce the birthrate within the black population.

Genetic diseases and disorders are transmitted within all racial groups. In general hospital populations, approximately 10 percent of all adult admissions and 30 percent of all pediatric admissions are related to genetic conditions.[25] As health costs rise, it is easy to target the elimination of genetic diseases and disabilities as a solution to the financial burdens we face in medicine. The obvious moral challenge is what the "elimination" of genetic disorders should involve. Preconceptual family planning for couples unwilling to parent a genetically disabled child could spare them from facing the moral dilemma of abortion. After conception, most people are morally amenable to the responsible use of prenatal genetic testing, either to terminate certain pregnancies or to prepare appropriately for difficult births.

Once these babies are born, however, the elimination of genetic diseases and disabilities involves the quest for treatments and cures, and that is often a costly process. The public resentment of reproductive choices by parents with known genetic risks at the time of conception is closely tied to the belief that the financial burden of caring for the children who inherit the disability will ultimately be shifted to the public.

The responses from participants in my survey reflect conflicting views. Most people want to retain the freedom to choose whether to have children but do not want to suffer penalties for their choice in the form of lost health insurance or government benefits. Furthermore, they do not want to pay higher insurance premiums or taxes to cover the expenses of caring for the children born with genetic disabilities about which their parents had been forewarned.

As you will remember, a significant percentage of those taking the survey said they were either undecided or that they would not avoid having children even with the knowledge of genetic consequences.[26] When these same participants were asked whether they should be penalized for conceiving a child, in spite of such knowledge, by exclusion from health insurance coverage for the medical expenses of the resulting babies, only 18 percent answered "yes." Twenty-three percent were undecided, but most people, 58 percent, answered "no" to the loss of coverage.[27] Illogically, these same people expressed an unwillingness to pay higher health insurance premiums to cover the costs of the insurance coverage. Only 19 percent said they would pay the higher premiums, 26.5 percent said they were undecided about it, and 52.6 percent said they would not.[28]

A few more of the participants in the survey would deny government benefits to disabled children, but in general the responses were similar to those regarding health insurance coverage. Twenty-six percent answered "yes" when asked whether government benefits should be withheld for babies born even after parents had been told before conception of the genetic outcome, 27 percent were undecided, but 44.5 percent thought the benefits should be paid regardless of the prior genetic information.[29]

In short, the survey results indicate that people want access to genetic information in their family planning and might decide against a conception; however, if they choose to proceed, they expect the same benefits they would otherwise receive and at no additional expense to them through higher insurance premiums or taxes. This sort of thinking makes the development of appropriate strategies impossible.

Cystic fibrosis is another genetic disease that predominates within a certain ethnic group, specifically persons of European ancestry. About one in every twenty-two whites is a carrier of CF, and within this group, about one out of every two thousand live births has the disease. Since 1975 advanced methods of diagnosis and treatment have allowed most of those with CF to live beyond childhood, but special therapies, such as treatment with antibiotics and enzyme preparations at meals, are necessary. Some CF patients have lung transplants, or transplants of both heart and lung, all of which are expensive. Before 1930 most children with CF died in early childhood, and the costs of medical care were of limited duration. Today we have the technology to treat the disease, but not the knowledge to cure it, and the costs of medical care have grown not only as a result of expensive drugs and technologies but by the greater duration of the treatment.

The complex moral issue we are forced to address by incurable but treatable genetic diseases such as sickle cell anemia and cystic fibrosis is whether the shifting of financial responsibility for long-term medical care to others, through health insurance or government disability payments, affects the fundamental right of procreation.

We must be careful not to assume that all genetic disabilities involve extraordinary medical expense or that all individuals who inherit the condition manifest it to the same degree. Bree Walker was particularly angered by the radio talk show host's inaccurate suggestion that ectrodactyly is degenerative or precludes self-sufficiency. Bree says, "The radio talk show host saw our decision as fair fodder for her show, because from her point of view our children are a burden to society in that they may not be able to be gainfully employed because of their hands and feet. She was mistaken because she had not done her research well enough to understand that ectrodactyly is not a degenerative disease. It is pure and simple a shape deformity, and there is no reason our children won't be gainfully employed."[30] Jim and Bree do acknowledge that there will be expenses associated with surgery and special shoes that might be financially difficult for a less affluent family, however.

Lyndall Southern has also thought about the potential medical expenses of her daughters, even though none of them has shown any signs of the cancers to which Lyndall's family has been susceptible. "I do realize, having just had a hospital bill," Lyndall says, "that one time in the hospital can be a lot of money. But I look at my children in comparison to the children of people that I work with, and my children never even meet their deductible in a year. I have seen other people spend a lot of money on their children, not because they have any type of genetic illness, but they are just sickly." She concludes, "You cannot really say that because the chance of inheriting a genetic disease was there that the child is going to be sicker and cost more money in the long run than a child who doesn't have that chance."

Insurance companies see it differently, however. Insurance has functioned traditionally by collecting premiums from all of us and using that money, in turn, to pay claims to a few of us. Whatever the company collects in premiums that it does not have to pay out for claims is profit, but if there are more claims paid than premiums collected, the company loses money. Stated simply, limiting the number of claims allows an insurance company to increase its profit without having to raise the premiums.

With that simple explanation of insurance in mind, consider the impact of the life-prolonging treatments for such genetic diseases as cystic fibrosis and sickle cell anemia. Whereas in the past, claims for babies with these genetic diseases would have been made for only a very few years because of early deaths, today the claims are likely to continue into adulthood. If the parents choose to conceive more children, despite the genetic risks, the insurance company might very well end up paying claims for several children within one family at the same time. Although it is true that in the past, families might also have given birth to more than one child with these genetic diseases, it is unlikely that several of their children would have survived through childhood to make multiple-sibling health care claims against the family's policy.

Since technology has affected their obligation to pay for treatments, insurance companies believe that it is reasonable that they will be allowed to use the knowledge gained by that technology as well. The director of public health policy at the Health Insurance Association of America, Jude Payne, says, "We are not as interested in the technology as our critics would make one think, but we don't think it's fair for someone to get insurance at standard rates when they represent more than standard risk."[31]

Too many Americans forget how insurance works. The more claims the insurance company pays, the higher the premium rates will be. If we determine that it is discriminatory for insurance companies to use genetic information in setting rates for their insured, it almost certainly follows that all of us will make up the difference by paying higher premiums. How insurance companies and people buying coverage use our growing genetic knowledge is more likely to render the existing health insurance system obsolete than are the soaring medical costs that currently have the public's attention. Even modifying the system so that some of these costs are covered by government benefits rather than by private insurance, the fact remains that many parents who do not limit the births of children with serious genetic problems will be financially incapable of paying all the costs of caring for these children. If society frees these parents from the financial worries associated with the births of babies with a genetic condition, has society encouraged the parents to have more children, particularly if they choose to keep trying to conceive a child born without the condition? It is not as simple as saying that people should be left to decide such reproductive matters for themselves, for when society intervenes in even indirect ways, it influences the private choices individuals will make.

As a disability activist and the parent of a son with Down syndrome, Emily Kingsley believes that the emotional investment of the parents more than offsets any financial assistance from public funds. "Nobody goes out and says they are going to have a child to bilk the government for everything they can get. You have a child with a handicap and you make the best of it with the hand you got dealt. If it is tough, and it is difficult, and you get some assistance, I don't think that is such a terrible thing." The fact remains, however, that genetic technology now allows parents to see the cards before they are dealt, and the births of genetically disabled babies need not be a matter of blind chance.

Various opportunities for genetic testing exist. For example, if everyone were routinely tested at birth, preventive therapies could begin before symptoms appeared, and many disabilities could be avoided or lessened. Those with an inherited condition could adjust their diets and activities appropriately.

We could also test people when they apply for marriage licenses. Since few couples voluntarily seek preconceptual testing, a requirement that couples obtain genetic information from each partner at the time they marry would force them to consider this knowledge as part of their family planning. Fifty-three percent of those taking my survey responded favorably to this idea.[32]

Certain institutions have already begun to collect DNA samples. Among these are the Federal Bureau of Investigation, which collects samples from convicted criminals for use in future criminal investigations; the military, which collects DNA samples from service personnel for use in identifying war casualties; and employers who collect samples from consenting employees before assigning them to jobs for which people with certain inherited conditions might be particularly susceptible to occupational illnesses. While these are positive uses, the problem is that the invasion of privacy is so incredible that nothing in our past—not drug testing nor access to credit information nor law enforcement surveillance—even comes close. Whether a person is tested voluntarily or mandatorily, the genetic information that is gathered must be safeguarded. We must decide who should have access to that information. The evidence so far indicates that being labeled with a genetic condition may be more limiting to an individual than the actual disability is.

A young woman with a genetic condition known as Charcot-Marie-Tooth atrophy got a job from an employment recruiter at a company. Her symptoms were unnoticeable, but because she disclosed on her employment application that she has CMT, the company looked up the disease in a medical book and, relying on the textual information rather than her observable condition, decided to withdraw the job offer.[33]

Society must also prepare for the personal impact on individuals who discover or receive confirmation of the inheritance of genetic disorders. Theresa Morelli has learned to live with the possibility of having inherited Huntington's, but she is not prepared to have that possibility confirmed. Lyndall Southern believes it is good to have as much knowledge as possible about her family's genetic susceptibility to cancers, but she intends to withhold the genetic test results from her daughters so that they may each decide for themselves when they are ready to know their genetic inheritance. We cannot force people to face genetic realities without helping them deal with the information through appropriate counseling, education, and emotional support systems.

The genetic legacy each of us inherits includes diseases and disabilities just as it does physical strength and intelligence, and we must allow recognition of all those factors to be considered in the choices we make, whether we are deciding to employ a person or to have a baby. However, we must educate ourselves and recognize that individuals are more important than labels. Like so many new technologies, the new possibilities of genetic foreknowledge demand more from us. Parents must begin to assume more responsibility in the reproductive choices they make, but before we can expect people to be tested for genetic conditions, we must determine how to protect them from ruinous financial and social consequences. It does not seem unreasonable that insurance companies, employers, and other social institutions want to implement genetic factors in their policies and procedures, just as they do such other inherited traits as physical strength and intelligence, but the implementation must recognize variable degrees within each genetic disorder and must encourage responsible individual choices in noncoercive ways.

For example, perhaps Theresa Morelli was motivated to apply for disability insurance by her experience with disabled clients, but her case illustrates the potential for consumers to use genetic information in ways that could bankrupt the insurance system. Certainly Theresa's potential to be disabled by Huntington's in midlife is greater than the potential within the general population upon which premium rates are based. Consumers with knowledge of genetic inheritances that increase their chances of early death or disability might load up on life and disability insurance before symptoms of their diseases appear, putting the insurance companies that lack that genetic information in a disadvantaged position. Couples at high risk of transmitting a genetic disorder to their children might consider a second or third pregnancy in an effort to conceive a child without the genetic disorder because of having health insurance to pay the costs. Unless insurance companies are allowed to cap the amount of claims in some way, such a couple's decision could impact many other families, whose premiums are used to cover the costs for that one family's disproportionate claims. The examples of coercion and discrimination collected by Dr. Billings and others make it clear that present social policies encourage people to avoid genetic testing or keep results secret to protect themselves from financial and social penalties. But simply telling employers and insurance companies that they cannot use genetic information is too harsh a countermeasure.

Existing laws against discrimination in other areas have recognized that some differences may be taken into account. For example, the Americans with Disabilities Act permits pre-employment medical examinations and inquiries if they are job-related and necessary. Laws concerning gender discrimination allow strength requirements for certain jobs, even though the requirements disproportionately preclude women, if the strength standards are necessary in the performance of those particular jobs. Employers have been able to implement these laws and courts have been able to interpret them, although subjective judgments must be made among individuals with varying differences. We must learn to recognize the same sort of differences in ability among people with inherited disorders, and if legislation is necessary, it can benefit from the lessons learned in drafting and applying other civil rights laws.

Those of us with no family history of genetic diseases like Huntington's or sickle cell anemia may not have recognized genetic discrimination or may have criticized reproductive choices by genetically disabled parents because we have never experienced living with such a condition. Yet nearly all of us have family members with medical conditions we hope will not be passed to the next generation. Consider the warning of genetic counselor Cam Knutson: "Our choices in the future will get even harder, I think—when we get to the point where we can identify genes that cause heart attacks or diabetes, as two examples." Think of the medical problems that appear in your own family history and consider how it would affect your thinking if preconceptual or prenatal testing could identify the transmission of that problem to your own children. Is this technology going to be used appropriately by parents, or will we expand our intolerance for "imperfect" babies? As Dr. Billings says, "For genetic information to be used in an intelligent way, there has to be better public information about genetics," and he emphasizes that people must understand that "genetic technology cannot guarantee you a happy family."

There is certainly the risk that as the technology to control genetic inheritence increases, a corresponding parental obsession to have the "perfect" baby will occur. Man already thinks he can improve on nature through genetic engineering of plants and animals. For example, chicken genes have been added to potatoes in an effort to increase disease resistance, and DNA from an arctic flounder has been added to fruits and vegetables in efforts to protect these plants against freezing! Some may consider these developments creative solutions to human problems, but others fear that such tampering with nature may cause unforeseen and irreversible calamities. "What we must understand is that the larger pattern [of nature] is not of our making and we must accept that we depend upon it," says Wes Jackson, director of the Land Institute in Salina, Kansas. "Before biotechnology goes any further, we need to know why biotechnologists suppose they can avoid producing the negative impacts comparable to those created by chemical and nuclear technologies."[34]

It is difficult, however, to resist pursuing gene therapy research that promises treatments for medical disorders that are now incurable. This is how the process works. Each of our genes carries instructions for a single protein, and flawed instructions result in genetic disorders. Gene therapy attempts to correct these instructions by introducing a therapeutic gene that will carry the correct code for the protein. The process requires knowing the location of the flawed gene, and the mapping of all human genes which is under way in the Human Genome Project is a necessary part of the research. Diseased cells are removed, manipulated, grown in the laboratory, and returned to the body within viruses that have had their own genetic information replaced with the therapeutic gene. In this way, the altered virus delivers and deposits the therapeutic gene into the host cell in the same way viruses deliver and deposit infectious disease genes. Approximately four thousand disorders are caused by genetic defects, so the potential benefits of successful gene therapy are enormous.

The potential risks deserve equal attention, however, and these risks are compounded when the gene therapy alters the sperm or the egg, or alters the cells that are just beginning to divide after fertilization, so-called germ-line gene therapy. This form of gene therapy permanently alters the genetic makeup of the family; traits that have been passed down for generations will never reappear in that family line. Dr. Billings says, "I am concerned about a whole series of issues—about what we choose to change and what we don't, about what we do with the mistakes and the unexpected results of this kind of alteration—all sorts of things. I can see treating individuals, but this involves treating potential individuals yet unborn."

We can look to genetic experiments that have been done to animals for examples of how gene therapy can go awry.[35] Experiments at the Agricultural Research Center in Beltsville, Maryland, that were intended to produce a hog that gained weight faster with leaner meat involved splicing a human gene into the hog's own DNA, but the unexpected results included arthritis, crossed eyes, renal disease, and an enlarged heart. Perhaps human experiments will not be undertaken until scientists can control results more closely, but it is unrealistic to presume that there will be no mistakes if the technology is applied to humans. Even if the alarmist claims that the therapy may be applied to create a "master race" or "perfect" babies are exaggerated, very real and practical problems remain to be solved before rushing into unlimited use of the technology.

In only a few short years we have expanded beyond using genetic information to predict eye and hair color based upon observable traits of the parents to predicting unobservable genetic traits through preconceptual testing, and confirming the actual inheritance prior to birth through prenatal testing. Now we are on the brink of being able to manipulate that inheritance. Not only has genetic knowledge taken away the guesswork, it is also beginning to allow us to reshuffle the cards even after they have been dealt. Are young couples wise enough to use all this knowledge in responsible ways as they bear and beget children, or does our expanding access to genetic information necessitate a partial relinquishment of the fundamental rights of procreation that we privately exercised before we had this knowledge?

Of course, many pregnancies are unplanned, even careless, and without draconian measures to inhibit the ability to conceive naturally, regulations can do little to encourage responsible genetic choices in those cases of unplanned conceptions. In planned pregnancies, people generally give thoughtful consideration to genetic consequences—to the extent those consequences are understood by the couples. It seems, therefore, that the best strategy for implementing our expanding genetic knowledge into the reproductive choices of individuals is through education and not regulation. People make poor choices more from ignorance than from callous indifference to the consequences for their family, the resulting child, or society at large.

Genetic counselor Cam Knutson rejects the idea of regulation and reminds us how the public responded to information regarding the consumption of alcohol. "Everybody is aware now that drinking during pregnancy can cause problems. Something similar could be done to teach people that if their family medical history contains certain things, they should think about seeing a genetic counselor. There is too much room for abuse when something becomes mandatory."

Society cannot ignore the infinite possibilities available through expanding genetic knowledge. However, our quest for healthier offspring must not diminish our appreciation for those who are born different. We cannot safely absorb the new genetic discoveries without preserving our traditional American respect for privacy and our democratic recognition of the inherent value each individual possesses. As Bree Walker warns, "Physical perfection is a very empty goal."

If you could have a test to screen for genetic diseases you carry which might be transmitted to your child, would you take the test?

Do you think you should be required to take such a test, for instance, in connection with the blood test for a marriage license?

If the genetic screening showed that you and your partner had a high probability of conceiving an abnormal child, would you choose not to have children?

If the genetic screening showed that you and your partner had a high probability of conceiving an abnormal child, should the government prohibit you from having children?

Would you (or your partner) become pregnant when there was a likelihood of your having an abnormal child, with the intention of testing the fetus for abnormality and aborting any abnormal child?

If the genetic screen showed that you and your partner were certain to have an abnormal child, would you choose not to have children?

If the genetic screen showed that you and your partner were certain to have an abnormal child, should the government prohibit you from having children?

If you conceived a child knowing of the high likelihood or certainty of abnormality, should you be excluded from receiving health insurance proceeds for the medical treatment of the child relating to the abnormal condition?

Are you willing to pay higher health insurance premiums to cover the cost of extending health insurance coverage to pay the medical expenses of babies born with genetic defects, even when the parents knew of the high likelihood or certainty such defects would occur?

If you conceived a child knowing of the high likelihood or certainty of abnormality, should you be excluded from receiving government benefits for the child relating to the abnormality?

Are you willing to pay higher taxes to cover costs of government benefits for babies born with genetic defects, even when the parents knew of the high likelihood or certainty such defects would occur?

CHAPTER 9

THE STORY OF SARA COLLINS

The life of Sara Collins will never be quite the same. Although the felony charges of delivering a controlled substance to her newborn daughter were dismissed, the notoriety she acquired during the criminal proceedings refuses to evaporate. "When I enrolled my four-year-old daughter in school the other day, the women at her school said to me, 'You look so familiar.' I just told them that my daughter and I ride our bikes in the neighborhood a lot," Sara says, trying to protect her daughter from the hurt of reopening public discussion of her case.[1]

In 1990, when Sara was charged, many other new mothers all across America were facing criminal prosecutions for their prenatal substance abuse, but Sara received particular media attention. While most of these defendants were black, and many were unemployed, Sara was a thirty-six-year-old white attorney who had clerked for several circuit judges in the very county where she was facing prosecution. Sara believes she was chosen by the prosecutor because she was atypical. "He picked one black and one white. He wasn't charging everybody. I have been told of several women during that time that he didn't prosecute. So I am bitter, yes," Sara admits.

Prosecutor Tony Tague denies that Sara was targeted and claims that the circumstances leading to her indictment were simply a matter of timing. "The prosecutor's office had explored what was being done about the problem of pregnant addicts, both in civil court proceedings and by the medical community as a whole, and we found that everyone was ignoring the problem. We were having a difficult time getting people to focus on the problem and do anything about it," prosecutor Tague remembers. "We decided that at least criminal prosecution was a proactive step in trying to address the problem."[2] He claims that Sara's case just happened to be one of those he was evaluating at the time his office decided to proceed with prosecutions.

It is not a crime to be an addict.[3] What is criminal is conduct, such as possession, use, or delivery of illegal drugs. Even when Sara revealed her cocaine addiction to her obstetrician during the fourth month of her pregnancy, she could not have been prosecuted merely for being addicted. Unfortunately, Sara did not stop using, and her doctor's records were subpoenaed for her prosecution. "Frankly," Sara says, "I think my doctor betrayed me." Sara was charged with delivering a controlled substance to her newborn daughter through the umbilical cord during the brief moments after birth but before the cord was severed. Evidence of that delivery came from a urine specimen taken by catheter from Sara just prior to the baby's birth and from the positive test results for cocaine metabolite obtained from her baby.

The growing number of infants born with cocaine and other harmful drugs in their tiny bodies led the Muskegon County Prosecutor's Office to initiate a program intended to curb that trend. As drug-related crimes increased in his own small community, Tague feared that his county might follow the emerging pattern of the cities. He studied statistics from Washington, D.C., where one hospital reported that births to drug-addicted mothers had gone from 3 percent to 18 percent in less than a decade, and another hospital reported that while 30 percent of its new mothers had admitted to drug use during pregnancy, actual numbers might be as high as 50 percent. He read figures from New York City that showed births to mothers who abuse drugs were up by 3,000 percent in a decade. He worried about a report to the U.S. Department of Health and Human Services that by the turn of the century, about 4 million American citizens will have experienced in utero exposure to controlled substances, and he heard from special-education teachers that the delayed developmental, neurological, and emotional effects of prenatal exposure were already appearing among their students. In a public statement prosecutor Tague released during the legal proceedings against Sara, he concluded: "Our society is facing a national emergency and health care crisis. It is the firm belief of my office that we must take immediate action."

Although the appeals court eventually rejected the legal theory upon which Sara's prosecution was based, Tague says, "I still feel very strongly that a multidisciplinary approach should be taken and that prosecution should be available as a last resort. However, I also believe the other components—the education, the treatment, and the medical availability to the women—are a very important part of any comprehensive program."

Tague admits that he did not have universal support from the legal community regarding his decision to use the criminal courts against pregnant women. "I think what we were attempting to do was enforce a zero-tolerance policy for any type of use of controlled substances, as opposed to trying to be pregnancy police." But, he acknowledges, "I had many lawyers who voiced strong support for what I was doing, and I had many lawyers who voiced strong dissent."

Some of those who disagreed with the tactics of the prosecutor's office expressed their disapproval by assisting in Sara's defense. Sara relates what her lawyer told her when he agreed to defend her: "He took the case because he really believed that what was happening was wrong." Other lawyers assisted by contributing to the defense fund established to pay her legal expenses. "I tried to call each contributor to say thank you," Sara says. "One attorney made it perfectly clear that what he had given wasn't for me but because he believed Tony Tague was abusing his power."

The Michigan Appellate Court agreed that prosecutor

Tague had gone beyond the intent of the law. "We are not persuaded that a pregnant woman's use of cocaine, which might result in the postpartum transfer of cocaine metabolites through the umbilical cord to her infant, is the type of conduct that the Legislature intended to be prosecuted under the *delivery*-of-cocaine statute, thereby subjecting the woman to the possibility of up to twenty years in prison and a fine of $25,000. This, in our opinion," said the court, "would not be a reasonable construction of the statute."[4]

Tague does not regret his decision to prosecute Sara. "The case seemed to cause the entire political system to wake up to the problem of pregnant addicts, both the women and their children." What does concern Tague, rather, is the way the problem has slipped out of public focus since then. "One of the very important things we accomplished in connection with the two cases we prosecuted was ensuring that there was a treatment center in my county for these women. When state funding was cut, it meant the end to our local program," he laments. He does not criticize the appellate court for the legal outcome of the two cases, but he does criticize legislators for failing to confront the problem. "It is pretty unfortunate that a lot of our politicians are so short-sighted that they don't see that addressing the issue up front is going to cost the government and society as a whole much less financially."

Sara Collins is more interested in the enormous personal toll Tague's decision has taken on her. She lost her job with a firm during the prosecution of her case, and she has been unable to find a new position with a firm since. She avoided an attempt by the state bar to take away her license to practice law, but she has only been able to continue by practicing alone. "I do have my own caseload right now," she explains. "But . . . he really impacted my life, very much."

Her words are guarded, like those of someone who has lost confidence in knowing whom to trust. But her judgments about Tony Tague are certain and unforgiving: "I would like to walk my daughter into his office and say, 'I hope you are happy, because she doesn't have the life she would have had if you would not have pegged me as one of your victims to make new law.' "

He, on the other hand, thinks her blame is misplaced. "The destruction of her family is not because of any action of third parties. It is because of her decision to use cocaine," he says.

Since the criminal charges against Sara were dismissed, no other addicted women in Muskegon County have been criminally charged following the birth of babies who test positive for drugs. Today, pregnant women in prosecutor Tague's county who need a treatment center to help them battle their addictions must travel over two hundred miles to reach the closest center offering them treatment.

Sara refuses to talk about her own substance abuse, admitting only that she had a problem which she says she has since put behind her. Although Tony Tague believes it was the threat of criminal prosecution that forced Sara to enter treatment, she has a simpler explanation for what empowered her to overcome her addiction. "It was when juvenile court took my child away," she believes. "They told me to straighten out my life if I wanted to raise my own daughter, and that's what did it for me. Juvenile court already had all the legal power that was needed. The criminal case was brought for the benefit of the prosecutor's career, not for my daughter or me."

CHAPTER 10

SHOULD WE CRIMINALIZE PARENTAL CONDUCT?

Frustration with our inability to prevent the abuse and neglect of babies has tempted us to solve the problem in the manner of the Queen of Hearts in *Alice in Wonderland*. Like the Queen, who settled all difficulties, great or small, by shouting, "Off with their heads!" many Americans have begun declaring, "Punish the mothers!" We urge prosecutors to bring criminal charges against mothers of babies born addicted to cocaine or other illegal substances and want to prohibit these mothers from having more children.

In fact, when my survey asked whether mandatory birth control is ever appropriate as a part of a woman's criminal sentence, 81 percent answered "yes."[1] Actually, the behavior most often selected as justification for a court-ordered limitation on procreation was the woman's own abuse of her existing children, followed closely by neglect or abandonment of her children; substance abuse was participants' third choice among the five options.[2] Nearly all those surveyed said they would hold the mother and the father equally accountable for abusive behavior.[3] Interestingly, although the participants selected abuse of existing children by the mother above all other choices as an appropriate situation for imposing mandatory birth control in the sentence, they selected the failure to report abuse by someone else least often. In other words, while 85 percent approved of imposing mandatory birth control on the mother who abused her children, only 35 percent thought it would be appropriate in a case where she stood by and watched the children's father abuse them without reporting him for the abuse.[4]

On September 13, 1990, a twenty-seven-year-old California woman, pregnant with her fifth child, was arrested and accused of abusing two of her daughters, ages four and six, by beating them with an extension cord and the buckle end of a belt. When Darlene Johnson came before Judge Howard Broadman for sentencing on January 2, 1991, she had been in custody since her arrest and was seven months pregnant. Although she had a history of prior arrests for various thefts, this unmarried mother had never before been accused of abusing any of her five children, born of three different fathers. She pleaded guilty to the charges of abuse filed against her, saying she had become angry and spanked her daughters with a belt after catching them smoking cigarettes in a closet.

At her sentencing hearing, she and the judge had the following exchange.

Judge Broadman:	*Are you on welfare?*
Ms. Johnson:	*I was [before entering jail].*
Judge Broadman:	*Okay. And you will be again, right?*
Ms. Johnson:	*Yeah.*
Judge Broadman:	*Do you want to get pregnant again?*
Ms. Johnson:	*No.*
Judge Broadman:	*Okay. As a condition of your probation, you know, this new thing that's going to be available next month, you probably haven't heard about it. It's called Norplant.*
Ms. Johnson:	*No.*
Judge Broadman:	*It's a thing that gets put into your arm and it lasts for five years. You can't get—it's like birth control pills, except you don't have to take them everyday. If I order that as a condition of your probation, then maybe MediCal or Medicare will pay for that.*

Ms. Johnson raised only one question. She asked, "Is it harmful to the body?" Judge Broadman answered, "Well, it's like a birth-control pill. It's FDA-approved. It's not experimental. What do you think about that?" Ms. Johnson replied, "Okay."

Because of the nature of her crime and her prior criminal record, Ms. Johnson could have been sentenced to a maximum of seven years in state prison. Instead, Judge Broadman crafted a probation that not only included the provision for implanting Norplant but also required her to attend parenting classes and prohibited her use of cigarettes and alcohol for the remainder of her pregnancy. She was allowed to select her own physician for the Norplant procedure.

Within a few days, Ms. Johnson had a change of heart. Her court-appointed lawyer filed a motion to modify the judge's order, claiming that Ms. Johnson had been coerced into giving consent and no longer wanted to use Norplant as a condition of her probation. The case gained the attention of the media, and all across America newspapers ran editorials commenting on the Norplant as a part of the sentence. The originator of implant contraception and the director of the international team of scientists that developed Norplant, Dr. Sheldon J. Segal, joined in the debate with a letter that appeared in *The New York Times* on the Sunday after the sentencing hearing. "Hold everything!" he wrote. "I am totally and unalterably opposed to the use of Norplant for any coercive or involuntary purpose. It was developed to improve reproductive freedom, not to restrict it. My colleagues and I worked on this innovation for decades because we respect human dignity and believe that women should be able to have the number of children they want, when they want to have them. Not just educated and well-to-do women, but all women. Those who suggest using Norplant for coercive sterilization or birth control will find me leading the opposition."

Much of the public debate over defendants agreeing to use contraception during probation questions whether anyone can freely consent when the alternative is imprisonment. In other words, no matter how thorough the judge's explanation or how kindly his manner, are circumstances themselves coercive?[5] The reality in the Johnson case, and in most other cases unless the prison system allows conjugal visits, is that incarceration will preclude sexual intercourse, and thus pregnancy. The celibacy mandated by imprisonment prohibits conception even more completely than a probation with mandatory birth control. Unlike most prisoners, probationers are free to engage in sexual intercourse, and even court-ordered contraceptives sometimes fail. Both imprisonment and probationary birth control interfere with a defendant's right of procreation, but logic suggests that for most defendants counseling and rehabilitation outside prison walls would be preferable to the absolute loss of opportunity for coital relationships. Criticism on the basis of interference with procreation alone makes little sense.

Obviously, if the judge threatens an unusually harsh prison sentence to compel the woman to choose contraception, coercion exists. Likewise, orders that fail to allow the defendant's physician to determine whether the procedure is medically appropriate go too far. In Darlene Johnson's case, however, her crime of abusing young children, combined with the increasingly serious nature of her prior convictions and the fact that she had already served a prison term, supported imprisonment as an appropriate sentence, and provision was made in the order for medical consultation.

Before Ms. Johnson's appeal could be heard, she violated other terms of her probation and was sent to prison. The higher court dismissed her appeal, since her imprisonment made the issue of whether she should be compelled to comply with the Norplant provision during probation moot. However, in a similar case challenging Judge Broadman's inclusion of contraception as a condition of probation, the appellate court reversed the portion of his order requiring the defendant to use contraception.[6]

Although Darlene Johnson admitted that she had punished

her daughters too severely, another California mother refused to accept the state's judgment that her actions endangered her children, even though the consequences of her actions were far more apparent and long-lasting. When she was convicted of child endangerment, Ruby Pointer was given five years' probation that included one year in county jail and a prohibition against conceiving any children for the balance of her probation.

Ms. Pointer had a history of ignoring the advice of others about her ongoing neglect of her two sons, ages two and four at the time of her trial. Her doctor had pleaded with her to discontinue the strict macrobiotic diet she imposed on the boys, and the father of her older son had turned to the county Children's Protective Services for help. Her refusal to modify her own diet left her younger son, whom she was breast-feeding, severely malnourished. When he was hospitalized as a result, she defied the doctors and not only sneaked macrobiotic food to him but also breast-fed him, despite warnings of the danger from the high sodium levels in her milk. After her son was placed in a foster home for his own protection, she abducted him and resumed the dangerous diet. By the time their mother was prosecuted, one son was seriously underdeveloped and the other had suffered severe growth retardation and permanent neurological damage.

It was apparent to all those involved with the case that this mother was a danger to her children. The baby had been rescued only because a doctor had called the police when she refused to hospitalize the emaciated, semicomatose, dying infant. In addition, a psychologist at the trial testified that "any newborn child to Ms. Pointer would encounter similar risks as those of her previous children."

Faced with such tragic evidence of Ruby Pointer's inability to safely parent, the judge expressed his feelings at her sentencing hearing: "I have never considered imposing as a condition of probation the requirement that someone not conceive during the period of probation, and I have never considered requiring as a condition of probation that a defendant not have custody of her children without approval by the sentencing court following a hearing, but that's certainly what I intend to do in this case. This is an extremely serious case." Although she was free to choose her own birth control method, Ruby Pointer appealed the prohibition as an unconstitutional restriction of her fundamental rights of privacy and procreation.

Many of us would applaud the commonsense approach of the judge in ordering that she avoid having another child until she completed the probationary counseling intended to reform her criminal behavior. The California Appellate Court in the Pointer case concluded, as the appellate court had in overturning Judge Broadman's orders, that the prohibition against conception was intended to protect her unborn child rather than to assist her rehabilitation, and that it thus violated her fundamental rights. Instead of prohibiting conception altogether, the appellate court reasoned, pregnancy testing could have been required, with mandatory prenatal and neonatal treatment should she become pregnant, and since a less restrictive alternative to the one ordered by the court was available, the appellate court reversed that portion of her sentence.[7]

Remember that neither of these decisions called for sterilization or even mandatory contraception of such long duration that the woman's childbearing years were likely to expire during the probation. Furthermore, both mothers were convicted of criminal acts directly connected with parenting. As precious as our fundamental rights of procreation and privacy are, there would seem to be room enough under existing legal precedent to allow judges to implement probationary birth control during counseling intended to reform and rehabilitate abusive parents.

Certainly other rights under the constitution are limited by probationary conditions, such as restricting travel or with whom the probationer can associate. Shouldn't judges also be able to temporarily limit a woman's right to conceive a child when she is before the court for her criminal behavior toward children she already has? In Judge Broadman's words, "The birth of additional children until after she has successfully completed the court-ordered mental health counseling and parenting classes dooms both her and any subsequent children to repeat this vicious cycle. This is unconscionable and something the law should not countenance."[8]

In the Pointer case, however, the California appellate court reversed the trial judge's probationary requirement of birth control, even though they agreed that "the record fully supports the trial court's belief that [Ruby Pointer] would continue to adhere to a strict macrobiotic diet despite the dangers it presents to any children she might conceive." The appellate court suggested instead periodic pregnancy testing, and in the event of pregnancy, intensive prenatal and neonatal treatment monitored by her probation officer and a physician, with removal of the baby from her custody and its placement in foster care following birth. Aren't the measures they propose at least as intrusive as requiring her temporarily to avoid becoming pregnant while she receives counseling intended to reform her criminal behavior? Legal precedents that limit the infringement of fundamental rights do not require the suspension of common sense.

The danger is, of course, that if we begin to weaken the protections surrounding the fundamental right to procreate, even more reasons for encroachment may be found. For example, although poverty is not a crime, people frequently criticize women for having children they cannot afford, and the most common reason given by survey participants for limiting the right to conceive was financial considerations. If the fundamental right of procreation is not strictly protected, judges might begin to consider noncriminal factors, such as financial ability, in deciding whether to order birth control. Darlene Johnson's lawyer accused Judge Broadman of doing exactly that, and although the judge denied that her economic status had any influence on his ruling, he certainly inquired about her receipt of welfare before suggesting Norplant as a part of her probation.

In an appearance on the television program *60 Minutes,*

Darlene Johnson told interviewer Ed Bradley that while she did not want to have more children right now, she did want more in the future. When he asked whether she could take care of more than she already had, she replied, "I feel the Lord will provide a way for me." At that time, only one of her children lived with her. Three lived in foster homes, and one lived with her mother. If she saw this as divine Providence, then the vehicle He used to care for her and her children was the charity of others, and especially the financial provision made possible by taxpayer dollars.

Financial irresponsibility was not her crime, however, and without the act of child abuse for which she had been convicted, the court would have had no legal basis for limiting her right to have another baby, whether or not she could afford the children she already had. In answering the intimation of economic bias by Johnson's lawyer, Judge Broadman said, "I can say without equivocation that [in] an appropriate case on similar facts it would make no difference whether the defendant was rich or poor. The abused and neglected children of the world are always poor. The economic status of the parents is irrelevant." Such disregard of wealth may be possible in Judge Broadman's courtroom, but in other courtrooms across the nation justice has not always been so blind to economic factors. Whether social welfare reforms are needed to discourage financial irresponsibility on the part of parents, the criminal courts are certainly not the proper arena in which to implement such reforms. That fact should not foreclose, however, a judge's ability to include temporary birth control with the defendant's consent in certain circumstances, and even without the defendant's agreement in extraordinary cases, as an aid to rehabilitation.

And it is already being done. Judge Broadman believes the Darlene Johnson case received media attention not because birth control was included in the probation order but rather because Norplant was a hot news item at the time. "As to the publicity," he said, "all I can say is that I have made similar rulings without Norplant and have received no publicity." One female judge who was interviewed during the furor over the Johnson case commented that women defendants sometimes have drug habits that impair their ability to use contraceptives. "Many defendants would like not to have more children but can't seem to implement traditional birth control. They would welcome Norplant," the judge observed.[9]

It is noteworthy that Darlene Johnson's abuse of her existing children justified ordering birth control as a part of her sentence to more survey participants than did any other wrong behavior.[10] Ruby Pointer's macrobiotic diet was more life-threatening to her children, but participants in my survey did not regard practicing a harmful lifestyle as critically.[11]

Ordering the temporary use of birth control to facilitate rehabilitation is not the same thing as using it as a form of punishment. In Tennessee, a twenty-six-year-old woman was convicted, along with her husband, of molesting her two sons, and they were each sentenced to ten years in prison. One week after her sentencing, Barbara Gross gave birth to the couple's fifth child, and although the state had begun proceedings to acquire permanent custody of all five children, the judge was troubled by the prospect of sexual abuse of any future children the couple might have. Court documents revealed that the woman herself had come from an incestuous family. "It's abundantly clear to me," criminal court judge Lynn Brown said, "that if she has any more children, it is very likely that they would be victimized."

In an effort to avoid that possibility, Judge Brown urged Mrs. Gross to have a tubal ligation, and it appeared that the sterilization was intended as a condition of probation. Although she wanted to avoid jail, she was concerned about having the tubal ligation and chose not to have it done. Her probation was not revoked, and Judge Brown told her attorney that sterilization was never intended as a condition of probation. Rather, the judge said, he was only expressing his opinion that the procedure would be best for her and her family.[12] Although the public defender appointed to represent Mrs. Gross accepted the explanation Judge Brown gave, many others wondered whether she might have been coerced into having the tubal ligation without the intervening public criticism of the judge's remarks.

Some of that criticism arose because Judge Brown had directed his comments to Mrs. Gross rather than to her husband; however, both men and women have faced the choice of relinquishing their ability to have children in order to avoid imprisonment. The 1982 Michigan conviction of Upjohn heir Roger Gauntlett for the sexual assault of his fourteen-year-old stepdaughter required him to take the drug Depo-Provera. The drug, which is used for birth control in women, reduces the sex drive when administered to men. The case was particularly ironic because Upjohn manufactures the drug Gauntlett was ordered to take. In South Carolina the following year, a judge directed three men convicted of raping a young woman to choose between thirty years in jail and surgical castration. Appellate courts in both states later ruled castration to be cruel and unusual punishment, and thus unconstitutional. Periodically, however, headlines will report on some other defendant who has been asked, or who himself volunteers, to submit to castration in lieu of going to prison. In California recently, the state legislature even passed the nation's first law allowing judges to order repeat sex offenders to undergo chemical castration. A paroled prisoner in Texas who had been convicted of sexually abusing young boys made headlines for several days by asking to be castrated. At the time of his 1996 parole, Larry Don McQuay claimed he feared he would resume the abuse unless he was castrated. Although the state refused to comply with his request (stating constitutional prohibitions), officials assisted him in arranging for the procedure to be done voluntarily at no expense to him.[13]

In a poll of its readers published in 1992, *Family Circle* magazine reported that 64 percent of those responding would approve of a court-ordered vasectomy for a male child abuser. Judge Broadman commented in the Darlene Johnson case that although no implant contraceptive is yet available for men, if one were, he would not hesitate to use it in an appropriate case. Most temporary birth control exists for women rather than for men, but as technology develops temporary options for men, courts may begin to use it in criminal sentencing in cases for which permanent sterilization would be "cruel and unusual."

Any such use, as with women defendants, must be strictly scrutinized for appropriateness within a complete rehabilitation plan designed to reform criminal behavior. Restricting a rapist's ability to impregnate his victim does not reform his violent behavior. A vasectomy does not correct the psychological imbalance of a child molester. Permanently taking away a criminal's right to bear and beget a child is cruel and unusual punishment under our Constitution and by itself does little or nothing to reform the criminal behavior. Temporarily taking that right away must be regarded with equal suspicion.

Criminal courts' interference with defendants' rights to conceive involve complicated moral and legal issues, but after conception the role of criminal prosecutions becomes even more complex. More and more people are asking whether a woman who has decided to carry a fetus to term should be legally responsible for actions that she knows or should know will measurably damage the resulting baby. Obviously, criminal punishment would be directed toward women alone, since only they can be pregnant. Even if society is unwilling to prosecute women, should laws be passed to regulate behavior that we now know may be harmful? Or, if we believe the courts are not the proper places to reform harmful conduct, what can society do to protect the babies from harmful prenatal behavior by their mothers?

Pamela Rae Stewart Monson had given birth to two other children, but in the later part of her pregnancy with her third child, she was told by a physician that she suffered from placenta previa, in which the placenta may separate from the uterine wall and cause death to the fetus unless the mother gets immediate medical attention. The doctor told her not to take illegal drugs, to stay off her feet, and to avoid sexual intercourse for the remainder of the pregnancy. She was also warned to seek medical treatment promptly if she began to hemorrhage. On November 23, 1985, she noticed a little blood at about seven-thirty in the morning, but she said nothing to her husband, and they consumed some amphetamines and had intercourse. Soon after, the bleeding increased. Uterine contractions began by early afternoon, but it was evening before she told anyone about the vaginal bleeding. Her son, Thomas Travis Edward Monson, was born with massive brain damage that night, and he died on January 1, 1986.

In what is generally regarded as one of the first American cases in which a woman was criminally charged for her conduct during a pregnancy,[14] Pamela was charged with a misdemeanor, punishable by up to a year in jail and a $2,000 fine, when the county Child Protection Service Division reported to police that the baby was born with traces of amphetamines and marijuana in his blood. The 1926 law under which she was charged was generally used on behalf of pregnant women seeking support payments from fathers who had deserted them. In her case, prosecutors urged that Pamela's willful omission to follow medical advice and to seek treatment when she noticed bleeding violated the provision in the law criminalizing the willful omission, without lawful excuse, to furnish necessary medical attendance for a child.

Pamela Rae Stewart served six days in jail before making bail. Although the criminal charges against her were eventually dropped, her case is regularly cited as the beginning of an active period of prosecutions of women nationwide for various prenatal conduct. Lacking laws that hold a woman directly accountable for conduct harmful to the fetus she carries, prosecutors have relied upon a variety of criminal laws intended for other purposes, such as laws punishing child abuse, child neglect, child endangerment, delivery of drugs to a minor, assault with a deadly weapon, and manslaughter. To avoid the legal question of whether a fetus is a person entitled to legal protection, prosecutors often describe the criminal conduct as having occurred immediately after the baby was born, before the umbilical cord was cut. Most of the prosecutions involve the mothers' use of illegal drugs, particularly cocaine.

If what disturbs us is the damage to the baby caused by the mother's behavior during pregnancy, shouldn't we be equally disturbed by all harmful behaviors? Yet we know that smoking cigarettes during pregnancy increases the risk of miscarriage, premature birth, stillbirth, sudden infant death syndrome, infant mortality, and low birth weight. In addition, pregnant smokers are 50 percent more likely to deliver retarded babies,[15] and their babies suffer reduced respiratory function that leads to adult respiratory disease.[16] Even with such damning evidence against smoking during pregnancy, we have not begun to imprison the nearly one in every five pregnant women in America who smoke during their pregnancies. A state statistician in North Carolina examined 300,000 birth certificates in his state for a period from 1988 to 1990, and he found not only that the one-in-five national ratio of smoking mothers was representative of the women in his state, but also that the women who smoked were 46 percent more likely to have a baby who died before the age of one year.[17] If our concern were based solely upon the measurable harm to babies that the behavior causes, exposure to tobacco smoke by their mothers puts far more babies at risk than the estimated 4.5 percent of births in which the baby is exposed to cocaine.[18] If we were to include the effects of secondhand smoke upon pregnant women married to men who are heavy smokers, the fetal exposure rate would be even greater, yet fathers are rarely mentioned in the campaigns to stop smoking during pregnancy. Newborns of mothers who smoke are not labeled "tobacco babies," despite the presence of medical conditions traceable to their mothers' smoking. Contrast the 75 percent of survey participants willing to punish a mother for using illegal drugs during pregnancy with the 36 percent willing to punish mothers who smoke.[19]

That society condones one form of harmful behavior is not to suggest that we should overlook all other harmful conduct by pregnant women. It should, however, serve as a reality check—a reminder that our attitudes need to reflect consistency, both as to the understanding we extend to women battling addiction during pregnancy and as to the level of responsibility we demand from them. If we have comforted a friend, or a relative, or even ourselves for the loss of a baby whose life may have been complicated by a smoking mother, perhaps we should find a similar level of sympathy for women who pass other addictive substances to their babies. If we cannot imagine punishing a smoking mother for the harm she has done, perhaps we should question whether punishment is appropriate for the mother who uses cocaine. On the other hand, if we have urged increased accountability from pregnant women addicted to illegal drugs for the harm their substance abuse does to their fetuses, perhaps we should consider harsher social attitudes toward all harmful conduct, basing maternal responsibility upon the consequences of the conduct rather than the legality of the substance.

Participants in my survey reflect society's inconsistency on the issue of what maternal behaviors are excuseable. For example, participants were most willing to punish women for use of illegal drugs and alcohol but least willing to punish them for failing to eat a well-balanced diet or get adequate rest during their pregnancies; they were more willing to punish a woman for refusing medical treatment for herself which would have helped the fetus than for failing to obtain prenatal care, and they demanded more punishment for a woman who damages her fetus in an unsuccessful attempt to self-abort than for women who continue throughout their pregnancies to do things that expose their fetuses to known health risks, such as smoking, drinking coffee, and working in an unsafe environment.[20]

In Seattle, a woman in her ninth month of pregnancy decided that joining her friend for a drink to celebrate the approaching birth date would be a relaxing treat. She had not counted on the criticism of a stranger spoiling the occasion. When she ordered a daiquiri, her young waitress felt morally obligated to comment on the risks of drinking alcohol during

pregnancy. Instead of returning with the mixed drink, the waitress and a second waiter brought to the woman's table a bottle
of rum and showed her the warning printed on the label.
Angered by their judgmental intrusion, the woman complained
to the restaurant manager, and both the waitress and waiter
were later fired. Ironically, if her pregnancy had been in an earlier stage, and therefore less apparent to the waitress, the potential risk to the fetus would have been greater than the danger
posed when fetal development was nearly complete. The incident incited a national debate over whether the waitress had
exhibited appropriate concern or had sought to impose her own
viewpoint on the customer inappropriately. "I can picture it
now—," wrote a reader to the editorial page of *Glamour* magazine. "[A]ll women of childbearing years will have to take a
pregnancy test before being served in a bar or restaurant."[21]
     A nurse in the audience of an Oprah Winfrey show de-
voted to the incident commented, "It's her body. She can do
what she wants. She shouldn't drink or smoke, but no one has a
right to tell her that. I may sound confused, but I'm not."[22]
Like that nurse, many of us think legal substance abuse is wrong
but resist the notion of regulating the behavior. We imagine
ourselves having avoided liquor and cigarettes for nine months
and think how angry we would be if some young stranger criticized us for having one little drink near the end of our pregnancy. Our problem is that the freedoms we cherish require a
responsible citizenry, and irresponsibility during conception
and pregnancy punish not only the one acting inappropriately
but also the innocent child who is born. Not every woman who
drinks alcohol during her pregnancy limits her consumption to
a single congratulatory drink near the end of her term. No
wonder society in general sounds as confused as the nurse on
Oprah when we talk about the abuse by pregnant women of
legal substances.
     When Michael Dorris became a single father through the
adoption of a son, he had not heard of fetal alcohol syndrome,
or, as it is also called, FAS. He was perplexed by the problems

he was having with his beautiful, happy child. After years of talking with other adoptive parents and professionals, and enriched by his own loving sadness for his son, he is an eloquent spokesman for society's need to do more to save the disappointment of diminished lives caused by drinking mothers. Speaking of his son, he asks, "If his mother had been locked up, prevented from even one night of drinking, how much more awareness, how many more possibilities might he have had? If she had come after him with a baseball bat after he was born, if she had smashed his skull and caused him brain damage, would she have been constrained from doing it again and again? Was it her prerogative, moral or legal, to deprive him of the means to live a full life? I had no doubt that there were compelling reasons for her weaknesses, for her mistakes, but reasons don't equal rights."[23]

Assessing the extent of the damage caused by the abusive behavior is very difficult, despite the technological advances we have made in prenatal detection and neonatal treatment. Poor diet, failure to seek early prenatal care, the age of the mother, environmental pollutants, and a combination of legal and illegal substances the mother injests may be present in various combinations so that tracing cause and effect is impossible. Furthermore, the stage of fetal development at which the behavior occurs may be more important than the extent of the abuse. Even after birth, the baby's home environment—whether it is nurturing or neglectful, loving or abusive, safe or deprived—can make all the difference in the development of the baby.

The Georgia Addiction, Pregnancy and Parenting Project (GAPP) began in 1980, and Dr. Claire Coles and Iris Smith have been involved from its inception. Their research supports the role intervention can play in helping pregnant women who are abusing drugs or alcohol; however, they both warn against the dangers of coercive intervention that evidences a class bias. Dr. Coles repeats the comment a neighbor made to her: "He said, 'What's a few IQ points? I like to have a drink when I come home.' " She also describes a cocktail party she attended in a white, upper-middle-class home at which one partygoer observed that among the private-school-educated children of the party guests, many of those children were cocaine babies. In other words, the use of both legal and illegal substances exists at all levels of society, but social condemnation of individual pregnant women who are abusers tends to be directed at poor minority women.

Ms. Smith agrees. "Identification of substance abuse among more affluent women is less likely because their doctors are reluctant to recognize it. If the woman is discovered as an abuser, and she is uncomfortable with the doctor's conversation, she'll go find another doctor. Low-income people generally don't have that kind of option. They have to go to the public health clinic; there's no place else they can go." After years of working with pregnant abusers and following the development of the children to whom these women have given birth, Dr. Coles believes, "We need to be concerned about those people who are substance abusers, but we don't need to get hysterical. Today we have a lot of overcorrecting."[24]

Others disagree. They believe addicted women have shown themselves to be incapable of regulating their own behavior and that the intervention of the courts is necessary. South Carolina has been among the most aggressive states in prosecuting women who continue drug abuse during pregnancy. The solicitor involved in a program for criminal prosecutions in Charleston expressed his frustration that medical caregivers and social workers are so ineffective in reaching pregnant drug abusers. "The only way we could begin to solve this problem was to make the individual accountable for her own actions. Otherwise, why would they stop?"[25] An assistant district attorney in Cobb County, Georgia, agrees: "We want the same thing the other side wants. We want these women to get help." But, he adds, "We are involved because there's no one to speak for the baby. We don't want to see another baby born this way."[26]

The charges of class and racial bias in criminal prosecu-

tions in these cases are not without merit; disproportionate
numbers of poor minority women are defendants in these cases,
and studies show that these defendants do not reflect the racial
and economic ratios among pregnant substance abusers in society as a whole. A study of 715 pregnant women in one county
in Florida showed little difference in the number of positive
drug tests between women who went to public clinics as compared to those who went to private offices, and the frequency of
positive results was similar among white women and black
women.[27] The differences appeared in the type of substances
the women abused. Black women more frequently tested positive for cocaine use, while white women more often tested
positive for cannabinoids. The most startling differences were
in how often the drug use was reported to health authorities.
Although the rates of substance abuse among black and white
women in the study were similar, black women were reported at
approximately ten times the rate for white women, and poor
women were more likely than others to be reported. Thus, the
findings of this Florida study support both economic and racial
bias by health caregivers in reporting substance abuse to governmental authorities.

The 1992–1993 National Pregnancy and Health Survey
reflects that more than half the women using illegal drugs among
those surveyed were white, although the percentage of abusers
was higher among blacks.[28] White women were far more likely
to drink or smoke during their pregnancies.[29] The highest illegal substance abuse occurred among unmarried women, the
unemployed, those with less than a college education, and those
who relied upon public financing to pay their hospital bills.[30]
Statistics about substance abuse by pregnant women are not always consistent. A government study reported in the fall of
1996 found that welfare recipients are no more likely to abuse
drugs and alcohol than the general population.[31] While the statistics may vary, the studies consistently show substance abuse
by pregnant women across racial and economic lines.

As Americans, we want solutions. We see ourselves as

problem solvers, not problem managers. Iris Smith suggests that this approach is counterproductive in addressing the problem of substance abuse during pregnancy. "I don't think there is a solution," she says. "I think there are strategies that we can implement that will have an impact on these problems."

When she was in high school, Cecelia Lyles was voted most likely to succeed, but her life took a dreadful detour. "I wanted to do what the crowd was doing. I got involved in the nightlife, the excitement of the whole drug arena, and it just progressed from one extreme to another," she remembers.[32] During this time she became pregnant. "I didn't get prenatal care until my seventh month. . . . Bad diet . . . [I wore] tight clothes because my family didn't even know I was pregnant until I was seven months."[33] As much as she loves her son, she admits that she used drugs during the pregnancy, and even his birth was not enough to make her stop abusing. By the time he was three, she had relinquished legal custody to her family. Cecelia explains why it took her so long to admit what drugs were doing to her life: "One of the things that I took the most pride in and had the most denial about was my job. Not too many women eighteen, nineteen years old had a decent job around my hometown, and that kept me in so much denial."

Eventually, drug abuse jeopardized her job, and forced her to enter treatment. "I never got in trouble with the law, thank God, but I was in trouble with the community as a whole because of a lot of behavior that I'm not proud of. As for my self-esteem and my self-worth, I didn't have any." She believes, "I got clean and I stay clean because I didn't have any other choice. I'm being honest. I didn't have any other choice."

Today Cecelia's life is back on course. She has regained custody of her son and is a counselor with two Atlanta agencies, working for addiction recovery and AIDS prevention.[34] The director of programs at one of the agencies says Cecelia has lived up to the success her high school classmates predicted. "There are probably very few people who graduated with Cecelia who do something that helps themselves but also helps other people. Because she has been so vulnerable, has had so many experiences—not always good—she has been able to reach many people in a very different way, people whose lives were hopeless." The chief social worker for the intensive care nursery of Atlanta's public hospital echoes this endorsement, praising Cecelia's ability to get pregnant and AIDS-infected addicts into treatment.

Cecelia is modest about her accomplishments but agrees that her own experiences help her reach addicted women who might be resentful of others. "I use leverage—anything that is hanging over their heads that I can use as a motivator," she says, remembering the social and economic pressures that motivated her own recovery. "Not in a negative way, like threatening to call the police, but sitting down with my patients and talking about reality, getting past the denial. The things that I say to my patients are repetitious, because I know that in spite of them being on drugs . . they are able to retain and hold some of that information, and it could be a motivator."

Cecelia believes we must involve whole communities if the cycle of addicted mothers is going to be broken. "The only way we are going to deal with it is when we start educating one another and reaching out to one another—not running in the house, closing the blinds, and saying 'It's not my problem.' " How can we involve people, especially elderly people—the ones that have the wisdom and knowledge—without fear? People need to feel freer to reach out, not feel fear that if they reach out that there's a drug dealer on the corner."

Instead of the model neighborhood she envisions, Cecelia knows what a pregnant woman or new mother trying to break a drug habit faces today. "I put a lady in treatment and I sent her back to the same place that she was so screwed up in. No type of support there. It was like throwing her back, like taking her to treatment and dropping her off at a drug house, because it's right next door." Cecelia believes that punishing women for drug use during pregnancy ignores the more damaging reality for many babies born to abusers. "A lot of the babies are born healthy. It's just the fact that they go into the home, and the mother needs treatment she can't get, particularly if she doesn't have insurance. She takes care of her child the way she learned from her mother, and what she gets from her community. If what she sees is everyone drinking and using and hollering and screaming at the kids, then the fact that the children have emotional problems when they enter school is not just because their mothers used drugs during pregnancy."

Cecelia Lyles and her son are only one success story, but she believes their success could be repeated by many other addicted women and children if communities became involved. In short, the attitudes of our families, our neighbors, and our coworkers are more likely to change behaviors than policemen, prosecutors, and judges.

Education is the best strategy for reducing harmful conduct during pregnancy. Once most Americans know that certain behaviors jeopardize the birth of a healthy baby, all of us can discourage those behaviors, not only in ourselves but also among our families and friends, in ways that are personal but persistent, motivated by concern for the women as well as for the fetus she carries.

However, education fails when society is unwilling to assume its own role in helping individuals face responsibility for their actions, and recently we all seem unwilling to demand individual accountability. Jurors deadlock over finding guilt even when the defendants' violent acts are undeniable, sports fans applaud poor sportsmanship and many of us turn away from problems within our own families and communities. We confuse explanations for bad behavior with justification for it, and the result is a declining regard for individual responsibility. Why should we be surprised when pregnant women act as irresponsibly as the rest of us?

Iris Smith urges us to look for strategies rather than solutions, and it is good advice, for it suggests roles for individuals rather than big government. For example, instead of urging laws intended to rescue all babies harmed in the womb, we should be more interested in helping the women among our own acquaintances who are battling addictions and ignorance. Moral accountability does not come from lecturing strangers, lobbying for warning labels, or campaigning for legislators who favor regulations to protect the unborn. If we really want to make a difference, we must be willing to care—not only about the unborn child but also about the woman unable to give her baby the best possible beginning, for whatever reason. Most of us would not have to look far to find someone needing our personal interest to help with their pregnancy, if we were willing to invest our genuine concern. But many of us prefer to delegate our role to social workers or other professionals, doubting our own power to make a difference. Demanding that authorities prosecute a stranger for delivering an addicted newborn is far easier than confronting your sister about a drinking problem you have both pretended not to recognize, easier than encouraging a coworker to stop smoking during her pregnancy, and far easier than involving yourself in the troubled personal life of an unmarried, cocaine-addicted woman who has come to your church for help.

Abortion politics has worked against society's ability to consider ways to assist in healthy births, and the intransigence of both sides has contributed to the problem. Consider this possibility. Assume that every pregnant woman were free to decide whether or not she wanted to carry her baby to term and give birth. This assumption would require the pro-life advocates to compromise: Women who determined that their addictions, abusive relationships, financial deprivation, or whatever other problems in their lives prohibited responsible gestation, would be free to obtain early abortions. Next, assume that a woman's decision not to abort were deemed an admission that she willingly assumed the role of responsibility gestating the fetus during the pregnancy. This second assumption would require the pro-choice advocates to compromise: A dual legal status of woman and child-to-be would be recognized, allowing legal protection of the unborn fetus. In sum, abortion opponents would give up absolute protection of fetal rights from the moment of conception to gain greater protection of fetal rights after an election to abort was waived by the woman, and pro-choice advocates would limit the individual rights of a gestational woman in exchange for her freedom to decide for herself whether it was appropriate to carry her fetus to term.

Neither group has been willing to accept such compromises, but if both were, then we could focus on the healthy births of babies whose mothers chose to give them life. In those circumstances, intervention to protect the fetus if the woman ignored medical advice or continued to smoke, drink, or use drugs would be imposed only upon mothers-to-be who chose to proceed with their pregnancies. The decision to continue the pregnancy would give rise to legal obligations to the fetus similar to the parental obligation of care owed a baby after birth. Extreme cases of prenatal abuse or neglect might involve the sort of guardianship and involuntary commitment proceedings already legally available to supervise people mentally or emotionally unable to conform their behavior, but because these women had elected to continue their pregnancies, it is more likely they would welcome voluntary programs of counseling, treatment, or residential care to help them provide their babies with a healthy start. The important distinction from what exists under current circumstances (in which there are financial, social, and legal impediments to early term abortions) is that prenatal intervention, voluntary or involuntary, would be imposed upon a population of pregnant women who had declined to abort because they willingly chose to gestate their fetus to term. At least theoretically, that willing choice should indicate their desire to do what was necessary to ensure a healthy gestation for their baby. Current attempts to mandate healthful behaviors during pregnancy too often include women who may have had little say, due to their own addictions, in having become pregnant in the first place, little ability to conform to the behaviors demanded from them, and little likelihood of mothering adequately after their babies are born.

Any future legal trend toward regulating the conduct of pregnant women must be limited in its scope. Just as we do not inject ourselves in unwise—though not neglectful or abusive—parenting, we should not consider injecting judges and social workers in each case of thoughtless pregnant conduct. Society cannot presume to control every activity known to pose dangers to the fetus, activities that have nothing to do with substance abuse, such as continuing to change cat litter or soak in extremely hot tubs, both of which pose fetal risks. Nor can we confine a woman for continuing to enjoy an occasional glass of wine with dinner or a cigarette with her morning coffee.[35] Such a change in the law would, however, provide a legal basis for protecting a fetus from ongoing substance abuse or medical neglect that the mother-to-be seems unable to control. Certainly there would be subjective tests applied in many situations, but just as authorities have distinguished between parents who spank their children and parents who beat and abuse their children, distinctions could be made in evaluating prenatal behaviors as well. Whatever restraint or control were exercised, however, would have to be for treatment and fetal safety, and never for punishment.

The current demand for criminal accountability punishes the mother after the damage is done. Not only does criminal prosecution following a positive drug test of a newborn fail to rescue that particular baby from prenatal exposure, it may also increase the risk of more such births in the future if pregnant addicts fear detection and prosecution. Subjecting pregnant women to drug testing, with or without their consent, is enough to cause many addicts to avoid prenatal care. A program that reduces the likelihood that women will receive early and regular medical care throughout their pregnancies defeats society's goal of enouraging healthy births. For that reason, medical associations and public health organizations, such as the American Medical Association and the March of Dimes, are nearly universal in their condemnation of criminal prosecutions.[36]

Our inconsistent attitudes toward legal and illegal substances, affluent and poor, friends and strangers, and whites and minorities should cause us to observe, as Alice did about the Queen of Hearts and her subjects: "I don't think they play at all fairly, and they all quarrel so dreadfully one can't hear oneself speak—and they don't seem to have any rules in particular: at least, if there are, nobody attends to them." We must begin examining our own rules about maternal responsibility during pregnancy and encourage the same standards of moral accountability among all women. Expecting the courts to be our moral guardians isn't working.

Should mothers who deliver babies damaged by the actions of the mothers during pregnancy be punished by law?

If they should, what actions justify punishment:

- Using illegal drugs?
- Using alcohol?
- Smoking?
- Attempting to self-abort?

What should be done for or to mothers whose conduct during pregnancy damages their babies?

Is mandatory birth control ever an appropriate part of a woman's criminal sentence?

Is mandatory birth control as a part of the sentence appropriate in response to convictions involving

- abuse of existing children?
- failure to report abuse of existing children by someone else?
- substance abuse during pregnancy?
- neglect or abandonment of existing children?
- practice of a lifestyle harmful to her children?
- prostitution?
- other occasions?

Is birth control a more appropriate part of a woman's sentence if she agrees to it as part of a plea bargain than when it is imposed by the court as a mandatory part of her sentence?

Should the criminal sanctions involving birth control be applied to male defendants in a similar manner as they are to female defendants?

CHAPTER 11

THE STORY OF GUY AND TERRI

If Guy Walden is the head of his family, then his wife, Terri, is the heart. His conversation is filled with talk of congressional hearings, genetic research, and Bible study; she is more likely to talk of the joys her children give her, of the loving support of friends, and of telephone calls from other parents of children with disabilities. Their responses to the challenges with which life has presented them are different, but the merging of their differences is the source of the strength their special family requires.

They named their first child Jason. At first they had no reason to suspect that their hopes for his future were threatened, but when he was only a few months old, unexplained symptoms began to appear. A doctor in Costa Rica, where they were serving as missionaries, suggested they return to the United States for medical tests, and at the University of Alabama they learned that Jason had a genetic disease called Hurler-Scheie compound. Children who inherit this disorder cannot produce sufficient enzymes to break down the complex carbohydrates formed in cells. As the carbohydrates accumulate, the characteristic symptoms begin to appear: stunted growth, defective organs, clouded eyes, severe mental retardation, and the facial deformities that gave the disorder an earlier name, gargantuism. Children suffering from Hurler's rarely live past the age of ten years.

The diagnosis was a cruel blow to the young couple. Terri recalls, "We found out when Jason was about fifteen months

⊥ that he had the disease. We were devastated." They did not want to accept such a tragic diagnosis for their son, and they sought other medical opinions. Before they had come to grips with the reality of their son's condition, they learned that Terri was pregnant with their second child. Prenatal testing revealed that this baby had also inherited Hurler's from her parents. Although they could have aborted when they learned the news, that choice was unthinkable for Guy and Terri. "I personally am against abortion," Terri says. "Totally. For any reason. And I've lived it, because I knew Angie had the disease when I was carrying her." Almost simultaneously they were forced to accept the news that both babies were born with a fatal disease.

Although they had not known it, both Guy and Terri carry the recessive gene for Hurler's, a tragic genetic coincidence that Terri sees as a blessing. "The moment we found out Jason had the disease, both families started blaming the other family. Now, everybody's part of it so nobody can point the finger at anybody." Terri laughs, "I say, Lord, thank you."

Although she can find a blessing in it today, at the time that they learned of their mutual genetic legacy, Terri and Guy struggled with whether it meant an end to their dreams of raising a family together. "For a full year we searched and sought counsel about having more children, and it was a terrible strain on our marriage. Sexually, I didn't want to get near Guy, because I was afraid I'd get pregnant. We were both trying to stay away from each other until we could make our decision." During that year they sought the advice of others. "We got as many different opinions as people we asked," Terri says. "We thought, we can't live our lives this way, based on an opinion poll."

At last, Guy and Terri came back to the same source that has always guided them: the Bible. "We searched every single verse in the Bible about abortion, about birth control, about children, families, everything," Terri remembers. "I was kind of looking for something to tell me that I could stop," she admits, "because I didn't want to go through this anymore. But I couldn't find it. It says that children are a blessing, the fruit of the womb is your reward. It doesn't say only if they are healthy." Together, Guy and Terri concluded that the birth of their children should be left to God, despite the strong possibility that future children would inherit the same fatal disease they had passed to Jason and Angie.

People cannot understand why they take such reproductive risks, and they are criticized, even by Christians who share their pro-life beliefs. Terri says one doctor told her she needed a hysterectomy, not because it was medically necessary but because he was opposed to her having more babies. "He said, 'You've got this problem and you need a hysterectomy.' I said, 'I don't feel like I have any problem, and I want a second opinion.' The second doctor told me there was nothing wrong with me, and I think the motive of the first doctor was to do anything he could to stop me from having more children. That's not right."

As they adapted to the special demands of caring for Jason and Angie, Terri gave birth to two more children who were both born without the disease. First came Hannah, and then John. In the meantime, they learned more about Hurler's, they networked with other families raising disadvantaged children, and they became acquainted with medical professionals who specialize in treating children with Hurler's.

Jason was eight years old when he died. Guy and Terri knew that Angie's death would follow soon. "I think the hardest thing about having a child that has a disease of this type is the anticipation of their death, wondering when it's going to happen, hoping it never does, but knowing in your heart that it probably will," Terri believes. Two years after her brother's death, little Angie died, and Terri recalls that despite knowing their deaths were inevitable, she and Guy were shocked each time death came. "With both of them it was a very happy and healthy time. They were playing thirty minutes prior. Then, just all of a sudden gone, that quick."

When Angie died, Terri was pregnant with their fifth

child, and prenatal testing had already revealed Hurler's. For the first time, however, medical science had a potential solution to offer, but the experimental treatment doctors proposed raised new challenges to the couple's religious beliefs. The future life of the fetus Terri carried might be saved by transplanting cells from a fetus who was aborted. Guy and Terri, who oppose abortion, were asked whether they could consent to the use of aborted fetal tissue to save their unborn child.

Ironically, Guy and Terri's pro-life position made Terri a particularly appropriate candidate for the procedure. Most couples choose to abort when prenatal tests disclose the presence of Hurler's, and doctors needed to know that the couple they selected for the experimental transplant surgery would not decide to abort prior to birth. Guy and Terri were committed to the birth of their son, regardless of the outcome of the surgery. When doctors selected Terri for the procedure, all the other pregnant couples elected to abort.

Just as they had done in reaching their decision about having children, Guy and Terri turned to Scripture to evaluate their consent to the procedure. They were concerned not only because of their personal beliefs but also because of their responsibilities as examples to members of the church in which Guy served as pastor. Guy explains, "When we made the decisions that we did, we asked, not Can we do this? but Can I do this and still be a Christian? Can I do this and still say I am being obedient to God in all the areas of my life? Can I do this and still be a proper example unto my flock?" When Guy explained the scriptural basis for their decision to the members of his church, they accepted what he and Terri had decided, and even after Guy left their pulpit, members continued to extend moral support to Guy and Terri during difficult times.

Terri believes God's hand was present not only in the conception and birth of their son but also in the technology they utilized to try to save his life. "People say that God isn't in such things, but I remind them of all the doctors that came together, all the circumstances that came together—fetal tissue that came from an ectopic pregnancy (which took some of the pressure off us), all the cells being 100 percent viable, everything going fine, and the baby absorbing it. I think God orchestrated it."

They know that consenting to participate in a medical experiment using fetal tissue might seem to have involved them in a practice that, if successful, could lead to a growing demand for fetal tissue for therapeutic use, and, theoretically, more abortions to supply the demand. Guy and Terri counter such theoretical arguments with accounts of their own experiences and those of others, and they insist that in the case of Hurler's the therapeutic use of fetal tissue would reduce elective abortions. "The problem that parents in our situation have always faced is if you are pregnant and the baby has the disease, do you abort the baby—which is a negative choice—or do you have the baby and live with the problems—which is a negative choice? There has never been any positive choice for parents, and that is what this technique offers that is so important. Giving parents a positive choice will save many babies from abortion," Guy insists. Terri knows couples who have chosen to abort when prenatal testing revealed the disease, as all the other candidates for the experimental surgery did after Terri was selected. She also knows many couples who have given up their plans for raising families together. "A lot of people have one child with the disease and they don't want to have any more children. They miss out on having healthy children because the fear is so great that they will have another one with the disease. Fetal surgery would let them get pregnant, and if it had the disease, they could do the procedure. It takes the fear away."

The transplant of aborted fetal tissue into their fifteen-week-old fetus was the first surgery of its kind to be done in the United States. Guided by a sonogram, Dr. Nathan Slotnick inserted a needle filled with fetal cells from the aborted fetus through Terri's abdomen and into the abdomen of the fetus. The objective was not to replace all the defectively encoded cells but rather to implant healthy cells that would grow alongside the defective ones. Doctors believed that if only 5 to 10 percent of the transplanted cells survived and began producing enzymes, the effects of Hurler's would be averted, or at least reduced.

Nathan Adam Walden, named after his pioneering doctor, was born on October 30, 1990. The specialists began regular testing of his enzyme levels to evaluate whether the procedure produced the desired effects. Guy and Terri waited anxiously for the results of each test, not only because of their hopes for Nathan but also because they wanted his experience to advance the technology and help other families.

Their desire to help others also led Guy and Terri to speak publicly about their decision. Today Terri says, "We did what we did and what God gave us peace about doing. We didn't realize some of the things it cost us—when we did it. But I guess I'd do it all over again in a heartbeat."

They had certainly not intended to enter the national spotlight as spokespersons for lifting the federal-funding ban on fetal tissue research, but because Nathan's surgery was the first of its kind in this country, they were asked to testify before Congress. The hostility their testimony evoked was especially hurtful because it came largely from people whose moral views they shared on most other issues. They were troubled to find themselves testifying in opposition to other pro-life witnesses, and when they were pressured by Christian groups to recant their testimony, Guy and Terri questioned once again whether their use of the technology was misguided. Briefly, the pressure overwhelmed them, but finally, Terri says, they regained their confidence in the scriptural interpretation upon which they had based their decisions and found the strength to confront the angry voices with compassion. "If we find something in the Bible, and the Bible says it, we'll do it."

When Nathan was one year old, the tests finally showed enzymes at therapeutic levels, and the transplanted tissue appeared to be helping Nathan produce the missing enzymes needed to lessen the symptoms of the disease. The doctors were cautious but excited by this indication of success. For Guy and Terri, it

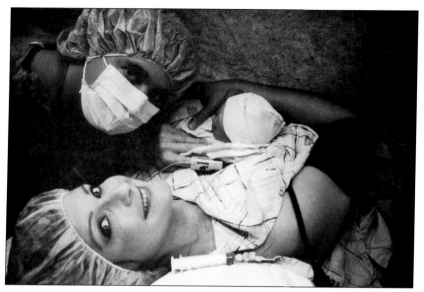

Proud parents Lisa and Gary Childress with newborn daughter,
Christina, only moments after her birth.

The medical necessity for a donor sibling had a happy ending
for Brad and Lea Ann Curry and their three daughters,
Emily, Audrey, and Natalie.

PAT FARRELL, THE MIAMI HERALD

Laura Campo and Justin Pearson
grieve for their baby, Theresa Ann, below.

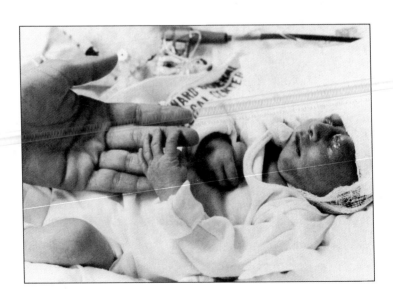

Postmenopausal mother Mary Shearing and proud father
Don Shearing show off their twin daughters, Amy and Kelly.

DAN SCHWEITZER

Christa Uchytil holds son Chad and Arlette Schweitzer
holds granddaughter Chelsea for a Christmas portrait
two months after Arlette's surrogacy birth of twins
for daughter Christa and her husband Kevin.

Since coming to the Center for Surrogate Parenting to do research for her doctoral thesis, Dr. Hilary Hanafin has devoted her professional career to protecting all the participants in the surrogacies arranged by the center, especially the babies born from such arrangements.

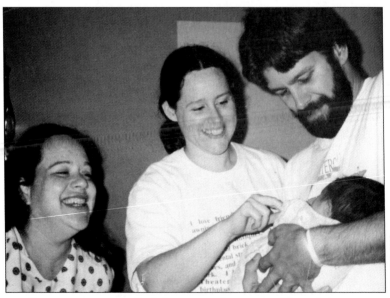

PAT AUTON

Surrogate aunt Julie Johnson and parents, Janet Johnson and Mark Wittle, admire John Wittle soon after he is born.

Emily Perl Kingsley
and her son,
Jason Kingsley, enjoy
a moment together.

Without innovative surgery
allowing the correction of a
congenital problem while
Michael was still within
Mioko Shinn's womb,
mother and son could never
have shared this moment.

Lyndall Southern finds
time in her busy life to
pose with daughters,
Desiree, Genevieve,
and Miranda.

Deborah Hecht and
Bill Kane at their home
in Malibu the year he
took his own life.

Cynthia Hallvik
is a busy wife
and mother to her
family, Carly, John,
and Preston, despite
being HIV positive.

Mary Ann Hughes's legacy, twins Joe and Megan with big sister Amanda.

Cecilia Lyles at work as a health education and outreach specialist on the streets of Atlanta.

SEARS PHOTOGRAPHY STUDIO

Guy and Terri Walden pose with children
Nathan, Hannah, David, and John.
(Not pictured are Amanda Grace, born a
year after the picutre was taken, and Jason
and Angie, whose lives were cut short by
Hurlers Syndrome.)

Nancy Becker Kennedy
believes her life has been
enriched by the quadriplegia
that resulted from an
accident when she was
twenty-one years old.

was an incredible birthday gift for Nathan, and they looked forward to an end to further progression of symptoms, and even a slow reversal of existing conditions. Unfortunately, the therapeutic enzyme levels that appeared at one year did not continue, and the promise of a normal life for Nathan faded.

Nathan's health was complicated by problems not directly related to Hurler's. Early in his life, doctors recommended inserting a feeding tube to help him gain weight. During that procedure his esophagus was torn and his lungs were punctured, causing permanent damage. "Nobody could tell if the problems were because of the operation or due to the disease," Terri explains. "I kept telling the doctors they could separate the two, if they would try, but I know he was not the candidate they had hoped to study." Terri compares Nathan's symptoms to those exhibited by her first two children at the same ages, and she believes Nathan's were less severe. "His stomach was not nearly as enlarged as theirs were; his nose didn't run as much; his heart seemed to be better. I know what's different, and if nobody else does, then I have to be satisfied with knowing for myself that what we did improved his life a little bit."

Their goal of helping other families through the knowledge scientists gained may have failed, but Guy and Terri have succeeded in helping families in other ways. Guy's congressional testimony was pivotal in opening the eyes of antiabortion congressmen and others to the view that using fetal tissue to save lives can actually be a pro-life position, provided safeguards are implemented to separate a woman's decision about whether to abort from her subsequent decision to donate the fetal tissue. As a result of his lobbying efforts, Guy was asked to serve on the board of the Parkinson's Action Network, and his work today extends beyond helping families with Hurler's to those facing other genetic diseases.

Terri has focused her efforts on helping individual families. "Four hundred families have called us," she says. "Sometimes it just helps to talk. When I know of another family that has been through something and overcome things, I give them a few names to call." She pauses. "I can't take the disease away from these children, but I can talk to their families on the telephone and send them birthday cards. That's what I like doing and what I know more about than anything else."

Although the public attention has allowed them to reach out to others, they have paid a personal price for their notoriety. The church that had been their spiritual home for twenty years excluded them from holding any leadership positions because of the controversy associated with Nathan's treatment. "We have gone through a grieving process. I love the people there. They are the ones who gave us the strength, the support when our children died. But how can we attend a church if we aren't allowed to use what God has given us to use?" Terri asks.

A year and a half after Nathan's birth, Guy and Terri had another son, David, and three and a half years later a daughter, Amanda Grace, both born without Hurler's. "I am so thankful we did not stop having children after Jason and Angie, even though everyone wanted us to. If we had stopped, we would not have these children, and that would be far worse." Terri remembers what they have been through because they chose to raise a family together, and is confident that they made the right decisions.

In making the decision to continue having children in spite of the genetic trait they share, Terri and Guy believe they are obligated to shoulder the greater responsibilities that have resulted from their decision. She explains, "We have not asked anybody to raise our children. We knew they had the disease. There were consequences to our decisions, but there were also a lot of blessings." Terri continues, "I think you need to make a conscious decision that these are the things that are going to happen and you will have to live with them. That is what we have tried to do, and not ask anybody to take all these things on for us."

Guy and Terri admit that the constant demands imposed on parents of children with disabilities can be overwhelming. Guy explains, "There are no mechanisms to help parents with genetically problemed children. There are none. I mean, government doesn't help. One of the parents has to be with them constantly, or you have to pay a registered nurse, which most people can't do." Terri remembers her delight in discovering the Children's Circle of Care Foundation, which arranges child care to allow parents one night out during a year. "I read in their brochure—'one night out a year'—and I thought, 'I guess it's a start!' " she laughs. "I also suggested to the Foundation Board having a maid service come in and help families. Sometimes you want to be with your child, and you just can't get all the housework done."

Guy and Terri hope that knowledge learned through the removal of the ban on federal funding of fetal tissue research will spare other parents from having to face such tragic disabilities in their children. As Guy says, "We've had to watch our children die. We've had to live with the tremendous cost and the difficult situations. My wife and I have our faith, and for that reason we've been able to endure the storms. But the pressures are overwhelming others, adding to the divorce load and destroying the other, healthy children's lives." It is for all the members of the families, and not just for the children with genetic disabilities, that Guy and Terri urge pursuing the promising therapeutic use of fetal tissue. As Terri sees it, "Sometimes you have to say, if God opens the door and keeps the door open, I'll walk through it."

Despite the high hopes of his parents at the time of his birth, Nathan's life was even more brief than those of his two older siblings who shared the same genetic disease. After two weeks of hospitalization with a lung virus, four-year-old Nathan died on December 10, 1994. Yet Terri remains convinced that his Hurler's symptoms were less severe, and she attributes his earlier death to the damage to his lungs that occurred during the insertion of the feeding tube.

For the first time since becoming parents, Guy and Terri have only healthy children, something Terri admits has been a big adjustment. They are both active in organizations assisting families dealing with disabilities, but perhaps the special legacy left to them by their children lies in the simple words of compassion they, as parents who have struggled with caring for children with such compelling needs, can share with other parents facing similar struggles of their own.[1]

CHAPTER 12

FETAL TISSUE USE AND
SIBLING DONOR CONCEPTION

If you grew up in the 1950s, you will remember the fear that a single word could cause. *Polio.* For Americans of a certain age, the word evokes memories of swimming pools closed for the summer, of leg braces and iron lungs, and of the helplessness that struck entire communities when a child was diagnosed with the virus.

But if you are just a few years younger, polio is only a word on your vaccination schedule. Practically overnight, this dreadful disease was reduced to a rarity because research using fetal tissue led to the discovery of a vaccine.

Fetal tissue is unique because of its greater potential to grow and its smaller potential for rejection compared to those of adult tissue. For over thirty years, researchers have benefited from knowledge gained with fetal tissue, and there are promising signs that this research will lead to treatments of common diseases. Yet in 1988 the federal government banned funding of medical research that used fetal tissue obtained from abortions. The list of organizations that pleaded with the government to lift the ban included the most respected groups within the medical and scientific communities, including the American Cancer Society, the American Heart Association, the American Diabetes Association, the National Arthritis Foundation, and the Alzheimer's Association, to name only five.[1] When the Department of Health and Human Services convened a panel to help decide whether scientific and medical use of fetal tissue is ethically appropriate, the panel concluded that such use is "morally acceptable." But President Ronald Reagan and his successor, George Bush, ignored the thoughtful pleas of researchers and health care providers and the recommendation of the government-appointed panel, and continued the ban.

Support for the ban came almost entirely from outside the medical and scientific communities, from such groups as the National Right to Life Committee and the U.S. Catholic Conference. The ban did not extend to research using tissue from spontaneous abortions, a so-called compromise approved by most of the right-to-life groups. Use of such tissue is not an acceptable scientific solution, however, since researchers fear that chromosomal abnormalities are a greater possibility in tissue obtained from miscarriages and stillbirths. Reagan and Bush continued the ban on federal funding of fetal tissue research because they believed a positive medical use of fetal tissue might induce women to choose to have an abortion. Abortion politics rather than scientific merit gripped the National Institutes of Health, the federal body that administers funding of medical research.

On the second day of his presidency, Bill Clinton signed four executive orders, among them one ending the ban imposed on the use of fetal tissue in federally financed medical research.[2] As he signed the executive orders, President Clinton said, "Our vision should be of an America where abortion is safe and legal but rare." By selecting the twentieth-anniversary date of legalized abortion for the signing, President Clinton aligned himself with pro-choice factions as strongly as his predecessors had aligned themselves with pro-life groups.

So long as fetal tissue research remains entangled in abortion politics, treatments for such diseases as diabetes, cancer, and Parkinson's will be imperiled with each shift in the political balance, and the long-range planning necessary for many research projects will be impeded by uncertainty. Is the politicizing of fetal tissue research unavoidable?

Participants in my survey were asked to select the characterization that best described their views about abortion. Sixty-four percent said they were "pro-choice," 25 percent said they "oppose abortion," and 10 percent were undecided.[3] The answers participants gave to other questions contained in the survey revealed no fixed pattern reflecting their characterizations of abortion opinions, however.

Thus, while policy statements and statistics are important, more influential for individuals considering the use of fetal tissue in research and treatment are the people they know who may be helped. Senator Strom Thurmond, who is strongly pro-life, surprised many by voting to lift the ban on federal funding for fetal tissue research, a vote that must have been influenced by his having a daughter with diabetes. In her lobbying efforts in favor of lifting the ban, Anne Udall credits the respect for her father, Morris Udall, who represented Arizona in Congress for thirty years before Parkinson's disease forced his retirement, with allowing her access to many offices that might otherwise have been closed to a lobbyist urging her position.[4]

The Reverend Mr. Guy Walden opposes abortion and twice rejected it as an option when two of his unborn children tested positive for Hurler's syndrome during his wife's pregnancies, but he also supports the use of fetal tissue in medical research and treatment. He knows that many think his beliefs about abortion and the subsequent use of fetal tissue are inconsistent. He and his wife find their answers in Scripture. "When my wife and I made the decisions that we did, we asked, Can we do this and still be Christians? Can we do this and still say we are being obedient to God in these areas of our lives?" The irony of a pro-life, Baptist minister having consented to the first American fetal tissue transplant on his own fifteen-week-old fetus and then having become a lobbyist for lifting the ban on federal funding is not lost upon Rev. Walden. "The problem is, too many people deal in theoretical absolutes, when life is not a theoretical absolute. They say, if you're basically against abortion, you're pro-life, and if you're for abortion, you're pro-choice. With that one toggle switch—since most people cannot understand all the issues involved—once they switch that one toggle switch, then they start buying hook, line, and sinker all the rest of the presumptions. My wife and I don't fit the paradigm." Rather than allowing their opposition to abortion to determine their attitude toward the experimental medical procedure their doctor suggested, Rev. Walden and his wife returned to Scripture for fresh guidance on this separate issue. He is saddened when attitudes about abortion preclude others from making separate evaluations of related issues and says, "Every day in this country there are children dying needlessly. Pro-choice, pro-life, all that stuff—they are arguing what I call 'ivory-tower theory.' We don't live in that kind of world where it's one extreme or the other."[5]

Use of fetal tissue from aborted fetuses is a difficult issue for many people, regardless of their views about abortion, and participants in my survey reflected that uncertainty. More approved than disapproved of the use of the tissue, but many remained undecided. They viewed its use in treating living people slightly more favorably than its use in research. And their responses reflected no pattern related to their opinions concerning abortion.[6]

Although common sense shaped by personal experience allows many ordinary people to weave through the complicated moral issues, public officials and organized groups have historically viewed opposition to abortion as encompassing opposition to any use of fetal tissue derived from an abortion. In 1971 four doctors in Boston undertook a study to determine how pregnant women metabolize common antibiotics. Because fetuses were routinely incinerated by the hospital following the abortion procedures, it did not occur to the doctors to seek the consent of the women whose aborted fetuses they used in their research. Their actions were within existing hospital practices at that time. From a scientific viewpoint, their study yielded valuable information, but when their findings were published in the *New England Journal of Medicine*, abortion opponents were incensed. Angry demands for an investigation of hospital practices led to the indictment of the four doctors under an 1814 law prohibiting grave robbing.[7] The fact that pregnant women would benefit from the knowledge gained by the doctors was less important to abortion opponents than the fact that aborted fetuses had been used in the study. On the other hand, the doctors did not recognize the fact that the material they used in their research might have become a baby but for the abortion as an appropriate reason to obtain permission from each woman before using her aborted fetus in their study. The research technology had overtaken the evolution of corresponding ethical responses.

In Robin Cook's best-selling novel *Coma*, published in 1977, a young doctor is stunned to hear the chronic-care nurse attending a room filled with brain-dead patients say they were no longer people. Standing in a ward filled with comatose patients, the fictional nurse says: "They *were* people; now they're brain stem preparations. Modern medicine and medical technology have advanced to the point where these organisms can be kept alive, sometimes indefinitely. The result was a cost-effectiveness crisis. The law decided they had to be maintained. Technology had to advance to deal with the problem realistically." The terrible prospect of a world in which caregivers no longer recognize the humanity of their patients, as depicted in the novel, is not so different from the world pro-life advocates predict if fetal tissue becomes an increasingly valuable commodity on the research market.

The very number of diseases represented by advocates petitioning Congress to lift the ban evidences the enormous potential use of fetal tissue in research. For each successful discovery in the laboratory, hundreds or thousands of patients are waiting for treatments to correct or relieve their suffering. Today's demand for fetal tissue in research may become tomorrow's demand for fetal tissue in treatment.

There are about 1.5 million elective abortions in the United States per year, and the supply of tissue to satisfy foreseeable research seems abundant. However, if the goal articulated by President Clinton "of an America where abortion is safe and legal but rare" is achieved through encouraging more responsible sexual activity and family planning, the number of abortions may decline as the demand for fetal tissue increases.[8] It is the corrupting influence of a growing need for the tissue that frightens many opponents rather than any absolute objection to using fetal tissue. As Stephen G. Post, chairman of the American Academy of Religion's Medical Ethics Group, warns: "Absolutely no one can reasonably doubt that the medical-industrial complex would be set in motion were elective aborted fetuses found to be of therapeutic use." He continues, "Biomedical science will depend on a steady supply of elective abortuses. Research interests could become a powerful voice in the abortion debate."[9] Other opponents are more absolute. They not only fear a growing demand for fetal tissue but urge that the wrongfulness of abortion in itself should preclude any positive use of the resulting tissue.

Both of these concerns exist with regard to organ donation, but that has not stopped Americans from accepting the morality of families donating the organs of a dead loved one to save the lives of strangers. Despite a chronic shortage of organs for transplant, we have adhered to the 1984 law that makes the sale of organs illegal in the United States. Despite the violence that causes the deaths of many organ donors, we have declined to taint the lifesaving act of donation with the wrongful reason for the donor's death. Joan Samuelson, the brave attorney who so effectively worked to lift the federal-funding ban by organizing patients and caretakers to lobby Congress and by speaking so movingly of her own daily battle with Parkinson's disease, asks, "What if we evaluated the cause of death of organ donors, and rejected those that result from murder, or drunk drivers, or suicide? We wouldn't bring any of those people back, and we would lose the opportunity to help people in need. Punishing me . . . or any of the other million other Americans, for another's moral choice—a choice that will be made anyway—doesn't even out the equation. It just harms more people."[10]

Rev. Walden believes that opponents of abortion are trying

to impose a burden upon fetal tissue recipients that society does not ask of recipients of organ donations. "Under the donation laws for organs and tissues of a nonfetus, we don't make the recipient sign any acknowledgment of the source, for instance, whether the donor was murdered or it was a wrongful death. Legislation to require acknowledgment that fetal tissue is being used, particularly if it says aborted fetal tissue, is urged by some opponents in order to make it more distasteful to people." He adds quietly, "The situation is already hard enough."

There is one undeniable difference. Family members who donate the organs and tissue of deceased relatives are not the ones to have caused the deaths. Women who consent to the use of the fetal tissue are the same individuals who chose to abort the fetus. Special provisions must take this difference into account.

In addition to compliance with the Uniform Anatomical Gift Act, which has controlled ethical organ donation in this country, special safeguards are necessary to shield a pregnant woman from the influence of knowing that the fetal tissue could be put to a beneficial use should she choose to abort. Her decision to terminate her pregnancy and the procedures involved in the abortion should be kept separate and independent from the retrieval and use of fetal tissue. No payment should be allowed, except for reasonable expenses related to the actual retrieval, storage, preparation, and transportation of the fetal tissue. Her decision and consent to abort must precede any discussion of possible use of the fetal tissue. The timing and method of aborting the fetus should not be influenced by the potential subsequent use of the fetal tissue. Although fetal tissue from induced abortions should not be used in medical research without prior consent of the woman, she must not be permitted to designate the recipient of the tissue.

These safeguards would protect against women becoming pregnant with the specific intention of aborting and selling the fetal tissue, or donating it to a relative in need of a transplant. It's more difficult to guard against the subtle influence the knowledge that aborted fetal tissue may be put to a beneficial use has on a woman as she decides whether to abort. It is unrealistic to argue that such general knowledge among women of childbearing ages might not occasionally tip the balance in favor of abortion for certain women. However, in her testimony before Congress, the director of the National Institutes of Health, Dr. Bernadine Healy, acknowledged that she disagreed with the President and the Secretary of Health, Education, and Welfare (HEW) under whose administration she served: "My personal views are that the issues that surround abortion are so complicated and difficult and so emotionally driven for a woman that it was unimaginable to me that there could be incentives." The American College of Obstetricians and Gynecologists stated strongly in their statement to Congress, "As physicians, we know that women have abortions for a variety of medical and personal reasons, and concern that they will have this procedure to support medical research is totally unfounded."

People in their thirties and forties are more willing to donate the organs of loved ones than are older generations, and a study conducted by Dr. John A. Morris, Jr., at Vanderbilt University found that families asked to donate organs from infants who had died were more likely to agree than families asked to donate organs of deceased adults.[11] While findings from this study might suggest that a large percentage of women would be willing to donate the fetal tissue following abortions, such willingness says no more about a woman's decision to abort in the first place than a mother's willingness to donate organs says about her decision to seek medical treatment for her baby prior to its death.

The horrors depicted in the novel *Coma* have been averted by the Uniform Anatomical Gift Act. The abuses feared by opponents of fetal tissue donation can also be averted by appropriate legislation. The watchfulness of pro-life groups has served to remind scientists of the dignity to which human life is entitled, whether the tissue on which they conduct their research comes from a life lived fully or briefly, or one extinguished

before birth. Ethical standards today require scientists to implement procedures that respect the dignity to which human tissue
is entitled, but public demand for ethical standards does not
reflect disapproval of use of the tissue. In fact, the trend toward
acceptance of organ donation has led states to establish procedures for electing organ donor status at the time of driver's
license renewal and has led lawyers to include discussions of
organ donation as a part of estate planning with clients.[12] The
distinction between broad public acceptance of tissue donation
after death in contrast to the opposition fetal tissue donation has
aroused is explainable only with reference to abortion.[13] Concerns about women holding both the power to consent to abortion and the subsequent power to consent to use of the fetal
tissue are legitimate concerns, just as there were legitimate concerns about abuse of organ donation prior to passage of the
Uniform Anatomical Gift Act. Directing our efforts toward
enacting safeguards against abuses protects women, fetal remains,
and potential recipients, as well as protecting the continuity
of ongoing research with legally acquired fetal tissue. Furthermore, conceding the need for safeguards does not require any
concession regarding opposition to abortion. As Guy and Terri
Walden said in their statement to Congress: "We do not agree
with abortion, but it is legal in this country. My wife and I want
to see it become illegal, but until it is we must make decisions
about the use of fetal tissue."[14]

The federal-funding ban delayed not only the discovery of
therapeutic uses for aborted fetal tissue but also the development of alternate sources of fetal cell material. For example, scientists are attempting to grow fetal cells in the laboratory so
that one fetus can supply additional generations of cells. Another
line of research is exploring the growth of tissue from different
human organs in mice. Scientists are also evaluating whether
tissue from spontaneous abortions may ever be appropriately
used in research or therapy without jeopardizing results. By
pursuing alternatives as they continue fetal research, scientists

lessen the risk of abuses should the demand for fetal tissue from elective abortions eventually exceed the supply.

In a society in which abortion is legal, developing safeguards against abuses and encouraging alternate sources of material seem more consistent with our attitudes toward organ donation, and yet allow room for ongoing political debate concerning abortion. Withholding federal funding of fetal tissue research did not cause any measurable reduction in the number of abortions during those years. It did, however, dim the hopes of countless Americans suffering from diseases in which fetal research offers great promise, and it may have unalterably diminished or shortened their lives by postponing therapeutic discoveries.

At the time of her wedding in 1986, Joan Samuelson's orthopedist had told her the swelling in her left knee was caused by torn cartilage, a logical diagnosis for a patient who loved aerobics. By their first anniversary, Joan and her husband knew differently. She recalls, "In our first year of marriage it became clear that there was a neurological problem, and it was serious. For a few years we were coping with trying to get a clear diagnosis and understand what it meant in our lives."[15] Eventually, Joan learned that she had Parkinson's disease. She told Congress, "It first took my ability to run, and hike, and backpack; then to play the piano; now it makes walking more than a block a grueling challenge, and makes the stresses of work as a trial lawyer a physical struggle to continue."[16] What she did not tell the congressional committee was that the disease had robbed her and her husband of something else. "The bottom line is that we don't have any children right now, and this disease has probably made it impossible." Although her Parkinson's would not necessarily preclude conception and pregnancy, she fears that the demands of caring for an infant and raising a child would be too great for her as the physical handicaps of the disease progress.

She was also concerned about genetic transmission of the disease. "Because I knew my [paternal] grandfather died of

Parkinson's, one of the first questions I asked following my diagnosis concerned that genetic link," Joan recalls. "The doctor told me it was an old wives' tale that there was any family connection. Now they are revising that medical view." Like many families with genetic diseases and predispositions capable of transmission to succeeding generations, Joan's family deals with the unspoken guilt parents often feel. "I would imagine that tortures my dad a bit, but we don't talk about it."

Despite the enormous personal effort that the campaign to restore federal funding required, Joan believes she was right to devote so much of her strength to the work. "One of the awful things about Parkinson's is its progressive and incurable nature. It's difficult to have so little control over your own fate—to watch the disease develop inch by inch, with nothing you can do to stop it. I'm sure that I have really seized on this thing as one way I can try to do something to control my own destiny— to try to save myself." Although she and the other patients and caregivers she mobilized did not succeed during the Republican administrations, one of President Clinton's first acts was to lift the ban. As Joan told a reporter the day the executive order was signed, "It may make the difference whether my life is saved or not."

On January 4, 1994, the government approved the first new grant for fetal tissue research, awarding $4.5 million to three institutions to study the effects of implanting fetal tissue into the brains of patients with Parkinson's disease. In the research, tissue about the size of a grain of rice, taken from the brain structure of a fetus aborted after seven to eight weeks of gestation, will provide about a half million cells for injection into the brains of patients. In the laboratory, fetal brain cells can survive for a week, while adult brain cells die within ten minutes, which explains why fetal cells are essential to the transplant research involved with Parkinson's. During the ban, the University of Colorado Health Sciences Center had injected fetal brain cells into sixteen Parkinson's patients, but because much of their work was funded by the patients themselves, there was no funding to support necessary scientific control procedures, such as injecting a control group with placebos. This early private and patient-funded research showed real promise. About a third of the sixteen patients showed significant improvement; another third improved somewhat. The federal grant will now allow researchers to implement controls and make more precise evaluations of the transplant effects. Joan Samuelson and about 500,000 other Americans with the disease have new reason for hope.

Aside from the seemingly irreconcilable differences surrounding the definition of when life begins, nearly everyone agrees that once life exists, no one life should ever be sacrificed to provide the materials to save another. There are instances, however, when tissue can be donated from one living person to another without sacrifice of life. For example, organs may be redundant, as a pair of kidneys are, or regenerative, as bone marrow is. Society approves the voluntary donation by one person to another in such instances, although the law will not compel it. When redundant or regenerative tissue is needed by a child, parents may be motivated to conceive a sibling to supply that need. Is it a moral choice by the parents when they conceive a baby to create a living donor?

When Anissa Ayala was sixteen years old, she was diagnosed with leukemia. Her parents chose to conceive a baby, hoping a bone marrow match could be created through the miracle of birth after their nationwide search for a donor had failed. When news of their decision became public, opinions were divided.[17] Once again, those critical of the Ayalas' decision raised fears that women and the babies they conceived would be exploited by financial incentives or emotional pressures. Critics made sensational predictions that babies would be bred like animals in order to harvest their organs.

Anissa's transplant specialist, Dr. Stephen J. Forman, sees little reason for such concerns, because of the complexities of matching donor and recipient. "The circumstances make it unlikely," he believes. "Marrow is about the only thing you can conceive for with any degree of real possibility." He believes that the probabilities that the organs of an infant would be too small, the odds of a match too remote, or the delay in awaiting conception, birth, and sufficient maturity too extensive to encourage commercial abuse.[18]

Dr. Forman also feels we should resist the temptation to second-guess the motives of parents like the Ayalas. "You really have no idea why it is that a child is brought into the world by a couple on any given day. We may know what we hope is the reason, but is bringing a child into the world so another child can have a brother a good enough reason? Is having it to save a marriage, to start a marriage, to run the family business? People don't really question it a lot."[19] However, while Dr. Forman does not object to a conception motivated by the desire to create a tissue match, he feels that the new baby must be wanted, not solely as therapeutic material for its sick older sibling but also as a member of the family in its own right. "If you had a situation where parents clearly were doing it for the express purpose of providing a donor, without any interest in the child they were conceiving as an individual being in itself, I would not be involved. I doubt many of my colleagues would either."

The obstacles Anissa's parents overcame to create a sibling donor cannot help but call to mind Terri Walden's belief that God is a participant not only in the pregnancy of each woman but also in the technology itself. Without incredibly good luck or some divine intervention, it did seem impossible that they could succeed. One writer described the odds Anissa's parents, Abe and Mary, faced: "First, Abe had to have his vasectomy surgically reversed, a procedure with a success rate of just 40 percent. That done, Mary Ayala ventured to become pregnant at the age of forty-three. [Then], the odds were one in four that the baby's bone marrow would match her sister's."[20] Amazingly, the Ayalas overcame all these odds.

Dr. Forman is correct that such odds would never support

a commercial venture, but incredible odds may not deter parents desperate to save the life of a sick child. Even if the commercial abuses predicted by opponents are unlikely, do we risk a growing trend among parents like the Ayalas toward conceiving donor siblings? One primary concern is that their desperation might lead parents to test and abort any fetus that failed to create a match. Although Dr. Forman refuses to participate in donor conceptions in which the fetus is regarded solely as therapeutic material, loving parents faced with the death of a child might be pressured by their own emotions to conceive and abort a series of fetuses. The Ayalas challenged the odds and won. In the race to conceive a donor match in time to save a sick child, not every family could expect such immediate success.

Lea Ann Curry remembers the day the doctor delivered the news that her daughter had Fanconi's anemia.[21] "It broke his heart to give me that diagnosis," she recalls. When Natalie Curry was born on January 11, 1985, it was immediately apparent that something was wrong. Her left thumb was missing, her right thumb was useless, and her left arm had no radius bone. As countless doctors tested to find an explanation for Natalie's illness, Lea Ann and her husband Brad felt helpless. "We needed a diagnosis to know what to fight," Lea Ann says. "Until we had the tools to be able to fight some kind of war, we felt like we were searching." Even though the diagnosis of Fanconi's anemia meant that Natalie faced a brief life of severe anemia and possible retardation unless medical treatment could rescue her, it also meant the enemy had been identified. "When the doctor gave me the diagnosis, I got up and went to the bathroom, wiped a few tears away, and then walked back into the room and said to him, 'OK, that's the bad news. Now, what's the good news? What can we do? What are we going to do?'" Lea Ann's questions made it clear to the doctor that what she wanted was a battle plan for the defense of her daughter's life.

He told her then that Natalie's best hope was to receive a bone marrow transplant. "He knew that children with Fanconi's anemia had a much higher success rate—almost the only successful survival rate at that time—using a matched sibling donor," Lea Ann recalls. Because she was their first child, thirteen-month-old Natalie had no sibling. "I was pregnant within four weeks after that," Lee Ann acknowledges.

Bone marrow registries were fairly new at that time, but Lea Ann and Brad initiated donor drives to get more people registered. Although they hoped to conceive a sibling donor for Natalie, they realized that a donor outside their family might be necessary. Whether or not it helped Natalie, they wanted to encourage donor registration, and even today they are active in that effort. "A lot of people are not aware of how important it is to register as a donor. When you need it the most is when you recognize the importance of it," Lea Ann says.

The pregnancy, on which Brad and Lea Ann were placing such hope, ended in a miscarriage only about one week after they learned she was pregnant. "A lot of doctors told us we would never be able to do what we had planned on doing—our dream plan of conceiving a match. They said we would run out of time," Lea Ann explains. On the advice of her doctor, Lea Ann waited only one month following the miscarriage before becoming pregnant again. Natalie was two years old when she was joined on January 4, 1987, by her sister, Audrey, and although the new baby was healthy she was not a match.

Fanconi's anemia had never appeared in either of Lea Ann's or Brad's families, but Natalie's diagnosis revealed that her parents have a one-in-four chance of passing Fanconi's anemia on to any child they conceive. When Audrey was born, Lea Ann and Brad focused on her good health rather than on the absence of a match. "We never wanted an only child. Our first priority was hoping for a healthy child. Number two was our hope that maybe she could give Natalie a second chance at life, but when she wasn't a match, that was OK. That would have been just another, special blessing if she had been," Lea Ann says.

The absence of a match forced them to challenge the odds once more, and within twelve weeks of Audrey's birth, Lea Ann was pregnant again. Their third daughter, Emily, was born on January 14, 1988, within days of her sisters' birthdays, and at last there was a sibling donor match. Brad and Lea Ann have chosen to have no more children. "We would like to have a fourth child, but we don't want to push our luck. With the risk we carry of having another child with this dreadful disease, three is enough."

Within less than two years of the date Lea Ann was told of the need for a sibling donor, she conceived three times and gave birth twice. She admits the emotional pressure is intense for parents in their circumstances. "I would have given my life for [Natalie] to have hers. You love them so much. If right now she had to have a heart so she could live, I would give her mine. I think that is a motherly instinct. It is something no geneticist could ever understand." She is convinced, however, that parents must be free to make their own decisions in such circumstances and believes that the best protection against abuses is professional counseling. "I think what society needs to focus on is giving these families support rather than criticism. Families in these situations are not bad people. They are trying to save a child. A lot of them don't understand all the technology. They are confused. They need to be counseled in ways that will help them make the right decision within the circumstances they have been given."

During her pregnancy with Emily, Natalie was seriously ill, and the match resulting from Emily's birth may have come just in time. Both Audrey and Emily underwent prenatal testing, not so their parents could abort them if no match were found, but to implement appropriate procedures for saving the transplant material at the time of birth if a match were found. Lea Ann is adamant that they never considered abortion when tests showed that Audrey was not a match, but neither was Natalie's life in imminent peril at that time. Although they never considered an abortion, they did discuss how many children they were willing to conceive in their effort to give birth to a match, and

Lea Ann says, "We would have lost Natalie trying. We wouldn't have stopped with number three. I know that."[22]

As for the impact on her children of their donor-motivated conceptions, Lea Ann discounts it entirely. "Emily didn't choose to be a match and Audrey didn't choose not to be. It was kind of a gift from God." In fact, because the transplant material came from the umbilical cord rather than having been retrieved from her body, Emily has faced no risk or discomfort. Lea Ann would have considered more invasive donor procedures had they been necessary, however. "I think you have to keep in perspective that your ultimate goal is to save a life. You don't want to cost another child theirs, but if it would not cost one child her life to save the other, I would consider the give-and-take, the balance to both of them. Absolutely." Even though all three of her daughters are aware that Emily's cord tissue probably saved her older sister's life, Lea Ann sees no indication that the girls' lives are different because of it. "They are so well adjusted. They are just three little girls that argue and play together, the same as any other family."

Because she and Brad had received so little public comment when they chose to conceive a sibling donor, Lea Ann was surprised by the criticism of the Ayalas and spoke out in their defense. "We live in America, and we can conceive a child for any reason that we choose. How dare anybody judge us for wanting to conceive a child to help save the life of another one!"

At about the same time the headlines proclaimed the success of the Ayala sibling-donor story, sadder headlines reported the results of a legal battle involving a different family. A twelve-year-old boy died of leukemia when the mother of his half-siblings refused to allow her twin children to be tested as possible donors. Existing laws allow donation of regenerative and redundant tissue but will not compel it. When the former girlfriend of the dying boy's father refused parental consent for her minor children to be tested, the court upheld her decision. Regardless of the minimal medical risks to her children as balanced against the potential lifesaving treatment for the dying boy, the court left the mother's decision undisturbed.

As harsh as the outcome of that case was, the law is intended to protect all of us from being compelled to donate lifesaving tissue unless we choose to do so. By law, our individual rights to control our own bodies are greater than the rights of others to demand lifesaving tissue donations from us. When parents are the source of legal consent for all their minor children, it is obvious that therapeutic tissue transplants are likely to involve conflicts of interest between recipient and donor children. Loving parents are placed in the position of deciding whether a healthy child should sacrifice in some way, physical or psychological, for the potential benefit of a sick child. The reason for entrusting a parent with the power to consent is society's belief that a parent will act in the best interest of a child, but when the interests of two children conflict, how can a parent choose? Lea Ann Curry's explanation that she would balance their respective needs is the likely response of a loving parent, but the result of such balancing in lifesaving transplants is nearly always going to favor the dying child and demand sacrifice from the healthy child. In effect, the life-or-death benefit to the sick child is going to outweigh anything less than a life-threatening risk to the donor. On the other hand, who is in a better position to make this sort of decision than the parent who loves both children?

The only certain way to protect minors from the physical and psychological risks of being donors, at a time when they are too young to consent or refuse for themselves, is to completely prohibit tissue donation by minors, and such an absolute ban would sentence many sick children like Anissa and Natalie to brief, pain-filled lives. That seems to be a high price to pay for protection of donor children who do not appear to be unreasonably exploited under the current system. Since many adults choose to be tissue donors to their siblings, removing this medical option from minors might actually cause more trauma to them and their families than does our present practice of entrusting parents with the power to decide.

Physicians like Dr. Forman already recognize the importance of avoiding conceptions in which the parents value the matching tissue above the baby itself. Professional guidelines must continue to warn health care givers against their participation in donor conceptions undertaken without sufficient regard for the donor baby as well as for the tissue it may provide.

Since we do not question the motives of other parents when they decide to conceive children, it does seem illogical to criticize parents who are motivated by the desire to create a donor match, so long as the baby is welcomed into the family, regardless of whether the tissue match occurs. The real moral issue arises when prenatal testing reveals that there is no tissue match and the parents consider aborting a healthy, planned fetus simply because it cannot supply the lifesaving tissue for their dying child. If they choose to abort, it is obvious that this fetus was conceived solely to provide tissue and without respect for its independent claim to life. This is troubling even among people who favor a woman's right to choose for herself whether she should continue a pregnancy. In donor-conception situations, it is even more complicated because of the extreme emotional pressures placed on the parents by the desperate medical condition of their dying child. Are these circumstances so unique that society should limit the legal right of the mother to initiate and terminate a series of pregnancies in an attempt to create lifesaving tissue?

The United States Constitution protects the fundamental right of procreation, and any limitation of that right must be as narrow as possible. One solution for protecting the right to conceive a donor sibling while restricting the ability to selectively abort nonmatching tissue would be to withhold the results of prenatal tissue analysis from the parents until after birth. By receiving all other prenatal test results, these parents would be in the same position as all other couples with regard to making decisions about the well-being of the fetus. With-holding information about the tissue matching would, how-ever, restrict the parent's ability to abort a healthy, planned pregnancy solely on the basis of transplant-material suitability. Since the physician, but not the parents, would have full ac-cess to the test results, appropriate preparations for collecting matching tissue could be made prior to birth. Such a narrow limitation would respect the couple's fundamental rights to bear and beget children and to choose abortion for any reasons unrelated to tissue matching while taking away the potential for treating the womb as a laboratory for the creation of therapeutic material.

Each year, expanding transplant technology will present parents with increasingly complex decisions. Knowing that some-thing is medically possible is only one consideration among many when parents determine what is right for their families. The obvious moral danger is that the emotional pressure to save a dying child may tempt not only parents but all of society to sanction any lifesaving option that technology allows.

The surgical procedure with which Amy and Angela Lake-burg's parents were confronted was so morally controversial that the hospital where the conjoined twins were born declined to do the surgery. The parents transferred their babies to Children's Hospital of Philadelphia and authorized doctors there to deter-mine, based on strictly medical criteria, which of their daughters would survive the surgery. Baby Amy died on August 20, 1993, when the shared liver tissue and malformed heart were given to her sister, Angela.

Even with the surgery, Angela was given less than a 1 per-cent chance of surviving, but she battled the odds until a few days before what would have been the twins' first birthday, when she could struggle no more. Her short life was lived inside a hospital, attached to a lung machine and attended by nurses who gave her their love and affection as part of their routine care. Expenses exceeded one million dollars.

In death, as in life, Angela continues to raise questions

about the costs to her sister, to hospital and state assistance programs, to Angela herself, as well as to those who loved her—costs measured in both dollars and human suffering—as a result of the decision to employ technology in a desperate effort to save one of the conjoined twins.

After the deaths of both Amy and Angela, Joey Lakeburg appeared on *Good Morning America* with her only remaining daughter, a happy six-year-old who was eagerly describing some recent school achievements for the camera. Gently reaching out to touch her daughter, Joey said, "I'm proud of all my girls. They did the best they could."

The parents of another set of conjoined twins decided against surgery when medical necessity did not compel their separation. Together, Abigail and Brittany Hensel can do nearly everything, a situation their father sees as preferable to surgery that would have left his daughters with "half a body each."[23] The parents' decision to reject a technological solution for the Hensel twins avoided benefiting one daughter at the expense of the other or leaving each girl with severe physical limitations after surgery, but it also sacrificed an independent life for each twin.

There are no easy answers to such complex questions, and the decisions parents make do not always have happy endings. Angela's life was not saved by Amy's sacrifice for her, and Nathan Walden was not spared the suffering of Hurler's syndrome by the fetal transplant of tissue from an abortus, but other children like Annisa Ayala and Natalie Curry have been given a chance at life by the courage of their parents and doctors, and the precious gifts of donor tissue.

Lea Ann Curry treasures the gift one of her daughters gave to the other. "When you have seen it, have gone through it with other parents of children with the disease, life is just not something that you take for granted," she says. "It is a gift. Every day should be something that everybody is very thankful for." Neither, however, can adults take for granted the wisdom of using organ and tissue transplants to save one child when the donor of the gift is another little child.

Are your opinions regarding other reproductive issues dictated by your attitude toward abortion?

Should cells or tissue from aborted fetuses be used in the treatment of diseased or disabled people?

Should aborted fetuses be used in laboratory research conducted in efforts to discover possible cures of diseases and defects?

Should laboratory growth of embryo cells for medical use be prohibited by law?

Should experiments on unimplanted embryos from in vitro fertilization procedures which are conducted in order to gain knowledge to assist traditional pregnancies be prohibited by law?

Would you object to having your own organs removed after your death for transplantation?

Should the law be changed to presume consent to organ donation after death unless the deceased had declared opposition to becoming an organ donor prior to death?

Should there be a law requiring you to declare each time you renew your driver's license whether you wish to be an organ donor?

CHAPTER 13

WINTER WORKSHOP

It was such a cold January night that the program director wondered aloud whether many people would come. It was the first time Kinder-Mourn had sponsored a workshop on infertility, and she questioned whether people would actually gather to share their feelings of disappointment and loss. Long before the hour set to begin, people began filling the room, about half of them women who had come without their partners and the other half couples. Except for the struggle with infertility they shared, the participants and panelists were a varied collection of ages and social groups, although no minorities were there.

The program director began by reading published quotations from infertile women. Although everyone listened politely, their faces said more than the words she was reading to them. Finally, the panelists were allowed to share their stories.

Lane and Chet were the oldest couple on the panel, and she admitted that by the time they married, her biological clock was ticking loudly. Chet had children from an earlier marriage and wasn't even sure he wanted more children, but she persuaded him to try. Like many women today who have delayed childbearing for one reason or another, Lane had little time left.

She described the progression of steps they had taken, gradually escalating the technology and the expense. The multi-syllabic names of drugs and techniques were scattered so thickly through her narrative that sometimes it sounded as if she were speaking a foreign language, but the words were already familiar to this group. After relating setbacks and failures that would have defeated most of us, they described their joy in learning that Lane was pregnant. On her thirty-ninth birthday she gave birth by cesaerean section to twenty-four-week-old twin boys, one of whom lived fourteen hours, the other sixteen. Even before she interrupted her story, the muffled sniffling of nearly everyone present could be heard. Lane continued, "We went home with empty arms and wide-open belly to heal."

As difficult as the loss was for both of them, they were unwilling to stop trying, and a new round of infertility treatments began as soon as Lane was able. Both of them admitted the strain all of this put on their relationship. "We grieved so differently that we really couldn't help each other," Lane said. Her friends could not understand her obsession. "People ran from me," she admitted.

More disappointments followed, and in a way they couldn't explain, the option of adoption occurred to them like an idea they had never imagined until then. The journey to that moment was one they had to make before they were ready to see adoption as an appropriate choice. "You are the only ones who know when enough is enough. Don't let anyone else tell you, unless continuing to try is truly a danger to your health," counseled Lane. For them, the adoption of a little girl was the right conclusion to their story. Expressing the mixture of sadness and hope that everyone in the room shared, Chet said, "Given enough time and financial resources, something good is going to happen, as it did in our case. But we will always miss our little boys."

Rhonda began to share her experience. Her husband's health insurance through his job paid for infertility treatments, and because she was younger, she didn't feel quite the same urgency as each technique was tried. "As long as I was working on it and another treatment was available, if this one didn't work, I was OK." Once she became pregnant, there seemed to be no reason for worry. "We went and bought a crib at three months, because I wasn't having any problems." One day in her seventh month, she realized that she hadn't felt the baby move for many hours. She learned, alone at the doctor's office with her husband out of town, that she had lost the baby. "I had to call him on the telephone and tell him that my stupid body had done it again. First it wouldn't conceive, and now it had killed my baby," she said, turning her hurt into guilt and anger at herself.

She and her husband named their baby Samuel Nathan, after the biblical story of Hannah, whose baby was given up. Rhonda had continued teaching school during her pregnancy, and after the loss of her baby, she returned to the classroom. "I was the worst teacher. All of a sudden these kids that I had been teaching for so long were somebody's children."

Her husband could not understand her emotional struggle. "He just wanted me to 'straighten up.' That was it."

When she became pregnant again, she was terrified of losing the baby. "I had to learn progressive relaxation because I would sit there and just buzz from the stress." Not only did this pregnancy end happily, but also a second, unplanned pregnancy quickly followed, so that Rhonda's happy ending was the birth of not one but two children of her own.

The youngest members of the panel, Tara and George, acknowledged up front that their financial circumstances limited the infertility treatments they could pursue. George was studying nursing and Tara was working when they decided to start their family. Tara described herself as a very determined person, the kind that confronts each personal challenge with a plan and an expectation of success. Each month she expected to become pregnant. "I was a home-pregnancy-test junkie!" she declared. Unfortunately, her pregnancy ended in miscarriage.

George expressed his surprise at discovering his own anguish over the miscarriage. "It never dawned on me that a guy hurt from this. When we had our miscarriage, I thought about all the guys I knew who had been through this that I hadn't gone to see."

When doctors told Tara that it was unlikely that she could
have children, she directed her determination toward adoption
efforts. She assembled a thick, three-ring notebook, filled with
forms and certificates and reference letters to convince any
agency that might have babies available what good parents she
and George would be, and this time her determination paid off.
They have now adopted two little girls.

George counseled the group that for them adoption was a
very good option. "They couldn't be any more ours. When they
say 'Daddy,' it's awesome."

The last couple to speak, Trisha and Steve, had been married for eight and a half years when Trisha became pregnant,
and at first she wasn't even sure that she was pleased about it.
Ironically, only after she became excited about the pregnancy
did she miscarry. After that, she was committed to starting their
family, and three months later she was pregnant again, only to
miscarry once more.

Like the other panelists, Trisha described the unintentional, hurtful comments people make in these circumstances.
In her case, it was her own mother whose comment caused the
deepest hurt. "She told me I shouldn't have gotten pregnant
again so soon." Her sister, who is a nurse, commented that
Trisha should have waited at least eight months, and her
mother repeated that opinion to her. "I felt so guilty."

Trying to follow the advice, they waited to try again, but
her third pregnancy also ended in miscarriage. "I didn't think
things like this happened. I've been a good girl all my life. Nobody in our families had ever miscarried." The loss disrupted
her emotions so much that she asked for a leave of absence from
work and withdrew from everyone, even refusing to answer the
telephone. When someone suggested that she attend a support
group for grieving parents, she said she didn't feel entitled to
participate. "I didn't feel like I was a parent. I didn't feel like I
was validated." Eventually, she and Steve did attend, as everyone on the panel had, and the support helped.

Trisha described how difficult it was to grieve the loss of a child that had never been born. At the suggestion of a counselor, Trisha created a symbol of her loss. "On the months that these babies would have been born, I got three birthstones. I put them in a pendant. It was very helpful." Later, after an unintended pregnancy ended in a miscarriage, a fourth birthstone was added to the pendant.

Steve remained quiet as she spoke, occasionally touching her hand when her tears spilled over or providing a word when she looked to him for help. When she had finished, he asked the program director if he could add something. He acknowledged his carefree bachelor years and then confessed his feeling that somehow God had brought the two of them together. His simple words conveyed the helplessness of many husbands at their inability to spare their wives the suffering, both emotional and physical, as they face infertility together.

The people in that room had come together at different stages in their emotional journeys, and the past and future decisions they reached would differ, but for two hours on a cold winter night, they had done what they could to help one another find their way.

CHAPTER 14

COMPLEX CHOICES
FOR INFERTILE COUPLES

For couples facing infertility it probably offers little comfort that they are not alone. Estimates range from as many as one in five to as few as one in twelve American couples who suffer some form of infertility. Not too many years ago, their only options might have been accepting childlessness or adopting. Today they may spend many years and tens of thousands of dollars before they achieve a pregnancy or exhaust the reproductive options available to them.

Infertility is generally defined as the inability of a couple to conceive after twelve months of sexual intercourse without contraception. The term does not exclude couples who may have conceived a child together at some time in the past, nor does it attempt to identify the cause of the couple's infertility or to determine whether they might conceive with different partners. The only consideration is whether the two of them can conceive a child now.

Over the years, the definition of infertility has changed. In the past, couples were not considered infertile after only one year, but for today's couples who have delayed starting their families, the image of the loudly ticking biological clock looms large. It is also likely that the couple's ages have reduced fertility, making it harder to become pregnant just when time is so urgent.

Age is not the only explanation for the number of infertile couples, however. Other possible causes are such common reproductive toxins as alcohol, cigarettes, drugs, or the environment, or in other instances, tubal blockage from sexually transmitted diseases or contraceptives.

Just as the definition of infertility has changed over the years, the procedures for treating it have also changed. Previously, treatment might have focused on the woman. Today doctors know that male factors are involved in the couple's infertility at about the same rate as female factors are, and several factors are involved about 25 percent of the time.

Because the sperm is easier and cheaper to access, semen analysis is often the first procedure for the infertile couple today. Technicians can determine the level of functional sperm the husband has. If it is appropriate, they can employ such techniques as sperm wash and artificial insemination to maximize the ability of the sperm to fertilize the woman's egg. Even when the woman's reproductive system is functioning normally, treatment may include giving her fertility drugs to increase the odds of fertilization by increasing the number of eggs available to the sperm in one cycle. During the analysis, genetic testing may even be done on the sperm, particularly if the man has a family history of some genetic disease or is a member of an ethnic group that is at high risk for a genetic disease.

All of this can be done without any invasive procedures, and if the semen analysis indicates that conception is possible, the couple will probably be advised to attempt four to six inseminations before doctors will examine the woman more extensively. If the woman does not become pregnant, then she will be evaluated for such female infertility factors as blocked Fallopian tubes, endometriosis, or endocrinal problems interfering with conception. Once these problems are corrected, doctors will perform another series of inseminations if the couple has not conceived through sexual intercourse.

Some religious denominations, like the Catholic Church, oppose assisted reproduction, instructing their members to avoid medical interference if it goes beyond enabling couples to conceive by "natural acts of conjugal love."[1] Even within the

Catholic Church, however, there is criticism of limiting too severely the medical assistance appropriate for their members. As one Catholic biomedical ethicist says, "A child should be born within a marriage from a loving act. Sexual intercourse is not the only loving act."[2]

The procedures described so far do not involve attempts to fertilize the egg outside the uterus or any invasive retrieval of eggs. No one other than the couple has been involved as a gamete donor or surrogate. While some churches would condemn even this much technological intervention, most people would proceed with drugs or surgery if their doctor recommended the procedure. Among participants in my survey, 77 percent said they would, 12 percent said they would not, and 6.5 percent were undecided.[3]

The decision whether to begin more invasive technologies raises new moral questions. Most couples who seek help for their infertility do not think in advance about the extent of the technologies they may utilize. Rather, a progression of procedures leads them into moral territory they might never have considered in the beginning. Some people draw the line when fertilization is assisted outside the womb, even if the egg and sperm are those of the couple.

In 1978, when the first in vitro fertilization baby was born, a Gallup poll asked: "Some people oppose this type of operation [IVF] because they feel it is 'not natural.' Other people favor it because it allows a husband and wife to have a child they could not otherwise have. Which point of view comes closer to your own?" In response, 60 percent favored, 27 percent opposed, and the remaining 13 percent had no opinion about IVF. The responses of participants in my survey, when they were asked whether they would utilize in vitro fertilization with their partner, were amazingly similar to the answers given in 1978, when the procedure was new. Fifty-nine percent said they would, 22.6 percent said they would not, and 13.5 percent were undecided.[4] Even among participants who had reservations about using the procedure themselves, very few thought laws should prohibit the practice.[5]

For the many people who have no moral objection to assisted fertilization using a couple's own egg and sperm, the determining factor is the couple's financial ability to pay for the procedure and support the resulting child. For many others, however, there are serious moral issues, particularly among people who believe that a human life exists from the moment of fertilization.

The arguments surrounding respect for human embryos in assisted reproductive technologies share many common points with those made in the abortion debate, but significant differences separate the two situations. Abortion is motivated by an intention to terminate a potential life; assisted reproduction is motivated by a desire to create a life that, in the absence of technologies to assist the couple, would probably not otherwise occur. Even when fertilization occurs through sexual intercourse, the birth of a baby does not necessarily follow. In fact, most of the time a live birth does not result. The numbers may surprise you. Seventy to 80 percent of all fertilized ova and 50 to 70 percent of all embryos fail to develop into a pregnancy that results in a live birth,[6] and the natural pregnancy rate is only one per every three or four cycles. Fertility specialists believe that the rates for assisted conception compare favorably with these natural rates for pregnancy, particularly when we remember that the technology is being used by couples whose natural ability to conceive has failed. Such facts allow many people who oppose abortion to accept reproductive assistance.

The motives and statistics make no difference to others. If their religion teaches that "the spiritual soul of each man is 'immediately created,' " the reproductive material is entitled to the same respect as any living person.

Solving this moral issue is not a simple matter of accepting or rejecting a religious definition. Not all religions assign the same moment to the creation of the soul. Religious individuals may reject theological teachings about reproductive matters in light of scientific knowledge. One author points to the division of cells in the development of identical twins to refute the existence of an indivisible human soul from the moment of fertilization.[7] Even without any consensus on the spiritual nature of the embryo, most people agree that a special respect is due the material that is, at least, a potential human life. And even if people disagree about whether the embryo is entitled to the same treatment as a living person, they may be troubled by the sacrifice of a potential life or the artificial intrusion into the process of life.

Here is how in vitro fertilization is done. The woman takes hormones to stimulate the ovaries to produce eggs, which are retrieved through a needle. The eggs are fertilized by the man's sperm in vitro, meaning literally "in glass." Fertilization usually occurs in a glass dish called a petri dish rather than in a test tube despite the common name of "test tube babies" used to describe the procedure (Today there is inconsistency in the terms applied to the fertilized egg, or zygote, once it begins to divide. The term "preembryo" is preferred until fourteen days after fertilization, after which "embryo" is used; however, that terminology is far from universal, and because many of the sources contained in this book make no distinction, the more encompassing term "embryo" will be used unless the source specifically used the narrower term.) The embryos are grown in laboratory incubators for about two days before being transferred through the woman's cervix into her uterus. The embryos must implant in order for the woman to become pregnant. It does so only about 13 to 21 percent of the time, according to national averages, and for that reason, more than one embryo may be transferred to increase the odds for a resulting pregnancy.

Dr. Roman Pyrzak at the Centre for Advanced Reproductive Technology in Atlanta cautions against applying national averages to predict the outcome in individual cases. "We know of at least fifteen female factors and about ten male factors. One infertile couple may have only one factor involved, while another couple has several. Statistical averages are very unrepresentative numbers for individual cases."[8]

Fertilization in the in vitro process is usually successful. The riddle of why so many embryos fail to implant remains to be solved, and that is the focus of much current research.

Lisa Fagg knows firsthand the stress the procedure can cause. She and her husband Bill tried unsuccessfully four different times with twelve embryos to achieve a pregnancy. "People put so much faith in it, even though the statistics are relatively low. You still say, I am going to be the one in four[9] for which this will work. You put all your hopes in that one situation, and when it doesn't work it really is upsetting."[10]

The procedures leading up to IVF also exact a heavy emotional price. Another woman describes her experience after five years of infertility treatments this way: "It is such invasive therapy. Every other day they are taking blood. It got to the point that my veins were callused and it really hurt. Then there were the vaginal ultrasounds—they are not comfortable, no matter how gentle the technicians are—and measuring the egg, and giving yourself shots. It is very emotionally draining."[11]

Despite the high emotional and economic cost, in vitro fertilization offers hope to patients with damaged or absent Fallopian tubes, endometriosis, low sperm count, sperm antibodies, or unexplained infertility, and for them a 13 to 21 percent chance is better than no chance at all. Even Lisa Fagg, who has suffered four disappointments, says, "I would do it again without any hesitation."

Cryopreservation, or freezing embryos that are not implanted, is now a common practice. When more eggs are extracted than can be used at one time, the eggs may still be fertilized to create extra embryos for later attempts if the first embryos fail to implant. It is an emotional cushion for the couple to know that more than one opportunity exists, and it saves the emotional and financial cost of repeated procedures involving hormones, retrieval, and fertilization for each separate attempt to implant an embryo. Freezing embryos does raise new ethical issues, however.

Since even in sexual intercourse most fertilized eggs do not result in the birth of a baby, the statistics reflected in technologically assisted reproduction may not be terribly shocking. Cryopreservation, while allowing certain advantages for the couple, adds to the negative statistics, for about half of the embryos are lost in cryopreservation. Unlike the losses in nature, freezing introduces a risk to the embryo dissimilar to any natural event. Therefore, cryopreservation may be unacceptable for some because it is "unnatural." Eliminating all "unnatural" procedures from pregnancy and birth, however, would exclude many routine medical procedures used in most doctors' offices and delivery rooms.[12]

For those who believe the embryo is entitled to the same dignity as a baby, cryopreservation is unacceptable because it exposes embryos to a freezing process that living people would not have to endure. Unless and until humans are cryopreserved as a part of medical treatment, freezing embryos will probably remain unacceptable to this group of people. However, among the participants in my survey, the majority would consider cryopreservation if they were facing a situation that might damage their ability to produce healthy egg or sperm in the future.[13]

Other problems have arisen from cryopreservation's unique ability to suspend time. Without cryopreservation, there can be only nine months between fertilization and birth. The ability to freeze the embryo allows that time to be extended indefinitely. The more time passes, the more things may change. By tampering with nature, technology has extended the period between the time the couple decide to have a baby and the point at which the baby is born; couples may have a change of mind or a change of their circumstances in the interim. Death or divorce has intervened several times while sperm or embryos were frozen.

Mario and Elsa Ríos were a wealthy couple from Los Angeles who went to Australia for in vitro fertilization in 1981, at a time when the procedure was quite new. Two years later, they were both killed in a Chilean plane crash, leaving behind two frozen embryos with no instructions for their disposition in case of their deaths. People all around the world debated the fate of the orphaned embryos. One law professor asked colleagues at a legal seminar to consider whether the embryos owned their parents' estate or the estate owned the embryos.[14]

The Ríos case is particularly interesting from a legal point of view because both a court in California, where the couple lived, and the legislature in Australia, where the embryos were frozen, considered the legal issues involved. The California court decided that even if another woman gestated the embryos, any resulting children could not inherit. The Australian legislature decided that the embryos should be donated anonymously for implantation. Although these two legal bodies deliberated separately and in different countries, both concluded that the legal relationship between the Ríoses and their embryos ended with the couple's deaths. Both of the decisions were necessary because Mr. and Mrs. Ríos had failed to make any provisions, however.

A decade later, another case made headlines. In December 1988 nine eggs were retrieved from Mary Sue Davis and fertilized by sperm from her husband, Junior. Two embryos were transferred to her uterus on December 10, but Mary Sue did not become pregnant. The Davises had attempted IVF six times in three years and had spent $35,000 in their efforts, but never before had enough eggs been retrieved from Mary Sue for any unused embryos to have remained after the IVF procedure. For the first time, the couple used cryopreservation, and seven embryos were still frozen on February 23, 1989, when Junior filed for divorce. Mary Sue sought custody of the embryos, but Junior opposed the idea of Mary Sue or anyone else bearing his child after the marriage in which the embryos were conceived had ended.

Their divorce was granted, and both had married other partners by the time the Tennessee State Supreme Court decided their dispute over the embryos on June 1, 1992.

The court established a framework to guide other courts in deciding such cases in the future, within which framework the unique circumstances of both gamete contributors can be considered.[15] Specifically, it provides as follows: First, allow their present agreement, if they can agree. Second, enforce their prior agreement, if one was previously made. Third, if there is no present or prior agreement, their conflicting wishes are to be weighed as follows: (1) Ordinarily, the party wishing to avoid procreation should prevail, assuming that the other party has a reasonable possibility of achieving parenthood by other means. (2) If no alternative means of achieving parenthood reasonably exists, then the argument of the party desiring to use the preembryos should be considered. (3) An intention to donate the preembryos to another couple should never prevail over an opposing gamete donor.

Since Junior and Mary Sue had no agreement, past or present, the court weighed their conflicting wishes. Mary Sue no longer wished to use the preembryos herself and was seeking custody in order to donate them to another couple, so Junior's opposition was given greater weight. Disposition of the preembryos, according to the terms of the court's opinion, was entrusted to the Knoxville Fertility Clinic, but Mary Sue carried her appeal to the United States Supreme Court, where the state court ruling was allowed to stand. In June 1993, Junior's wishes were finally carried out, and the embryos were destroyed more than four-and-a-half years after their creation.

In September 1996 the Israeli Supreme Court reached a different conclusion. Like the Davises, an Israeli couple had fertilized the wife's eggs in vitro with the husband's sperm prior to their marital separation. Ruti Nahmani had a hysterectomy because of a cancerous growth in her uterus, and so the couple had planned to use a surrogate to gestate their fetus. When they separated, Danny Nahmani opposed Ruti's desire to proceed with the surrogacy. Like Junior Davis, he no longer wanted his child to be born once the relationship from which the embryo was created had ended, and he asked that the eleven fertilized eggs be destroyed.

After four years of legal battles, the Israeli Supreme Court ruled in a 7-to-4 decision that the childless Ruti should be allowed to seek motherhood by having her frozen fertilized eggs implanted in a surrogate, despite Danny's opposition to becoming a father through such a procedure.[16] The Israeli majority opinion concluded: "A woman's right to be a parent prevails over the husband's right not to be a parent."

This preference for the rights of the woman over the rights of the man is contrary to the decision in the Davis case, but the outcome itself might not be different. Remember, the American court held that the party wishing to avoid procreation should prevail if the other party has a reasonable possibility of achieving parenthood by other means. Ruti Nahmani was forty-two years old, had undergone a hysterectomy, and was estranged from the man who opposed the procreation. The absence of any reasonable possibility of her achieving parenthood by other means would seem to have led the American court, had it been considering the dispute between Ruti and Danny, to move to the second part of the Davis test, allowing the argument of Ruti to be considered. The third part of the Davis test would not apply, since Ruti's plan to use a surrogate was not a donation of an embryo to another couple but rather a means of becoming a mother herself. Therefore, an American court using the Davis test might have considered Ruti's argument and reached the same outcome as the Israeli court did.

Today it is unlikely that clinics would perform cryopreservation without having first obtained a written agreement from the gamete donors. Apparently the Davises failed to execute the documents normally required by their clinic only because forms had been misplaced. While there is always the possibility of such mix-ups, the routine procedures used in most clinics now require agreements. There remain unknown numbers of frozen embryos in storage, however, that may have been placed there before the clinics required agreements concerning their disposition. Estimates of viability for cryopreserved emryos range from two to ten years. Therefore, written agreements signed by both gamete donors and the loss of viability of embryos frozen before agreements were required are likely to eliminate future disputes like the Davises'.

Only one state has enacted legislation to settle such disputes. A Louisiana statute requires unwanted embryos to be made available for "adoptive implantation." The state's legislators have prohibited the intentional destruction of a cryopreserved IVF embryo, directing courts to resolve disputes in the best interest of the embryo. The question raised by such a law is obvious: Should someone be compelled to become a genetic parent?

In Australia, where the use of IVF was pioneered, couples are required to donate unused embryos to childless couples. Laws such as these force a person to share himself or herself genetically with strangers. Couples willing to undergo IVF in order to bear or beget their own genetic children may find it morally wrong to entrust the genetic fruit of their union, in the form of unused embryos, to the care of strangers. Under laws such as these, helpless couples must permit their genetic offspring to be raised in an environment about which they know nothing and over which they have no control. Is such government meddling, no matter how well intentioned, more or less moral than the couple's own decision for a dignified disposal of unused embryos?

The British have dealt with the disposition of unused frozen embryos differently. They have passed a law requiring frozen embryos to be destroyed after five years unless couples consent to future storage. The deadline implementing the new law occurred on August 1, 1996, when thirty-three hundred frozen embryos belonging to nine hundred couples were destroyed. As the deadline approached, clinics attempted to contact the donors of all the embryos, and about half requested extended storage. A few donated their embryos to other couples or for research. Of the remaining nine hundred couples, about one-third received but did not answer registered letters. The rest could not be found.

Although frozen embryos are routinely destroyed by clinics at the request of donor couples or because defects are discovered, the large numbers destroyed because of the new law raised public debate. Despite its opposition to the production of embryos in laboratories, the Vatican condemned the British law, calling it "prenatal massacre." The highest-ranking Roman Catholic prelate in England and Wales publicly disagreed, telling a BBC interviewer that although he considered the embryos to be "frozen human life," he believed they should be "allowed to die and then disposed of in a dignified manner." The medical director of the fertility clinic where the world's first test-tube baby was produced expressed the emotions of many scientists and medical care givers at overseeing the destruction of embryos they had worked to produce. "We are unhappy we had to do it, but there is a sense of relief it is almost over," said Peter Brinsden when the Bourn Hall fertility clinic allowed about eight hundred embryos stored there to defrost.[17]

None of these legislative solutions is entirely acceptable. Moral arguments remain whether laws compel donation or destruction of unused embryos.

The Tennessee court concluded that Junior Davis had a constitutionally protected right not to be a genetic parent against his wishes. The court noted the regret expressed by some sperm donors and by some women who have surrendered children for adoption at not having contact with their biological children, and stated strongly in support of Junior's opposition, "Donation, if a child came of it, would rob him twice—his procreational autonomy would be defeated and his relationship with his offspring would be prohibited." Yet that is exactly what Louisiana has done by law! It seems unlikely that the Louisiana statute could withstand a constitutional challenge, but the British solution, even if it were to be passed by some state legislature here, would also raise constitutional questions.

If states are concerned about the fate of embryos for which no disposition has been made, it would seem wiser that laws be limited to requiring written agreement of gamete donors prior to cyropreservation but leaving the moral decisions to the gamete donors themselves. In fact, clinics seem to be doing this without the mandate of law.

This leaves the couple with the responsibility of deciding what is best for their unused embryos, and that is not an easy decision for many people. If they are not destroyed (as Junior Davis chose) or donated to another couple (as Mary Sue Davis had wanted and as the Louisana legislature mandates), another option is to donate the unused embryos for medical research. Lisa Fagg knows how difficult that choice can be. "I don't think I could ever donate them to science. I know somebody has to for progress for the future, but I don't want them to be experimented on and then destroyed. I don't think I could ever do that."[18]

Participants in my survey also found that option troubling. When asked a variety of questions about the scientifically valuable use of embryos in medical research, participants were divided, with a large portion undecided. The strongest approval was for medical use in the treatment of living persons at 48 percent, with less support for use in research to discover possible cures at 43 percent.[19] Slightly more approved of prohibiting laboratory growth of embryo cells for medical use than disapproved of it, and slightly more disapproved of prohibiting experiments on unimplanted embryos intended to gain knowledge to assist traditional pregnancies than approved of it, but approval and disapproval were so evenly divided in both situations that there was no clear majority point of view, and changes in opinion among those currently undecided will decide future majorities.[20] Couples making decisions about their unused embryos will find no broad public concensus to guide them.

During the years after the birth of the first in vitro baby, critics warned of possible abuse of the procedure. They suggested that wealthy individuals might attempt to create multigenerational dynasties by freezing embryos with instructions to thaw and implant new offspring every twenty years far into the future. Others foresaw IVF being used to exploit rather than assist women. In fact, most of these dreadful predictions of abuse involve the participation of donors or surrogates. Without the involvement of third persons as donors or surrogates, the actual births to couples using their own eggs and sperm do not seem much different from conceptions occurring naturally. Thousands of IVF babies have already been born in this country with little incident.

There have been, however, a few isolated uses of technology for the purpose of continuing the family line after the death of the father. For example, in June 1994, when twenty-two-year-old, University of Central Florida student Emanuele Maresca was declared brain-dead after a car wreck, his family had his sperm surgically removed and frozen. Manny's wife of only two weeks wanted to protect the possibility of becoming pregnant to allow "a piece of him to live on."[21]

Six months later, a twenty-nine-year-old man lay in the morgue undergoing an autopsy when his wife requested the extraction of his sperm. Anthony Baez and his wife Maribel had only been married two and a half years and had no children, although they had intended to start their family at some future time. During a visit to New York City to see his family, Anthony and his two brothers were arrested for disorderly conduct for tossing a football in the street in the middle of the night. He died from asphyxiation during his arrest, and thirteen hours later a urologist used a needle, inserted into the tube that carries sperm from the testes, to retrieve viable sperm.[22]

These two cases did not involve wealthy men scheming to conceive a future dynasty—just two young widows hoping to ease the premature loss of husbands they loved by conceiving a child. Since viable sperm can be taken from the testes up to twenty-four hours after death, and since sperm can be frozen for perhaps twenty years, this may be a tempting procedure for grieving families anxious for offspring of deceased loved ones.

An English widow who attempted to conceive a post-mortem baby with sperm taken from her husband as he lay in a coma was prohibited from doing so by the court. Diane Blood's husband contracted bacterial meningitis, and while he was on life-support machines she asked his doctors to take samples of his sperm. After Stephen Blood died in March 1995, Diane sought artificial insemination with her dead husband's sperm. The procedure, within the regulatory jurisdiction of the British Human Fertilization and Embryology Authority, was ruled unlawful unless the deceased had given written authorization, and although Diane argued that her husband had approved of artificial insemination and had wanted children, she could not produce written consent. The Family Division of the High Court empathized with Diane Blood but upheld the ruling of the regulatory authority prohibiting her use of the sperm.[23]

There is no comparable regulatory authority within the American judicial system, and unless families oppose the postmortem insemination or unless financial claims are asserted, our courts are unlikely to become involved. A well-publicized case in New Orleans exemplifies how financial consequences to the public can bring a widow's decision to conceive a child after her husband's death into the American judicial system.

Ed and Nancy Hart had tried during four years of marriage to conceive a child, but Nancy was still not pregnant when Ed was diagnosed in March 1990 with cancer of the esophagus. Knowing that the chemotherapy his doctors recommended might make him sterile, Ed deposited sperm at a fertility clinic before beginning the cancer treatments. When the chemotherapy failed to arrest the cancer and the couple realized he would not recover, Ed asked Nancy to use the sperm he had deposited to conceive a child. Ed died in June 1990, and in September Nancy became pregnant. Baby Judith was born one year after her father's death.

Louisiana refused to recognize the baby as Ed's child because Ed was not alive when his child was conceived. Because Social Security follows the law of the state, the state's refusal to name Ed as the father on Judith's birth certificate meant Judith was ineligible for survivor's benefits. Nancy Hart sued both the state and the federal government, and five years after her birth, little Judith's entitlement to Social Security benefits was finally recognized.

Certainly the emotions that motivate women like these to consider using sperm from their deceased husbands do not spring from greed, but knowing that benefits such as Social Security are available might provide some financial incentive for a young widow to proceed with a pregnancy that she might otherwise find unaffordable. If more families become aware that sperm can be retrieved after death, might more women decide to conceive the child of a man they loved, even after his death? Should we as a society be willing to underwrite survivors' benefits for children who did not actually survive their fathers' deaths but rather came into existence after death? So far, these cases remain exceptional.

Recent research appears to be expanding the potential for storing sperm far into the future. With present technology, sperm cells can be frozen, but they cannot duplicate themselves. Eventually, the frozen sperm will lose its viability. Now scientists are developing a way to freeze stem cells which can generate not only new sperm when thawed but also new stem cells. In this way, fresh reproductive material could be produced indefinitely. Among the less futuristic uses for the technology would be providing patients about to undergo radiation treatment or chemotherapy with a means to reimplant their own stem cells after treatment.

As a related part of this research, scientists have implanted stem cells from rats into mice, and the mice have then produced functional rat sperm. If one mammalian species can host the stem cells of another, biologists may be able to preserve genetic material from an endangered species in a different host species. More troubling, however, is the possibility that animals might also be used to host human stem cells. One California sperm bank already specializes in offering the sperm of men they deem extraordinary. What if this experimental technology were used to preserve the stem cells of this century's most accomplished men for use by future generations? We may wonder whether

Einstein might have discovered even more with computer technology, whether Babe Ruth would still make the team, or whether George Washington would be elected today. Future generations might actually test similar possibilities with the offspring of great men of our own time whose stem cells had been preserved.[24]

For now, postmortem conceptions and biological immortality may not warrant concern, but perhaps the warnings about one use to which IVF procedures have been put has received too little attention. The long-term effects of fertility drugs upon the patients and the children they conceive are too little known. Only a limited time has been given to research before implementation of promising procedures. There is precedent for such concerns. Prior to 1971 the synthetic hormone DES was widely prescribed for pregnant women to help reduce miscarriages and make their babies bigger and healthier. Only after their babies grew to puberty was it recognized that cancer, infertility, and birth defects in the children could be traced to DES use by their mothers. Thalidomide was another drug prescribed for pregnant women as a cure for morning sickness before it was recognized as the cause of missing or malformed limbs, facial deformities, and defective organs in twelve thousand babies. Thalidomide was banned worldwide in 1962.[25]

One expert in reproductive health law, Lucinda Finley, worries, "I have become very concerned that the fertility drugs of the 1980s and the 1990s will become the next DES story. Women are being pumped up with these without really knowing the long-term effects."[26] The trouble is, of course, that women who hear their biological clocks ticking increasingly louder do not have time to spare while lengthy tests assess the long-term health risks of the drugs they are taking. Couples may be warned of potential unknown dangers, but with no time to waste and no alternative to substitute, most will proceed in spite of the warnings.

Even women who believe the health risks are a real threat have proceeded with the drug therapy. A cancer specialist who

conceived her own twins after three cycles of in vitro fertilization admits, "I think we may find that a lot of women who go
through this will have a higher risk of breast cancer, leukemia,
lymphomas, or other cancers of the reproductive system." Yet
she assumed the unknown risks. In addition to her fears for the
women who consent to the treatments, she also fears for their
offspring. "I look at my little babies and I think: Well, they are
healthy now, but what about in twenty years? I worry about
them."27

It is difficult to calculate the number of women and babies
who may be affected, nor is it just those women who achieve a
pregnancy who have exposed themselves to such risks. There
are also at least an equal number of women who go through fertility treatments without becoming pregnant, and probably
many more. One of those women says, "I had decided to do
one more in vitro cycle and had actually gone in for the medicine. Then I thought, 'I don't want to do this right now. I'm
going to take six months off.' I got off all the drugs and all the
hormones and discovered—golly! I'm a real person again. Now
I focus on what I have in life as opposed to what I don't have,
and on what I missed those five years by wanting something I
didn't have."28

The description of the procedures Mary Sue Davis
endured in her quest for a baby exemplifies the courage women
bring to the treatments. "Despite her fear of needles, at each
IVF attempt Mary Sue underwent the month of subcutaneous
injections necessary to shut down her pituitary gland and the
eight days of intermuscular injections necessary to stimulate her
ovaries to produce ova. She was anesthetized five times for the
aspiration procedure to be performed. Forty-eight to seventy-
two hours after each aspiration, she returned for transfer back to
her uterus, only to receive a negative pregnancy test result each
time." In declining to rule for Mary Sue, the court admitted,
"We are not unmindful of the fact that the trauma (including
both emotional stress and physical discomfort) to which women

are subjected in the IVF process is more severe than is the impact of the procedure on men."

Yet women consent to all sorts of procedures, the full impact of which may be delayed for years. The difficulty of tracing the cause, with records lost or destroyed, memories faded, and participants dead or vanished, may further complicate making the connection between the fertility treatments and their effects. Legislation may be needed to ensure that full records, including all of the drugs that are administered, are taken at the time of the treatments and are preserved for a sufficient time afterward to be available if unanticipated results occur in the future.

Early critics of technologically assisted fertilization also raised fears about another procedure. When gender preselection became possible, critics warned that couples would favor one sex over the other and gender imbalance would result. While that result does seem likely in some societies, it has not happened here. As the office manager of a clinic that has done gender preselection since 1985, Vicki Ofsa has observed, "Most of our patients come to us because they have one or two children of the same sex and they want the next to be different. They can't afford large families, and they want to increase their chances that second or third time for having a child of the sex of their choice. We don't usually see sex selection for firstborn children."[29] While studies show that most American couples would prefer a birth order of boy first and girl second, there is no finding of total gender preference. Rather, consistent with Ofsa's observation, "Many couples indicate they would not use sex preselection for their first child but would use it for sex preselection of the second child in order to achieve a balanced family."[30] Contrary to her experience with American couples, however, Ofsa adds, "We see a lot of foreign couples. In their societies, I think, having a male child is very important, so we do have a lot of foreign patients."

In addition to the use of gender preselection in order to have children of both sexes in their families, couples may use the procedure for genetic reasons. Some genetic diseases occur in only one gender. In order to avoid having a child with the disease, the couple may use gender preselection to reduce their chances of conceiving a child of that gender.

Critics point to the possibility of yet another unacceptable consequence of fertility treatments: when more fetuses are created than a woman can safely carry to term. Multifetal pregnancies increase both the medical risks for the mother and the risks of fetal deaths and impairments. Couples facing this situation must choose to (1) abort all the fetuses, (2) attempt to carry all the fetuses to term with the attendant risks to the woman and the fetuses, or (3) terminate some of the fetuses for the benefit of the surviving fetus or fetuses. The particular agony of the decision is that couples who most desire children are asked to terminate pregnancies, in effect choosing favorites among children yet unborn.

Today doctors are better able to control the risk of multifetal pregnancies. The dosage of fertility drugs can be monitored to reduce the risk of excessive egg production. Blood tests can measure the hormone levels to determine how many follicles are developing eggs, and ultrasound allows technicians to see this development occurring inside the ovary. If the specialist sees several follicles and the woman's hormone levels are high, she can be advised to avoid insemination or sexual intercourse during that fertility cycle.

Even with this greater knowledge, however, multifetal pregnancies do occur. Some women do not respond to treatment with the more effective drugs and must be treated with stronger drugs that stimulate the ovaries in less controllable ways. Other women want a child so badly that even when their doctors recommend against insemination or intercourse, they say, "I don't care. I want to get pregnant."[31]

The American College of Obstetricians and Gynecologists emphasizes the importance of preventing the problem through the appropriate fertility treatments, but since multifetal pregnancies can occur despite the best efforts of specialists, ACOG also emphasizes the need to counsel couples about the risks and benefits, including asking them to consider avoiding treatment. With these precautions, they conclude that the benefits of assisted reproduction outweigh the discontinuance of technologic assistance.[32]

As doctors unravel the secrets of ensuring successful implantation of IVF embryos, the need to transfer more than one embryo in order to increase the chances that at least one will implant decrease. So long as multifetal pregnancies are a possibility in connection with any treatment for infertility, advance counseling emphasizing the risks must continue, and women unwilling to abort any resulting fetuses should be directed away from procedures in which the creation of an unsafe number of fetuses is likely.

A British woman attracted worldwide attention by ignoring medical advice and hiring a publicist to market the story of her multifetal pregnancy. Thirty-one-year-old Mandy Allwood was told that she was carrying eight fetuses and that she would probably lose all of them unless she aborted some of them. Instead, she sold her story exclusively to Britain's largest-selling tabloid. In August 1996 front-page headlines announced WORLD EXCLUSIVE: I'M GOING TO HAVE ALL MY 8 BABIES, and Mandy's publicist boasted to the press that he intended to arrange $1.5 million in deals involving the pregnancy. The morality of the commercial arrangement seemed particularly unsavory when it was reported that the price Mandy was to be paid involved a sliding scale, with an increasing amount for each child born. Although antiabortion groups supported her refusal to abort, most of the public comments questioned whether she was motivated by respect for the individual fetuses or desire for more money, and nearly everyone criticized the exploitive journalism surrounding the case. Just as the doctors had warned, on September 30, 1996, in the nineteenth week of her pregnancy, she began miscarrying, and by the night of October 2 Mandy had lost all eight fetuses. Whatever had motivated Mandy Allwood to attempt to carry all the fetuses to term had resulted in the tragic consequence that none of them had survived the doomed pregnancy.

With the improvements of in vitro fertilization technology have come new techniques. Gamete Intro-Fallopian Transfer (GIFT) involves the assisted transfer of the woman's eggs and the man's sperm to her Fallopian tubes, where fertilization may take place naturally. Zygote Intro-Fallopian Transfer (ZIFT) is similar to GIFT except that the egg and sperm are allowed to fertilize before being transferred to her Fallopian tubes. Techniques are also being improved to allow microsurgery on the egg. Such surgery could be used to facilitate penetration by the sperm to permit fertilization, as well as surgical micromanipulation of the embryos themselves. In September 1993 a baby boy born in Atlanta became the first U.S.-born child to be conceived through the injection of a single sperm into the mother's egg. These technologies do not raise significantly different ethical questions from those surrounding IVF, however.

If all of this technology sounds expensive, it is! Lower-income couples have been unable to afford many of the treatments. This may seem unfair, but it is important to remember that treatment does not guarantee a successful pregnancy, and unlimited funding could not accomplish the truly equitable result of ensuring that all couples who want a child could have one. During his term of office, President Jimmy Carter was asked by a newswoman whether he agreed that unequal access to abortion in the family planning of women of differing economic means was unfair, and he replied: "Well, as you know, there are many things in life that are not fair, that wealthy people can afford and poor people can't. But I don't believe that the federal government should act to try to make these opportunities exactly equal, particularly when there is a moral factor involved."[33] This comment came from a President who has, in his private life, devoted himself to helping poor people through such charitable programs as Habitat for Humanity. But his life as well as his words distinguish between public and private assistance.

No one can argue that the present birth rate is too low, here and abroad. Rather, more social and environmental problems are associated with overpopulation than with population shortages. Infertility may be a personal crisis for the couples affected, but it is not a national emergency. In fact, the impact on society as a whole can be considered beneficial. Population growth is slowed. Infertile couples may, as the Vatican has suggested, actually use their circumstance as an opportunity to adopt or to assist other needy families or children.

Although the specific need for funding for infertility seems more personal than public, groups have lobbied aggressively for financial assistance for infertile couples. Some have tried to obtain state laws requiring health insurance coverage for infertility treatments and technologies. Among the first states to require such health insurance coverage was Massachusetts, which implemented its law in 1988. A decade later, as many as twelve states have mandated varying levels of coverage for infertility treatment, and several other states have considered it. Since health care costs are soaring and universal health care is such a volatile political issue, we must ask whether it is appropriate to funnel limited resources into infertility coverage. Without much government funding, the technology has nevertheless advanced so rapidly in the last decade and a half that it is difficult for practitioners to keep up. Couples seeking the benefits of the technology have been the ones to bear the costs of it. In an unusual inversion of the class exploitation some critics of reproductive technology predicted, the more affluent members of society have assumed the risks associated with experimental technologies and have paid the economic costs as well. Certainly many couples unable to afford the treatments have suffered personally from remaining childless, but it is difficult to see that the absence of public funding for research and development has seriously impeded the technology itself. Before we ask society to pay higher taxes or higher insurance premiums in order to give more Americans access to fertility treatments lacking any guarantee of success, we must decide whether society is willing to underwrite the costs. Most Americans are not.

My survey asked participants whether they would be willing to pay higher health insurance premiums or taxes to share the costs of nontraditional reproductive technologies, and although slightly more expressed a willingness to bear higher taxes than increased premiums, in both instances the overwhelming response was "no."[34] A follow-up question asked what amount they would be willing to pay, if any, and many of those who had already expressed their unwillingness nevertheless wrote "none" or "0" in the space to emphasize their disapproval. Among those who were willing to share these costs, the amounts cited were generally $200 or less annually.[35]

Regardless of public disapproval of having these costs shifted to them through taxes, direct and indirect government expenses have been incurred because of nontraditional reproductive technology. As one example, state legislatures have spent countless dollars considering whether to regulate the infertility industry. Many of the practices that legislators debated have already been implemented voluntarily by clinics and recommended to their members by professional organizations like the American Fertility Society and the American College of Obstetricians and Gynecologists. Thus, even without laws having been enacted, early abuses and mistakes have been corrected.

Since the patients and the professionals who treat them are so focused on a successful birth as the end of the matter, often too little attention is paid to the long-term effects of fertility procedures. In early 1993 a group of researchers published their analysis of data from case studies suggesting a link between certain fertility treatments and ovarian cancer.[36] Although their conclusions were valuable, the data available to these researchers limited their findings. In 1994 both the National Institute of Child Health and Human Development and the National Cancer Institute funded studies to expand knowledge of the possible risks to which women and their offspring are exposed as a result of fertility treatments.[37] Because there is little profit incentive for private money to be directed toward such studies, the funding by government and publically supported groups such as these offer the only likely source of research money. Unless recognizable side effects in sufficient numbers attract the attention of the medical or legal communities, we may not learn of long term consequences to the women or their children.[38] The most likely source of grant funds for this research is the public, whether paid through taxes or charitable contributions.

Another way public funds could be spent to benefit the society at large rather than individual infertile couples is for research into the underlying causes of so many cases of infertility, such as sexually transmitted diseases and environmental toxins. Correction of these problems would save future couples from infertility and eliminate their need to undergo the financially and emotionally costly treatments.

Technological assistance in achieving a pregnancy is least controversial if no donors or surrogates are involved. When an infertile couple use their own egg and sperm, and technology is employed only to assist what would otherwise be a traditional union, the primary issues are moral and economic. At a time when we are unable to resolve our political differences concerning women's access to abortion and are struggling to reduce the national debt to which well-intentioned social programs have contributed, most Americans are willing to leave the private, moral choices involved in treating infertility to the individuals and their doctors, so long as the rest of us are not asked to open the public purse for assistance.

If you desired a child and you (or your partner) were unable to become pregnant after over a year of trying, would you try drugs or surgery to correct a medical problem?

In those same circumstances, would you try in vitro fertilization with your partner?

Would you consider freezing your egg/sperm if you were facing a situation that might damage your ability to produce healthy egg/ sperm in the future?

If you had frozen eggs/sperm or an embryo, what should happen to the cryopreserved reproductive material in the event of

- you or your partner's death?
- both of your deaths?
- divorce?

Should unimplanted embryos from in vitro fertilization procedures be used in laboratory research for possible cures of diseases or defects?

Should unimplanted embryos from in vitro fertilization procedures be used in the medical treatment of diseased or disabled living persons?

If you were unable to conceive a child with your partner after over a year of trying, would you consider accepting infertility and redirecting your desire to have a child to other pursuits?

Should in vitro fertilization with your partner be covered by health insurance?

Should drugs or surgery to correct medical problems related to infertility be covered by health insurance?

Would you be willing to pay higher health insurance premiums to cover the costs of extending coverage for in vitro fertilization to all policyholders?

Would you be willing to pay higher health insurance premiums to cover the costs of extending coverage for drugs and surgery related to infertility to all policyholders?

Would you be willing to pay higher taxes so the government could assist in paying for in vitro fertilization treatments?

Would you be willing to pay higher taxes so the government could assist in paying for drugs and surgery to treat infertility?

If you are willing to pay higher premiums and/or taxes to cover the costs of treating infertility, how much more would you be willing to pay annually?

Whether or not you would personally utilize in vitro fertilization with your partner, should such procedures be prohibited by law?

CHAPTER 15

THE STORY OF ARLETTE SCHWEITZER

When Christa was told at age fifteen that she had been born without a uterus, she and her mother devised a plan. Although it had never been done, they decided that when the time came for Christa to have a baby, her mother, Arlette, would carry Christa's baby for her. Over the years, they held to their plan, believing the technology would catch up with their dream. When Arlette Schweitzer finally became the first American grandmother to give birth to her own grandbabies, people were amazed, but she does not see herself or the surrogacy itself as particularly remarkable. "I was just a mother helping her daughter. It was more like donating a kidney,"[1] she says.

In fact, her first offer had been to donate her uterus for transplanting into Christa, but doctors told them this could not be done. Although Christa was born without a uterus, she has ovaries and they produce healthy eggs.

"We had read that there was a test-tube baby born in England, so we thought of doing this. We were aware that it had never been done, and I guess we knew that our chances weren't really good. But I am the kind of person that puts the cart before the horse," Arlette admits. "I just expect things to work out. Even when the odds are against me, I expect them to turn out the way I want."

Among the few people with whom they shared their plan were husband and father Dan and several other members of their close-knit family. Dan supported the idea, but the rest of the family did not take their plan too seriously. "I don't think anyone ever believed we really would do it. Christa, Danny, and I all had the impression over the years that they all felt it was just something we were saying to make ourselves feel better."

Certainly the most important person to join in their plan was Kevin Uchytil, the man Christa eventually married. Christa told him about what she and her mother planned to do very early in their relationship, even before she and Kevin became seriously involved, and he was pleased about the possibility it offered. When Kevin and Christa finally married, they quickly decided to start their family.

As a Catholic, Arlette knew that the Church opposes surrogate births, and although she was committed to carrying Christa's baby, she admits to having struggled with her conscience. "I knew that I wasn't going to change my mind, but I prayed about it and put it in the Lord's hands. From the beginning, Christa and I believed the Lord would decide what He wanted for us, and if it didn't work, we would know it wasn't His will. We both have a strong commitment to Mary, and we also prayed to her."

Because of her respect and affection for their local priest, she never spoke to him about her decision. "I knew his position would have to be one of following the Church, and our position had to be one of following our hearts. I didn't want him to have to be torn."

Dr. William R. Phipps of the University of Minnesota performed the in vitro fertilization and implantation. Eggs were taken from twenty-two-year-old Christa and fertilized with Kevin's sperm before being transferred into Arlette's body. Biologically, the parents and grandmother are exactly as they would have been if Christa had been able to carry her own babies.

Four embryos were transferred, and Arlette explains, "Dr. Phipps warned us about the possibility of all four embryos implanting and told us that some people choose to abort one or two if that happens. We told him right off that whatever the Lord gave us we would accept." Arlette was warned that carrying four fetuses could be risky to her, but because both she and Christa are opposed to abortion, they were determined not to consider it. Only two of the embryos implanted, and within days Arlette had her first ultrasound. "If ever in my life I've thought about abortion, it was on that table at that moment—not thought about having it done—thought about how wrong it was. Because, there I am with these minute grains of rice, less than that, and we're seeing their hearts beating. It was the most profound, profound moment."

Although Arlette's pregnancy was considered high-risk because of her age (forty-two) and her health (asthma), and Arlette was already menopausal by then, physically the pregnancy felt no different to her than when she carried her own children two decades earlier. She acknowledges, however, "With this pregnancy, more than with my own, not only was I a little wiser but the world is a little wiser. We know so much more about the development of these babies. I tried to do everything right—not just the medical aspects but eating right and not taking a drink." She also felt that she had been entrusted with something that was not her own. "It's like comparing caring for your own children with caring for someone else's children. You feel this huge responsibility if something were to happen. I felt that greater responsibility."

Unlike most surrogacy arrangements, Arlette and Christa had nothing in writing. Arlette believes, "It was unwritten because it didn't have to be [written]. We know each other so well, and that is one of the benefits of not hiring a surrogate. Christa knew that I would do everything in my power to have healthy children for her. And I knew that no matter what, she would take these babies, even if they were born deformed or retarded. We went to all the medical examinations together, and I think that if anything would have cropped up, we would have dealt with it the best at that time."

On October 12, 1991, five weeks early, Chad Daniel was born to his grandmother by cesarean section, weighing six pounds and three ounces and measuring $20^1/_4$ inches long. One minute later, Chelsea Arlette was born, weighing four pounds

seven ounces and measuring 18 inches long. On their birth certificates, Kevin and Christa Uchytil are listed as the parents,
based upon the sworn statement of Dr. Phipps. Despite their
early arrival, both of the twins were healthy, with mature lungs.

Although the family had tried to avoid publicity, a few
weeks before the births, news had somehow leaked to the press.
With the arrival of the twins, headlines across the nation
declared, GRANDMOTHER GIVES BIRTH TO TWINS AS SURROGATE
FOR HER DAUGHTER. When Arlette left the hospital five days
later, she allowed pictures, but declined to answer any questions
except to say she felt fine.

While Arlette would have preferred no publicity, her typically positive attitude has allowed her to find some good in it.
"We did not ask for the publicity. It was thrust upon us, but in
some instances we can see the benefits of it. Christa has Rokin-
pansky-Kuster-Houser syndrome, and we have been contacted
by people with this syndrome from as far away as Spain."

We know little about Rokinpansky's, and it occurs in only
about one in every five thousand women. Since no woman with
Rokinpansky's has ever been able to carry her own child, no one
knows whether the syndrome would be passed by the mother to
her female offspring. One of the interesting medical benefits of
this surrogacy is that for the first time the biological daughter of
a woman with Rokinpansky's syndrome has been born, and
doctors may learn from Chelsea whether the condition is passed
genetically.

As far as publicity about her role as a surrogate goes,
Arlette is a very reluctant spokesperson. "I don't even consider
myself a surrogate. I was just a mother helping her daughter,
and I would never have considered doing it under other circumstances." Since the birth of the twins, she has talked to many
other couples considering surrogacy, and she sympathizes. "I
understand the need, the desire to want to have a child so desperately." She also recognizes that her own family has benefited
from the technology. "I sound so hypocritical, like I am turning
things for my own use, but I feel we must be careful of how we

use medical technology." Christa is equally certain that had her mother been unable to carry the twins, there would have been no surrogacy. For both of them, the process was a matter of family love and not based upon whatever was technologically possible.

Arlette expresses two particular concerns about surrogacy. First, she doubts whether a hired surrogate shares the same level of responsibility toward the fetus that is felt by a surrogate acting out of love and without compensation for the gestation. "I am not an advocate for surrogacy generally, and yet I am an advocate for someone that would do it because they cared about that other woman—for a sister, a mother, or mother-in-law, or even a very close friend who says, 'I care about you and I know that you need this help.' " She explains further, "A hired surrogate is going to get her money whether she delivers a four-pound, premature baby that hasn't been nourished correctly or whether she does everything exactly as she was supposed to. There's not as much at stake. They are just hired to do a job."

Her second concern involves the use of genetic material from someone other than the couple. Christa's ability to produce the eggs from which Chad and Chelsea were conceived was essential to their plan, and neither Arlette nor her daughter would have considered a surrogate birth using donated egg or sperm. "I think we are playing games with ourselves when we start borrowing the actual makings of the baby from other people and then saying this is my child. I think those are the cases where there are going to be problems."

A surrogate who gestates an embryo created from the egg and sperm of the parents for whom she carries the child normally has no genetic link to the baby. Arlette is different because she has the genetic link of a grandmother whose traits passed through her daughter's egg. As far as she is concerned, her love for Chad and Chelsea is no different from the love she feels for her other three grandchildren, although she admits that she worried a little before they were born about whether there might be a difference. "It's even strange to me. I cannot believe that there is absolutely no difference. I walk into a room, and whichever grandchild gets to me first gets scooped up first." As she struggles to explain how this could be, she remembers something. "It's like when you are expecting your second child. You worry, I love my first child so much that I can't possibly love this second one as much. And then the second one is born and ah! it all just fits into place and you love them both the same. That's the way it is with the grandchildren."

After the birth of Chad and Chelsea, Dan Schweitzer described his new grandbabies as "two little miracles." Grandmother Arlette agrees. "There is no way that anyone could look at Chad and Chelsea and not know that they certainly are a gift from Him." But then she adds, "Just as each child is."

Today the twins are happy, healthy six-year-olds, and Christa and Kevin are relishing their roles as parents. "Motherhood was Christa's vocation," Arlette believes, "and Chelsea is already just like her mom, trying to mother Chad all the time." Christa has decided not to have Chelsea tested for Rokinpansky's syndrome until she is older, but Arlette confides, "I am taking very good care of myself." For a moment the meaning of her comment isn't clear, until she continues: "I don't know if Chelsea will need me—and we all hope she won't—but if she has inherited Rokinpansky's syndrome and wants me to carry her babies for her, too, I will if my health allows it." Arlette is prepared for the skeptical reactions of people to her notion of a great grandmother surrogate. After all, she and Christa faced years of skepticism. She mentions the possibility of being a surrogate for Chelsea in a casual way, but her sincerity is apparent. "What else could I do if she asked me? I could never deprive her of children and Christa of grandchildren if it were in my power to make it happen."

CHAPTER 16

THE MORAL, EMOTIONAL, AND LEGAL
COMPLEXITIES OF SURROGACY

Unlike the quiet, often secret, acceptance of third parties as gamete donors, the participation of another woman in the pregnancy, as a surrogate, has received enormous public attention.[1] Certainly one explanation is the visible nature of her role. The surrogate's connection is not remote, either in time or in place. The couple can no more ignore the presence of the surrogate during the pregnancy and birth than the surrogate can ignore the creation of a real baby from her acts. She cannot be clinically removed from the picture in the same way donors disappear behind images of white laboratory coats, petri dishes, and stainless steel instruments, nor can the baby remain an abstraction to the surrogate. The physical proximity of the surrogate throughout the reproductive process seems to have forced a public consideration of her role in the conception and birth, unlike the tacit willingness to ignore the role of donors.

If the wife is able to produce eggs but is unable to carry the baby, a surrogate may gestate and give birth to the couple's own genetic child. These surrogates are called gestational surrogates or nongenetic surrogates to distinguish them from surrogates who provide both the egg and the gestational environment. Because the procedure for extracting eggs requires greater technology than sperm donation or artificial insemination of a genetic surrogate, gestational surrogacy is the most recent of the reproductive techniques involving third parties.

For women like Christa Uchytil, it is uniquely heartbreaking to know that their ovaries are producing healthy eggs but some other problem makes it impossible for them to gestate and give birth to their own babies. For these women, the only option allowing the birth of their own genetic offspring involves the cooperation of a surrogate.

In the future, ectogenesis may be an option for women without a uterus. The possibility of growing a fetus in an artificial environment outside the mother's womb seems less fantastic when we recognize that smaller and more premature babies are being saved with neonatal technology, and embryos are being created and observed in the laboratory in connection with technologically assisted conception. The time a fetus must be within a womb is being reduced from both ends of gestation. Considering the rate at which other reproductive technologies have developed during the past decade, we may be amazed by the development of artificial gestational environments at some future time. Such technology would present a philosophical challenge to both sides in the abortion debate. If an aborted fetus could be sustained in an artificial womb, the independent right to life of the fetus—without a corresponding dependency upon the mother—would clearly change. While we expect pro-life advocates to object to this, the potential to save fetuses from abortion through ectogenesis might eliminate such opposition. On the other hand, pro-choice advocates would be faced with deciding whether freeing the woman from her role during gestation should require women to consent to ectogenesis for the aborted fetus as a part of the abortion procedure.

Participants in my survey were asked whether research to enable the creation of an artificial womb should be prohibited, opinions favoring and disfavoring were nearly equal. Forty-three percent said it should be prohibited, 40 percent said it should not, and a small 14.5 percent were undecided.[2]

For now, laboratory gestation is still impossible. Couples whose infertility is caused by certain female factors must rely upon a surrogate to gestate their fetus if they are going to experience the joy of their own genetic child.

A gestational surrogate is generally used by a couple who

can provide the embryo conceived from their own egg and sperm. However, the gestational surrogate could just as easily continue the pregnancy begun with the egg of a donor. On January 14, 1993, James Alan Mack, Jr., was delivered by cesarean section to his Aunt Kathy. He was conceived from an egg donated by his Aunt Ann, because his mother, Linda, had been forced by severe endometriosis to have a complete hysterectomy fifteen years before his birth. Because the gestational surrogate is the sister of Baby Jimmy's father, she could not provide the egg. The egg donor is the sister of Baby Jimmy's mother, but she was emotionally unwilling to face the prospect of giving up a baby she had carried for nine months. Aunt Ann provided genetic material that continued the family line of Jimmy's mother, and Aunt Kathy gestated her own brother's fetus without contributing any genetic link. Their complicated arrangement illustrates why three different women might be involved as donor, gestational surrogate, and the ultimate nurturing mother of the baby.[3]

Bruce Wilder, who is both a practicing neurological surgeon and a lawyer respected for his writings on genetic and reproductive law, criticizes the general tendency to place emphasis on the genetic contribution in the conception of the child when third parties are involved. While he does not advocate ignoring the genetic contribution altogether, he does believe that, "using genetic origins (or lack of them) as a touchstone for determining legal relationships to the exclusion of other factors is unwise policy and is going to create more legal problems than it solves."[4]

His argument minimizes what is, in fact, a primary motivation for many couples seeking infertility treatment—specifically, their desire to continue the family line, to forge the genetic link between past and future. If the longing for a child had no genetic component, the empty place in their families could be filled from among those children awaiting adoption or foster care. While some of these children awaiting families are physically or mentally disadvantaged, couples who undertake infertility treatments are not guaranteed physically or mentally perfect babies, either. Yet the mother of an adopted Romanian orphan, who considered infertility treatments before deciding to adopt, says, "Adoption is nearly always a last choice."[5]

Most couples do not want just any baby. They want a baby genetically related to them. One infertile adoptive mother, who despises what she calls "society's romance with its own genes," says, "I think biological and genetic narcissism, not racism, is the true reason people don't want to adopt already homeless children. I think the human race will feel a responsibility to all children only when and if they lay this biological narcissism to rest." She continues, "Technology is only catering to it and reinforcing it."[6]

Others disagree. For them, the need for the genetic contribution from both the husband and the wife is not narcissism but rather the ethical justification for the assistance of technology or a third person in the creation of their families. What Arlette Schweitzer calls "borrowing the actual makings of the baby from other people" is the ethical line that many couples refuse to cross.

Like Christa Uchytil, Chrispina Calvert could produce healthy eggs but lacked a uterus in which to gestate her own fetus. Chrispina and her husband Mark contracted with Anna Johnson for the gestation of an embryo created with the married couple's own egg and sperm. Even before the birth of the baby the agreement had broken apart, and both the Calverts and Anna had brought legal actions against each other. Christopher Michael Calvert was born on September 19, 1990, and blood tests were used to exclude the possibility that Christopher was Anna's biological child. The case is particularly interesting because Chrispina is Asian, Mark is white, and Anna is black. Even after the blood tests determined that Christopher is the biological offspring of Chrispina and Mark and has no genetic relationship to the surrogate who gave birth to him, Anna continued to claim a legal right to be recognized as Christopher's mother. California law recognizes only one natural mother, but both blood tests and giving birth can be used as proof of motherhood. In this case, each woman met one of the judicially accepted tests. Therefore, the California Supreme Court devised a new rule to break the tie by looking to the intentions expressed in the surrogacy agreement. "[W]hen the two means [of proving maternity] do not coincide in one woman, she who intended to procreate the child—that is, she who intended to bring about the birth of a child that she intended to raise as her own—is the natural mother under California law." In addition, the court rejected any recognition of dual claims and refused to order visitation rights for Anna, saying: "Any parental rights Anna might successfully assert could come only at Chrispina's expense . . . [and] such an interest would necessarily detract from or impair the parental bond enjoyed by Mark and Chrispina." The California Supreme Court ruled that in the case of a nongenetic, gestational surrogacy, the surrogate's role in the life of the baby ends with the birth, if that was the preconceptual agreement of the parties.[7]

Consider the impact on the lives of the new family when a baby's birth involves a nongenetic surrogate. The couple gains a child genetically related to both of them. They will miss experiencing the pregnancy firsthand, and their baby may be exposed to unknown prenatal risks during the surrogacy, but once the baby arrives, the couple can enjoy a parenting opportunity nearly equivalent to the traditional birth.

The baby inherits the same genetic potential and enters the same home environment that would have followed an unassisted gestation and birth. There are no missing branches to the baby's family tree or any artificial grafts on the tree from outside the baby's natural family. Despite the fascination many people have for genealogy, few give much thought to their own gestation. Therefore, unless the baby suffers some prenatal consequence, such as adverse effects from substance abuse by the gestational surrogate, the distinct impact on the baby as a result of surrogate gestation is minimal.

It is more difficult to generalize about the impact on the

surrogate following the baby's birth. Obviously, for surrogates like Anna Johnson, the separation from the baby they have borne is heartbreaking. Other surrogates are content to accept their limited role of gestation, and they often describe themselves as a baby-sitter hired to provide full-time care for a period of nine months.[8] But when the surrogate provides not only the gestational environment but also one-half of the genetic heritage of the baby, different moral issues are raised. The genetic surrogate is both a donor and a gestational surrogate, for she contributes her own egg to be fertilized through artificial insemination with the husband's sperm.

Those taking my survey saw a significant difference between surrogacies in which a couple provide the egg and sperm, as opposed to surrogacies in which not all of the genetic material comes from the couple. Their responses reflect a general disapproval of all surrogacies, but survey participants expressed less opposition if the couple provide both egg and sperm. Their opposition increases when genetic material for the surrogacy comes from a donor or the surrogate herself; the extent of the disapproval is nearly identical whether the sole genetic contributor is the male or the female partner. Like Arlette Schweitzer, survey participants were troubled by the idea of borrowing genetic material and were less likely to consider that reproductive option for themselves and more likely to want the practice prohibited by law.[9]

In 1987 nearly everyone in America took sides in the battle for Baby M, and most people sided against the surrogate.[10] Mary Beth Whitehead was a married woman with two children of her own when she decided to become a surrogate. She met William and Elizabeth Stern through lawyer Noel Keane. The couple sought a surrogate because of Elizabeth's multiple sclerosis. At that time nearly all surrogates were artificially inseminated, and the pregnancy was achieved with the surrogate's own egg. After Baby M was born, Mary Beth refused to relinquish as she had agreed, and the legal battle for custody began.

When the trial court upheld the surrogacy agreement in favor of Baby M's father, Mary Beth told the press, "I will not give up. I will fight as long as it takes. She's my flesh and blood. No judge can change that. . . . I believe that there is something so wrong and so harmfully unnatural about the surrogate practice that our courts will return Sara [*sic*] to me."[11] Eventually, the New Jersey State Supreme Court overturned the lower court deciding that Mary Beth Whitehead, as the genetic surrogate, was legally Baby M's mother and that she could not be forced to comply with the terms of her written agreement with the Sterns.[12] Mary Beth's legal prediction to the press came true—but at what cost?

Baby M will grow up in an environment split between her surrogate mother and her father, who have little in common except their love for her and their antagonism toward each other. Elizabeth Stern's dream of adopting Baby M is impossible, since there can be no adoptive mother without a termination of the natural mother's rights. Mrs. Stern is both a genetic and a legal outsider in her own family, and it must be difficult—at least some of the time—for her not to feel emotionally excluded as well.[13]

Baby M was not the only child in this case to suffer from the failed surrogacy agreement between the adults. In her book, Mary Beth describes a conversation with her ten-year-old daughter, Tuesday, who looked past all the legal technicalities of the surrogacy arrangement and warned her mother, "She will never forgive you if you give her up, and if she grows up and finds out you *sold* her, she will hate you."[14] Surrogacy affected her relationship with both of her older children. "I have also learned that older children can never believe and trust a mother who tells them that they are loved and valued and that it's only their baby brother or sister who had a price tag,"[15] Mary Beth says.

Another surrogate received early public attention by appearing on television to speak positively of her decision. After the birth of a baby boy, Elizabeth Kane (her pseudonym) honored her agreement with the couple who had contracted for the surrogacy but discovered too late the emotional cost to her entire family. In her own book about her surrogacy, she writes, "I do regret that what I had thought or intended to be a selfless act for an unknown family turned out to be a selfish act toward my own."[16]

A Wisconsin case involved three generations of one family in the emotional turmoil of the married surrogate's pregnancy. The surrogate's mother- and father-in-law were so upset by her surrogacy that they threatened to bring legal action to disown their son and to have her declared an unfit mother of her own children, conceived during her marriage to their son. Although the surrogate's husband supported his wife's decision to become a surrogate, it caused a schism in his relationship with his own parents.[17]

Psychologist Hilary Hanafin came to the Center for Surrogate Parenting in Los Angeles to study the surrogates for her academic dissertation and stayed to guide the surrogacy program through its early years and to help develop the criteria they use today in selecting participants. She points out that the surrogacies that go wrong are the ones that receive media attention.

The Center began arranging surrogacies in 1980. Unlike some surrogacy programs, the center sees an ethical responsibility to interview both potential surrogates and prospective parents and to refuse those for whom they believe surrogacy is inappropriate.[18] Much of the responsibility for making the decision to accept or refuse participants rests on Dr. Hanafin's shoulders.

As a result of criteria Dr. Hanafin helped develop, only about one in every twenty of the women who inquire about becoming a surrogate actually enters their program. As for the couples seeking a surrogate, Hanafin says, "An increasing number of couples who apply as prospective parents are rejected. The decision has nothing to do with demographics or some discriminating factor per se. Sometimes their attitude toward the surrogate is inappropriate or their grief is too heavy, and we must tell them that professionally and ethically, we don't feel we can do the best job for them."[19]

From 1980 when the center began arranging surrogacies until 1996, no dispute over custody had occurred in over five hundred surrogacies, as a result of their careful selection process. When one of the center's surrogates finally tried to avoid the terms of the agreement she had signed in order to gain custody or visitation of the baby she had borne, a California court awarded full legal and physical custody to the couple.

The single most legally unsettling consequence of surrogacy births is the custody disputes. It is certainly in the best interest of babies born through surrogacy arrangements not to be thrust at the moment of birth into a tug-of-war over custody. Unfortunately, there is no universal public or professional consensus regarding claims to the baby.

Many legal analysts emphasize the gestational mother's superior emotional claim to the baby because of the bonding that occurs during pregnancy, and they assume that such an intense relationship occurs for every woman. A lawyer in her thirties refuted that argument effectively, for as she spoke she was eight months pregnant with her second child and felt none of the emotions others were assigning to all women in her circumstances. "When I'm pregnant, I just feel like a container," she said. "I really don't feel anything for the baby I'm carrying. In fact, real feelings, for me, don't start until several weeks after he's born, when he gets big enough to do something cute. I can certainly see why women would be willing to carry another woman's baby."[20] Whether her feelings are the exception or the rule, her words make it clear there can be no fixed presumptions concerning the feelings the participants to the surrogacy will have for the baby at the moment of birth. Those who discount the emotional investment of the infertile couple are ignorant of the indignities and suffering involved in the infertility treatments that have in all probability preceeded the surrogacy, and they are insensitive to the hopes and dreams the infertile couple have committed to the pregnancy. Making the determination

of parental rights a contest of emotional investment ignores the
unavoidable reality that whatever the court decides is likely to
be emotionally devastating for someone. An unseverable emotional connection to the fetus has nothing to do with an umbilical cord.

Participants in my survey were given six factors to evaluate
regarding conflicting claims to the baby and were asked to rank
them in terms of importance. Two of the factors were given
clear prominence among their responses: first, the terms of the
surrogacy agreement and second, the genetic relationships shared
with the baby. Opinions about the other factors were far more
muddled. The third most popular factor was economic ability
to provide for the baby, but that same factor was picked as least
important by the second-highest percentage. In other words,
people were likely to rank financial considerations either in the
top three or dead last. Respondents were also inconsistent about
ranking the maternal feelings of the surrogate. Her feelings were
ranked least important by the greatest percentage of participants, but more people ranked her feelings most important
than ranked the feelings of the father or those of his wife
(whether or not the wife was genetically related to the baby)
highest among the six factors. The maternal feelings of the
father's wife least often ranked in the top three, but her feelings
were not ranked last as often as the feelings of the surrogate
were. The father's feelings were ranked first less often than any
other choice, but his feelings were ranked last less often than
those of either the surrogate or his wife. To summarize, participants tended to look first to the agreement that had been made
prior to the conception, second to the genetic relationships,
third to economic considerations, and then to the feelings of
the adults. The surrogate's feelings were generally regarded as
least important.[21]

In an effort to recognize the emotional investment of all
the adults involved, others suggest shared-custody arrangements
when disputes occur, as was the final result in the Baby M case.
This approach forces the baby into a broken-home environ-

ment from birth, and too many Americans already know how difficult that situation can be. Even worse, the baby is then split between adults who may lead very different lives and who are unlikely to cooperate in the raising of the child. From the example of the Baby M case, where the biological mother and father could not even agree whether their child's name is Sara or Melissa, and the child herself has invented the name Sassy (which sounds suspiciously like an effort to compromise the intransigence of the adults), we cannot help wondering what other compromises and unresolved conflicts children caught in court-ordered split arrangements might face.

Some legal authorities have suggested that the law should presume that the continuation of the baby's existing custody is best. Harvard law professor Martha Field admits that "in the context of disputes involving newborns, these presumptions would appear invariably to favor the woman who has borne the child."[22]

Another authority goes even further, urging that the gestational mother should be "irrefutably presumed mother for all legal purposes," whether she has provided the egg or is merely gestating an embryo created from the egg and sperm of the couple with whom she has contracted.[23] Five reasons for this inflexible rule are given: (1) This is the one participant sure to be present at birth; (2) Her identity is easy to determine, unlike the identity of the suppliers of egg and sperm, since the embryo that implanted may not have been the one intended; (3) She is there to care for the baby; (4) The child would be deemed the legitimate offspring of a certain person; and (5) The gestational mother would be given a final opportunity to revoke her agreement with the couple if the emotional bonds created during the pregnancy have become too strong to sever. This same authority also recommends that "the child's father should be presumed to be the husband of the child's mother" as a means of protecting both the baby and the integrity of the family unit.[24] If such a legal scheme were followed, the surrogate and her husband could be deemed legal parents of a child with whom they share no genetic connection while the couple who conceived the baby from their egg and sperm would be forced to watch their genetic child being raised by a woman who reneged on her promise to them. Any benefit such a scheme would have in terms of avoiding future custody battles is more than offset by its inhumanity toward the genetic parents and the baby itself.

Unless society determines that surrogacy arrangements should not be upheld under any circumstances, the primary consideration in determining custody disputes should be the intentions of the parties at the time they entered into the surrogacy agreement, except where it is not in the best interest of the baby to honor those intentions. Laws allowing the surrogate to revoke her agreement and keep the baby, sacrifice the feelings of the infertile couple in favor of the one who has breached the couple's trust, without any guarantee that the surrogate will be a better parent for the baby. Survey responses indicate there would be popular support for enforcing their agreement.

When the California Supreme Court decided the dispute between the Calverts and Anna Johnson, the majority based their decision on the intent of the parties as stated in their surrogacy agreement, prior to the conception. One justice dissented from the majority opinion, believing instead that even in a gestational surrogacy arrangement, the legal mother should be determined by what is in the child's best interests.[25] He was correct in emphasizing that courts must not appear willing to enforce surrogacy agreements harmful to the resulting babies, but his approach pays too little respect to the circumstances that lead to the birth of a child in the first place. Unless there is some proof that legal enforcement of the terms of the surrogacy agreement would be hurtful to the baby, the court should not even attempt to determine which of the two women would be the better mother. In other words, the legal balance should favor the couple, according to the agreement among the adults, even if the court believes the surrogate might be a better mother, *unless* there is evidence that the child needs the court's protection.

The use of surrogates has grown, but certain concerns remain. One woman acknowledges the injustice of infertility but believes, "Infertility, like blindness, or any other physical incapacity, is sad. But just as the blind have no legal or moral rights to be cured with another's eyes, the infertile have no right to cure their infertility with another's child. No child should be created as a product to be sold."[26] Following her reversal of attitude toward surrogacy, Elizabeth Kane wrote, "Surrogate motherhood is nothing more than the transference of pain from one woman to another. One woman is in anguish because she cannot become a mother, and another woman may suffer for the rest of her life because she cannot know the child she bore for someone else."[27]

In the Baby M case, the New Jersey State Supreme Court interpreted the surrogacy contract as "the sale of a child, or, at the very least, the sale of a mother's right to her child, the only mitigating factor being that one of the purchasers is the father."[28] Since baby selling is illegal in New Jersey, as it is in all fifty states, the court refused to enforce the contract against Mary Beth, ruling that the agreement was illegal and thus void. The court rejected the argument that her surrogacy payment could not represent the sale of a baby since Stern could not be accused of buying his own child.

Other states have not made these agreements void, but have declared them to be voidable at the option of the surrogate. In other words, the surrogate may enforce it against the couple but the couple may not enforce it against her to gain custody of the child she refuses to relinquish. Except as a way to discourage surrogacies altogether, making surrogacy contracts voidable is a poor legislative response to the issue. Refusing to enforce terms which were agreed upon by everyone before conception is an unfair treatment of the parties who entered into the arrangement in reliance upon its terms when they conceived the baby, and making the agreement voidable at the surrogate's option gives her both the legal right to revoke her agreement or enforce it, while the couple can do neither. The legislators would do better to require that both the surrogate and the couple be represented by separate legal counsel at the time the surrogacy agreement is signed so as to ensure that everyone understands the procedure itself and the terms of the contract, and to prevent any party from taking advantage of another. Or the state might require that psychological evaluations be attached to all agreements reflecting the emotional suitability of all parties to participate in the surrogacy arrangement. If the state is going to involve itself in surrogacies, it should implement requirements to assist in making them successful rather than facilitating their failure by making agreements voidable.

It is interesting to contrast how professionals regard a surrogate who changes her mind as opposed to how the general public sees her refusal to honor her surrogacy commitment. Professionals tend to show sympathy for the surrogate, like the New Jersey judges who refused to hold Mary Beth Whitehead to the terms of her own agreement. The American College of Obstetricians and Gynecologists endorses the idea of voidable contracts, expressing the view that a surrogate "should have a specified time period after the birth of the infant during which she can decide whether or not to carry out her original intention."[29] Professionals emphasize the unpredictable emotional bonding that may occur during the nine months of pregnancy and attach greater weight to the emotional investment of the birth mother as a result.

The general public, in contrast, is less willing to protect the surrogate from the obligations of her own preconception decision. During the Baby M legal proceedings, a *Newsweek* poll found that 61 percent of women thought the Sterns should get custody while only 22 percent favored Mary Beth. Among men, the percentages were 58 percent to 28 percent.[30] The public recognizes that the biological father and his wife may also have an enormous emotional investment anticipating the birth of the baby, which may extend through years of infertility treatments prior to the surrogacy, and the public attaches more importance to the agreement that created the pregnancy in the first place.

Negative publicity surrounded genetic surrogacies for years, but a story with a happy ending finally captured public interest. Deirdre Hall, a beautiful actress whom many viewers felt as if they knew personally after watching her portray a psychiatrist on daytime television for nearly sixteen years, disclosed to fans that the birth of her son was made possible by a genetic surrogate. Like many less famous women, Deirdre had endured whatever medical technology fertility specialists prescribed, from artificial inseminations to surgery to in vitro fertilization procedures. The September 28, 1992, cover of *People* magazine declared the birth a "miracle" and devoted six pages of pictures and print to portraying a positive surrogacy arrangement. If promoters of surrogacy as a positive alternative for infertile women had designed a recruitment poster, they could not have conceived a better image than the picture of a radiantly happy Deirdre holding her infant son; nor could they have devised the massive display that the magazine cover received on newsstands nationwide. The darkly brooding image of Mary Beth Whitehead that Americans had come to associate with surrogacy had been replaced in the public's eye by the maternal joy of an actress known for portraying confident, nurturing women. The era of media focus on the negative aspects of genetic surrogacies had ended.[31]

Today the media reports on surrogacy outcomes in a more balanced way, and the stories are less likely to be front-page news. Yet as the procedure becomes more commonplace, many concerns remain.

Everyone anticipates a healthy baby, but disabilities may occur. Couples must be prepared and obligated to provide for the child they create, regardless of the means of creation. Decisions about submitting to prenatal testing and choosing whether or not to abort a fetus found to be impaired must be resolved before the pregnancy begins. Because of legal disputes that arose when surrogacy agreements failed to provide for such contingencies, most written agreements today cover these possibilities, but informal arrangements among friends and family members still may not.

Another unintended possibility is having the "wrong" embryo implant. Most surrogates are married, and, having stopped taking oral contraceptives in order to become pregnant for the couple, the surrogate may unintentionally conceive a natural child with her husband if she miscalculates her fertile period or engages in unprotected sex inappropriately.

One tragic case involved both of these unintended consequences when a surrogate gave birth to a retarded child. The man whose sperm was used in the artificial insemination denied that he was the father. The surrogate, in disagreement, insisted that she had acted in accordance with their agreement and should not be expected to assume the responsibility for the resulting child. Eventually, blood tests established that the baby was the natural child of the surrogate and her husband, and she and her husband were left to assume the care of this child.

In addition to the unforeseeable risks to the baby are the risks to which the surrogate is exposed. The lawsuits involving conflicting custody claims to the baby have made the public aware of the emotional risks a surrogate assumes. These can be minimized by psychological screening to predict the surrogate's emotional capacity to relinquish the baby. Medical risks are harder to control, and certainly any reputable program must include medical screening of surrogate candidates, followed by appropriate prenatal care. Not every medical risk can be eliminated, however, and at least one surrogate has died during pregnancy.[32] The possible medical risks to the surrogate have led the American College of Obstetricians and Gynecologists to support the surrogate's right, in consultation with her physician, to be the sole source of consent for medical decisions regarding pregnancy and delivery.[33] As technology increasingly allows fetuses to be treated in the womb, the issue of how to balance medical treatment of the pregnant woman against that of the fetus she carries when the woman is a surrogate will become even more complex.

Even more difficult to resolve is determining who should bear the responsibility for long-term or permanent disability to the surrogate as a result of the pregnancy. The Center for Surrogate Parenting requires a couple to buy a life insurance policy for the benefit of the surrogate's own children should the surrogate die, but obtaining disability coverage has been more difficult. Instead, the center requires couples to pay for lost wages and all expenses for a fixed time after the birth, but permanent disability is a risk the surrogate assumes. "Luckily, we have never had a problem go beyond the agreed time, but it is a dilemma and a major risk for a surrogate," Dr. Hanafin agrees. Although it would be an ominous burden for the couple to assume a lifelong obligation of caring for a surrogate disabled during the pregnancy or birth, it seems equally unfair to abandon a surrogate who did nothing through her own neglect or disregard of medical advice to cause her condition. Predictably, it will result in litigation and heartache whenever a surrogate suffers a permanent disability for which she requires expensive treatment and care, unless adequate provision is made.

Lawyers attempt to draft contracts to cover not only the intentions of the couple and their surrogate as they plan for the pregnancy and birth but also unexpected emotional and medical possibilities that may result. To the extent that such written agreements force everyone to think seriously about the full effects of their decision and to determine certain obligations in advance, the contract serves an important purpose. But no document can anticipate every possibility or prepare everyone for the emotions they will face during the pregnancy and birth, and perhaps for the rest of their lives.

Hilary Hanafin says, "As a psychologist, I spend a lot of time helping couples work through their grief at losing the child they had imagined and hoped for. If they will not be at peace with where their child came from, who the birth mother is, or how the child was conceived, then they shouldn't proceed, because that could affect the child." She continues, "If the adults have a warm, caring, and mutually respectful relationship—not only throughout the process but afterward—have informed consent, have the same agenda, attitudes, and philosophy toward this procedure—*and* if they have uppermost in their minds that the guiding principle will be whatever is best for the children—the one being conceived and the surrogate's own—then we may not get everything right but we will be close."

The effect of paying surrogates for their role has been the subject of ongoing criticism. Some states prohibit surrogates from receiving a fee but allow payment of expenses. Such laws may actually provide a surrogate with more money in the form of reasonable living expenses than she would have been paid under a fixed-fee arrangement, and make the payments seem less like selling a baby. My own survey found that a slight majority of participants believed that payment of fees to surrogates should be prohibited (55 percent), but 29 percent said there should be no prohibition and 13 percent were undecided.[34]

Hilary Hanafin agrees that no surrogate should enter a program because she needs the money. "I am afraid that under those circumstances a surrogate would be more tempted to deny her psychological feelings. Most of our surrogates find the money helpful, but if they weren't a surrogate, it would not make a significant financial difference in their lives." Although Dr. Hanafin admits the corrupting influence payment can have, she also feels strongly that the public perception that women become surrogates for the money is wrong.

The amount surrogates receive varies from program to program, ranging from $10,000 to perhaps $20,000, or, in some programs, whatever the parties negotiate. A surrogate is likely to receive more if the couple asks her to carry a second child for them, just as she may receive more if twins are born. These amounts do not include other fees, such as those paid to doctors, lawyers, or the group arranging the surrogacy, and the total costs are likely to exceed $40,000.

While we might expect feminists to endorse a woman's determination to be a surrogate, instead they generally oppose the practice because of the potential for exploitation. The technology that allows the couple to use the wife's own egg for the procedure only increases the possibility that the couple will see the surrogate as nothing more than a womb; since a surrogate can provide genetic offspring for a woman who wants to avoid interrupting her career, risking her health, or diminishing her appearance with a pregnancy, surrogacy might be used for convenience rather than medical need. Feminists warn that surrogate brokers will create "stables of contract breeders" in Third World countries where poverty already degrades women, or will solicit poor women here to be surrogates for the wealthy.[35]

When the California Supreme Court upheld the surrogacy contract between the Calverts and Anna Johnson, one critic thought it was wrong to disregard the gestational environment. He wrote, "The growth and development of a fetus is a biological process and a non-genetic surrogate contributes a unique endocrine and gestational environment, and the resulting child's anatomy, physiology, mental capacity, and even genetic predisposition all depend to some extent upon gestational contributions from the surrogate. . . . A child has a right to know and be with the mother who created its life, and if more than one person is involved in that process he or she may have a right to a relationship with all those who contributed biologically to that life."[36]

Some also criticize brokers and other professionals who receive payment in connection with surrogacy arrangements. My survey found that while a slight majority felt fees to the surrogates should be prohibited, the number increased to 61 percent when survey participants were asked whether fees to third parties who arrange the surrogacies should be prohibited, yet 22 percent said they would not prohibit professional fees, and 13.5 percent were undecided.[37]

In 1988 Michigan passed the first state law making it a felony, punishable by a $50,000 fine and five years in prison, to arrange a surrogacy contract for money. This follows the example set by England, which punishes those who arrange, but not those who provide or utilize, surrogacy services. Both states that impose criminal penalties on those who arrange surrogacies and states that make contracts with surrogates legally unenforceable ignore noncommercial surrogacy arrangements while criminalizing or making legally unenforceable surrogacies arranged by a commercial broker. These laws reflect the public distaste for the idea that brokers enjoy the profits while surrogates assume all the physical and emotional risks, and it seeks to eliminate the exploitation feminists fear. It is also an effective means of curtailing the practice by making it more difficult for infertile couples and willing surrogates to connect. Unfortunately, it also eliminates the psychological and medical screening done by reputable professionals, as well as other practices they have implemented in order to avoid the pitfalls to a successful surrogacy.

On Mother's Day, 1993, Julie Johnson gave her older sister a very special gift. Julie gave birth to John Franklin Wittle as the surrogate for her sister and brother-in-law, who after eight years of costly infertility treatments were still without a baby.[38]

Julie admits, a little sheepishly, that she did not have a medical examination before her surrogacy began, nor did the family undergo counseling or sign a written agreement. "We intended to have a doctor do the insemination, even if it meant we had to go to another state. We knew that a doctor would want us to go to counseling and want me to have a physical and all that, so we figured all those things would eventually take place. But my sister Janet got this harebrained idea she had seen on a television talk show, and we decided, 'Let's just try it. What the heck. It's free.' We did it once and it worked!"

You might have expected more caution from this family trio. At the time, Julie Johnson was a thirty-three-year-old naval officer, teaching in a university NROTC program. Her sister, Janet, with a doctorate in mathematics education, and brother-in-law, Mark, a software engineer, were both thirty-six years old.

Janet's idea was to attempt insemination with a turkey baster. They had no specific idea how to proceed, and Julie remembers how inept they were about it. "It was a total fiasco, like an episode from *I Love Lucy.*" Since they had always intended to use a doctor, none of them was particularly disappointed when their awkward attempt to do it themselves seemed to have failed. Julie remembers all of them thinking aloud, "We are just going to have to find a doctor to do the insemination because *that* didn't work."

There were risks associated with the procedure they attempted. Too much air could have been injected, and if air had been absorbed into Julie's bloodstream, it could have traveled to her heart, lungs, or brain, and she could have died from an air embolism. In addition, they used raw semen that had not been tested for infectious diseases.

Julie's monthly cycles are absolutely regular, but when she did not start her period on the twenty-eighth day of her next cycle, she still refused to believe she might be pregnant. She decided to take a home pregnancy test for a very simple reason. She had promised Janet that she would drink no alcohol during her surrogate pregnancy. With a Labor Day party invitation ahead of her, Julie didn't want to feel guilty about drinking a beer at the party.

Julie laughs about her embarrassment when purchasing the home pregnancy kit. "I felt like the kids in the movie *Summer of '42* when they bought the condom. I picked up a few other things because I didn't want to go up to the cashier with just the pregnancy kit." She pauses to chuckle at herself and then continues, "I even put my topaz ring on my left ring finger and turned it around so it would look like a gold band. For some reason I had this feeling that the lady behind the counter was going to look at me with my home pregnancy kit and say, 'Hum, you little hussy!' "

When she got home and took the test, Julie left the color-coded indicator stick on the rim of the bathtub and forgot about it while she put away groceries and talked on the phone. When she finally returned to the bathroom to put away the other things she had bought at the drugstore, she was amazed to see that the indicator had turned purple. "I got on the phone immediately to call Janet and Mark. They did not believe me," she remembers. "I don't blame them. You know, doctors in white coats for eight years and all the high-tech, expensive nonsense, and then we come along with a turkey baster and it works the first time!"

Julie gets tickled thinking about their skepticism. "Their hopes had been shot so many times that they thought there was no way this botched-up artificial insemination that we did with a turkey baster we sterilized in the dishwasher and me standing on my head afterward was going to work." She remembers her brother-in-law challenging her: "You probably did the test wrong. Read us the instructions." With a comic's timing, Julie imitates her patient reply to him, "OK. Pee on the stick. Put the stick down. Read the stick three minutes later." She laughs raucously at her joke before adding the punch line. "They even had me take it over to a friend's house to have her look to see if it was really purple!"

Julie was particularly concerned that the news of her surrogacy be transmitted to the one hundred two midshipmen in the university program in a way that would not discredit the navy or her. She decided to relate the news to a few members of her class, trusting the grapevine to spread the information. The midshipmen she told held the news in such complete confidence, however, that when she first appeared in a maternity uniform, most of her class were surprised. She explains how she broke the news: "I just told the class that I taught, 'I am pregnant. It is my brother-in-law and my sister's baby. Biologically, it is mine and my brother-in-law's. It is not a secret. I am not ashamed of it, and I will answer any questions.' "

Mark and Janet attended Lamaze classes with Julie, and Mark was her push coach. Before the delivery, Julie worried about having Mark with her in the delivery room. "Gosh," she says, "my brother-in-law had never seen me naked, and I worried about the immodesty of that." When the time came, however, Julie was glad that both Mark and Janet shared the experience of labor and delivery with her. She recalls their joy as their son was born. "Mark wanted a baby during all the years of infertility, but Janet was the doggedly determined one. I think Janet was the one who wanted it most—until that baby was born!" Julie shared in their joy. "I thought I was a little disappointed that the baby was not a girl, but when I saw him, I knew right then—not only was I glad it was a boy, I was glad it was *that* boy. No other boy would do. I knew he was exactly what we wanted."

Julie feels entirely positive about her decision to be a surrogate for her sister. "The whole thing was planned to be their baby, so it was always their baby. John was their baby even before he was conceived. I didn't bond with John as a mother—but I think I did bond with him a little bit as an aunt."

Successful family surrogacy arrangements, like the birth of John Franklin Wittle as well as the births of James Alan Mack, Jr., and Chad Daniel and Chelsea Arlette Uchytil, have convinced many people that professional surrogacy brokers are unnecessary and pose greater risks of exploitation to couples and surrogates than the benefits they provide. But not all couples enjoy the loving generosity of family members or friends capable of serving as an uncompensated surrogate. Should laws or social attitudes distinguish between surrogacies solely on the basis of whether the infertile woman is fortunate enough to have among her family or friends someone willing and able to be her surrogate?

Before we sit in judgment on a couple's right to contract for the gestation and birth of a child, particularly when the egg

and sperm come from the couple themselves, we should be reminded that if fertility were not impaired, this same couple
would have the fundamental right to conceive an unlimited
number of children without any power of the government to
interfere in their decision. When government, by means of regulation, involves itself in determining the suitability of surrogate
parents, it holds infertile couples to a standard that does not
exist for fertile couples. Proposals involving home studies, psychological testing, and age requirements similar to those used in
adoption qualification might be unconstitutional limitations on
the right to bear and beget children, particularly when no donor
gamete is used. Government can stay out of surrogacies altogether, leaving it to the marketplace to determine how the trend
toward paid surrogacies develops and allowing the courts to
resolve legal disputes if and when they occur. Or state governments can prohibit surrogacy entirely on the basis that the fundamental right of procreation should not be extended to involve
a third person in the process, even though it is likely that a significant number of genetic surrogacies would quietly and privately continue to occur (as in the turkey-baster conception of
Baby John Wittle). When government decides to impose reasonable regulations intended to eliminate exploitation and participants for whom the procedure is inappropriate, legislators
face genuine risks of violating fundamental rights of procreation. Therefore, the difficulty state legislatures have had in
deciding how to regulate surrogacy contracts is understandable.
The focus on regulation of the brokers has occurred not only
because of the potential for exploitation and commercialization
but also because there are fewer risks that the laws will violate
fundamental rights of procreation.

Apart from concerns about commercialization and exploitation, and even if the potential for custody disputes were eliminated, there is another less tangible but very serious concern.
Our values are being reshaped without sufficient public debate.
Writer Katha Pollitt fears the danger of "disposable relationships" to all of society, even if practices by reputable agencies or

government regulations resolve the current legal and
issues. She writes, "In order to benefit a very small n
people—prosperous womb-infertile couples who shun add   —
paid surrogacy does a great deal of harm to the rest of us. It degrades women by devaluing pregnancy and childbirth; it degrades children by commercializing their creation; it degrades
the poor by offering them a devil's bargain at bargain prices. It
creates a whole new class of emotionally injured children rarely
mentioned in the debate: the ones the surrogate has already
given birth to, who see their mother give away a newborn, or
fight not to."[39]

Although Dr. Hilary Hanafin has reached the opposite
conclusion about surrogacy itself, she shares some of Pollitt's
opinions: "I tell prospective surrogates and couples two things
about each other—one, don't make a baby with anyone that
you don't like, and two, don't make a baby with anyone you
don't want to be in contact with for the rest of your life.
Because the child needs to know, and will pick up verbally and
nonverbally, your feelings about where the child came from. It
is important that those feelings are warm and loving, caring and
nurturing, and pioneering and respectful. If that is not relayed
to the child, there could be long-term psychological damage,
not only to the child you have with the surrogate but also to the
surrogate's other children." To combat the danger of "disposable relationships," about which Pollitt writes so convincingly,
participants in the center's surrogacy program with whom
Hanafin works are encouraged to maintain long-term relationships. Hanafin says, "It has changed quite a bit since the beginning of our program, but today it is more common to see
long-term relationships—similar to long-distance cousins."

In effect, Dr. Hanafin encourages the creation of a distant
extended family, with an end result similar to the loving and ongoing family relationships in which siblings have chosen to help
infertile family members have a baby. Obviously, this can only
occur when a couple reveals to the child the circumstances of its

birth and when the adults have a mutually respectful attitude toward the role each of them has played and toward each other.

There are ways society can reinforce those attitudes. First, the American College of Obstetricians and Gynecologists already includes among its guidelines for doctors assisting with surrogacies that the practice be limited to medical need and not mere convenience. The rest of us should apply that standard to our own reproductive choices and to our attitudes toward the practice. Wombless women like Christa Uchytil and Linda Mack, as well as women who have endured years of expensive fertility treatments, like Deirdre Hall and Janet Johnson, showed a medical need for their surrogacy-assisted births. The medical necessity is not always so absolute, but at least society should disapprove of the use of surrogacy arrangements for vain and selfish reasons having little or nothing to do with infertility, life-threatening medical conditions, or responsible reproductive decisions connected with genetically inheritable traits.

Second, the practice of leaving the surrogate to assume the risk of long-term disability related to the pregnancy or birth is contrary to the respectful, ongoing relationship that society should encourage. Imposing a shared liability with the couple not only would benefit the surrogate but also would encourage the couple to consider the impact their decision might have on the life of the surrogate and her family, even after the baby is born. A legal and moral obligation that extends beyond the gestation lessens the potential for dehumanizing the surrogate and regarding her as merely someone hired for nine months to do a job. The possible expenses of postnatal disability might deter some surrogacy arrangements, but it is more appropriate that these costs be shared by the couple who sought her services than that the surrogate be left to deal with them alone after the birth. The moral lesson for the resulting child would also be positive: the child would see that his or her parents care about the woman who cared enough to assist them.

The best protection for the well-being of future babies is neither laws nor professional guidelines but rather commonly held moral values. The involvement of third parties as surrogates and donors demands an adjustment of old taboos, though we must not forget why generations of our ancestors imposed certain limits on what even they, without the technology we now have, could have done and wisely chose not to do.

Should research to enable creation of an artificial womb be prohibited by law?

Do your feelings toward adopting, if you and your partner were unable to conceive a child after over a year of trying, depend upon the sort of child available for adoption, for example:

- A healthy, same-race baby?
- A healthy, different-race baby?
- A healthy, foreign-born baby?
- A physically impaired baby?
- A healthy, same-race older U.S. child?
- A healthy, different-race older U.S. child?
- A healthy, foreign-born older child?
- A physically impaired U.S. child?
- A troubled or abused U.S. child?

If you desired a child and you (or your partner) were unable to become pregnant after over a year of trying, would you use a surrogate to gestate your fetus if

- the surrogate gestated an in vitro fertilized embryo created by you and your partner?
- the surrogate gestated an embryo genetically related to the male partner only?
- the surrogate gestated an embryo genetically related to the female partner only?

Whether or not you would use the procedure, do you think it should be prohibited to use

- a surrogate mother to gestate an embryo genetically related to both parents but not to the surrogate?
- a surrogate mother artificially inseminated with the father's sperm?
- a surrogate mother to gestate the mother's egg fertilized with donor sperm?

Should the payment of fees to a surrogate for gestating a fetus be prohibited by law?

Should fees to third parties for arranging a surrogacy be prohibited by law?

In a dispute between the surrogate mother and the couple with whom she contracted, in what order of importance should the following factors be considered:

- Terms of the agreement they signed
- Genetic relationships of claimants with the baby
- Maternal feelings of the surrogate mother
- Paternal feelings of the father
- Maternal feelings of the father's wife (whether or not she is genetically related to the baby)
- Economic abilities of the claimants to provide for the baby?

Should health insurance cover the costs of

- in vitro fertilization with a surrogate?
- artificial insemination with a surrogate?

Would you be willing to pay higher premiums to cover the costs of extending coverage for surrogacy to all policyholders?

Would you be willing to pay higher taxes to cover the costs of government assistance in surrogacy procedures?

CHAPTER 17

THE STORY OF BABY WYATT

Her baby's name is Wyatt. Others may express uncertainties about the medical, moral, and legal outcomes surrounding her baby's conception, but for Deborah Hecht there is no doubt. "Our child already exists," she believes. "It is just a matter of when Wyatt is going to leave Bill's company to come and be in mine." What makes Wyatt's conception so controversial for many people is that the sperm of a dead man will be used to create a posthumous birth.[1]

When Deborah met Bill Kane, she was entering her thirties, and he was more than a decade older. Although they did not marry, they were definitely a couple, and Deborah says the decision not to marry was mutual. "We just didn't believe in the institution of marriage." She also says they shared common feelings about having a child. "We knew that we were going to have a child. It just wasn't the right time to do that."

When Deborah entered his life, Bill already had two teenaged children, a son and a daughter. Today his son Everett recounts a different version of his father's feelings about having a baby with Deborah. "He told me several times that he didn't want to have any more kids, and he sure didn't want to get married!"[2]

Trying to piece together the true motives of Bill Kane has never been simple. He was a Fulbright scholar and an honors graduate of Princeton University and Yale Law School who had practiced law in San Francisco and been involved in international banking in Tokyo and London before engaging in real estate ventures in California. College classmates considered the young Bill Kane so extraordinary that although his stories about himself seemed too extravagant to be true, listeners could not discount them entirely.[3]

Everett's mother, Sandra Irwin—the only woman Bill Kane ever married—remembers how he captivated her with his brilliance when they met in college. "Bill was a big talker, and he told some tales that I realize now were not true, but at the time I believed him. We met on a blind date when he was a senior at Princeton and I was a junior at Vassar, and we talked all night the first night we met."

Over the years, Bill's stories suggested daring exploits for the Defense Intelligence Agency, the Central Intelligence Agency, and the American military—covert adventures that are difficult to either confirm or debunk. Deborah believes these stories absolutely, but his family doubts much of what he claimed.

"During the time I was married to him," Sandra Irwin explains, "we had a very glamorous life. He was successful and we lived all over the world. He truly had accomplished a lot of things, but nevertheless, he had this great need to embellish. I believe he never matched up to what he thought he should be, and so he told stories to make himself more like he wanted to be."[4]

As a teenager, Bill's son Everett began to recognize inconsistencies in his father's stories, and they quarreled when he challenged his father's truthfulness. However, Everett concedes that there may have been a kernel of truth in his father's stories about service in the intelligence community. "He could have had some kind of employment as an analyst. He certainly had the mind for it, and the educational background in the area of Central American politics and U.S. policy. But there is a big line between that and running down there with a machine gun strapped to your back." Bill's power to mythicize his life lingers in Everett's admission that "the hardest thing to deal with in him was that he was clearly a brilliant and exceptional man.

That made anything that he said about what he had done hard
to counter."

Bill Kane's string of career successes began to develop
knots at about the time he met Deborah. Between his divorce
from Sandra and his relationship with Deborah, he had shared
a business and romantic partnership with a woman named Barbara Kelly, and the termination of their partnership was both
bitter and costly. Much of his wealth was drained by legal fees
and the oneway flow of living expenses, without a new source of
income. By the summer of 1991, Deborah was trying to help
Bill revive his stagnant career by planning a series of business
parties for him. "I hoped he would get back into a business that
he would enjoy and feel passionate about," she explains.

Ironically, Sandra Irwin's description of what her former
husband needed to do at that time in his life is quite similar.
"Bill had stopped working and had lived off his assets, and they
were running out. He needed to go back to work again. He
needed to turn over a new leaf and start a new life, but he was
very depressed and didn't seem to have the energy to do that,"
she recalls. One of the few things about which these two
women agree is that during the final months of his life Bill
seemed unable to focus his extraordinary mind on charting a
new economic life for himself.

Instead, he set into motion his most elaborate adventure.
He began to make parallel plans for the destruction of his own
life and the creation of a new life from his sperm, even after his
death. To accomplish his scheme, he recruited Deborah as his
accomplice, but first he made her promise she would tell no one
that he was considering suicide. Other than Deborah, only a
psychologist friend, with whom Bill agreed to counsel, knew his
intentions.

Bill's family does not doubt that he extracted a pledge of
secrecy from Deborah, but they believe she should be held
accountable for her decision to keep that pledge. "There is no
question that had she broken her word to Bill that he would
have ended his relationship with her," Sandra Irwin admits. "I

think there is no doubt in the mind of anybody who knew Bill that he was that kind of person. Her choice was to conceal this knowledge and let him die, or to tell somebody and try to prevent the death. His children don't agree with the choice that she made."

Money clouds the morality of her choice. In the last weeks of his life, Bill drafted a new will. Although his wealth was diminished, his net worth was still significant, and he made Deborah the primary beneficiary of this final will. His children see that as a clear motive for her silence. "We are angered by what happened with the suicide," Everett says. "We think it could have been prevented and that she participated in it in large part because she saw material gain." Obviously, Deborah denies their suspicions and says she did everything she could to dissuade him. "I did not facilitate Bill's death in any way. His children know in their hearts that their father was a man who made his own mind up about what he wanted to do!"

In his final weeks, Bill busied himself with compiling the documents necessary to allow the conception of his child after his death. The contract with the sperm bank where his sperm was deposited and frozen specifically authorizes the bank "to release my semen specimens (vials) to Deborah Ellen Hecht."[5] The will he prepared for himself expressly states, "I bequeath all right, title, and interest that I may have in any specimens of my sperm stored with any sperm bank or similar facility for storage to Deborah Ellen Hecht." A letter to his children, written a few days before his death, is addressed not only to his two living children but also to his unborn, unconceived child. "It may be that Deborah will decide—as I hope she will—to have a child by me after my death. I've been assiduously generating frozen sperm samples for that eventuality. If she does, then this letter is for my posthumous offspring, as well, with the thought that I have loved you in my dreams, even though I never got to see you born."[6]

On October 24, 1991, in a suite at the Mirage Hotel in Las Vegas, Bill Kane took his own life.

His son cannot reconcile these final directions for a post-humous conception with Bill Kane's earlier opposition to having another child. Everett admits, "Maybe he did feel that he was caught in some place that he couldn't get out of, either emotionally or because of his money loss, and that somehow the idea of putting out this new child as a last contribution to the world made it easier on him. I don't know."

Everett and his sister Katie turned to their mother for advice, and Sandra remembers their long debates. "Because the children believe Bill's attitude against having any more children changed only after he decided to commit suicide," she explains, "they feel that he was depressed—ill and suicidal—and that what he did was not himself. That is why they do not feel obligated to respect their father's final wishes."

Everett and Katie sought not only Sandra's maternal advice but also the benefit of her knowledge as a lawyer. Everett recalls seeing the need for legal advice almost immediately. "It was just the wildest thing to get to his house after he killed himself and see what had been orchestrated by this man. I remember I made a call to my mother within a day of being there, and I said, 'Get a lawyer!' " To avoid expensive legal fees, Everett and Katie asked their mother if she would represent them, and she agreed. That decision inevitably attracted media attention to the drama of the lawyer ex-wife battling to prohibit her former husband's girlfriend from bearing his posthumous child.

Everett imagines how his father might have regarded all the notoriety. "Part of his charm, and also the part that made him such a jerk some of the time, was that he would sometimes do something that was provocative just for the sake of the interesting scene that it was going to cause, not caring about who it was going to involve. In this last gesture of his, I see that part of him—throwing in this little twist and doing the Bill Kane kind of exit." Without bitterness, Everett adds, "It is really hard to resent. If you are in an emotional place where you are going to kill yourself, getting a little artistic about it is understandable."

Sandra Irwin believes Bill would have been delighted by all

the press coverage the case has received. In fact, she credits him with having built into his documents conflicts and contradictions that allowed the protracted legal challenges, citing as examples the absence of a no-contest clause in his will and the contradiction of deeding property to Deborah that his will left to the children. "He knew this was going to be a mess," Sandra declares. "He knew the position in which he was leaving Deborah. It was his final joke on her—paying her back for the fact that she didn't stop him from committing suicide."

Not surprisingly, Deborah finds that preposterous, but she does regret that Bill acted as his own lawyer in preparing all the documents. "I wish he had gotten some backup advice. Not that anyone would have ever heard of doing what he was doing, but at least they might have seen some things that he didn't, and maybe they might have made it more foolproof for me."

The legal battles have been extensive. In addition to the will contests, a criminal complaint was filed against Deborah for murder in the death of Bill Kane. When no criminal charges were brought against her, the family filed a civil suit for wrongful death. The family points to evidence that Deborah did more than remain silent. They believe she became an active participant in his death by driving Bill to the airport, buying him a one-way ticket to Las Vegas, and speaking to him in his hotel suite as he prepared to kill himself. They also describe active intervention by Deborah to avert outside contacts that might have led Bill to change his mind while he was alone in Las Vegas—falsely assuring Bill's secretary that her suspicions about suicide were misplaced, and also withholding news of a promising response from a potential employer.

Deborah counters by declaring her devotion to Bill, insisting that her actions are painful proof of her selflessness, since she was devastated by his decision. "Bill had a different idea of what suicide was. He was not afraid to die. His fear was of going forward in a way less than he would approve for himself." With no apparent recognition of just how true her words are, she adds, "Mediocrity scared him to death."

During the weeks before Bill's death, Deborah says he offered to conceive their baby in the traditional manner, but she says that was impossible for her to consider at that time. "I was a basket case dealing with his decision, and I knew that my body was not healthy enough to carry a child." It was then that Bill suggested depositing sperm for her to use after his death, according to Deborah. "When he told me to find a sperm bank, I had never even heard the term before. He said, 'Go research it and find me one. I want to do it.' " His decision to take his own life but to leave behind the means to create a new life became intertwined in Bill's mind, and that is what makes this case unique.

That is also what makes the posthumous conception so inappropriate from Everett's perspective. "This did not happen in an ordinary, happy-go-lucky family where there was a tragedy involved. It was very planned—inky, not even morally gray," emphasizes Everett. "I just think that the whole enterprise should not be condoned."

In opposing Deborah's access to the sperm, Sandra stated various public policy arguments to the court. She urged that posthumous conception should be prohibited because of its painful consequences for others—for the child who can never know its father and for the existing family members who are left to deal with the stress of an after-born child entering their family. Sandra Irwin bases those legal arguments on her belief that "a child should not be conceived to be a grave marker or to honor a dead person. The child has the right to be protected by having a father." She is unpersuaded by Deborah's legal position that the rights of the adults whose sperm and egg create life must be respected. "It's the child society ought to protect," Sandra insists, adding, "The constitutionally protected right should not be so much the right to procreate as the right to rear." In response, the court has stated that "it is not the role of the judiciary to inhibit the use of reproductive technology when the Legislature has not seen fit to do so."[7]

Everett is uncomfortable with abstracting the specifics of

their case to create broader legal generalities applicable to other cases. "It is a shame that the law in these uncharted areas is sometimes based upon freak cases," he believes. "I am not saying that I disagree with any of the public policy arguments we have made, but I am frustrated that the law is incapable of weighing the sides to this particular story and determining who is morally reprehensible, without having to force these peculiar facts into some recognized legal framework. If it were a King Solomon situation, we might be in better shape."

Deborah shares his frustration with the law, but she believes the real problem is litigating what should have remained a private choice. "It is always remarkable to me that people do think that there are two sides to this issue," she observes. "There are two sides to having a child, I suppose. The man and the woman's sides, but I don't think there is anybody else who should be involved. I still go into each court hearing in total amazement that someone can feel that they have the right to intrude on my right to have a child."

Like Bill's children, Deborah has found a legal champion to continue her fight for the sperm even after the exhaustion of her financial resources. J. R. Nerone and his wife were Bill's and Deborah's friends, but at the time of Bill's death, Nerone was not practicing law. After the suicide, he and his wife were there to lend Deborah moral support, but as he saw her money for legal fees being exhausted by the will contests and the wrongful death suit, Nerone knew he had to give Deborah more than moral support. "I am a real California story," he laughs. "I had dropped out of practicing law and had done some acting, writing, even driving a limousine. But when I saw that Deborah needed my help to continue this fight, I reactivated my law license and have been with her ever since."[8]

In the meantime, Deborah is preparing for Wyatt's birth. Friends and family have already given her baby clothes, and her car has been outfitted with an infant car seat. She has joined a support group, Single Mothers by Choice, and preliminary medical examinations have been done. She is confident of her decision to conceive Wyatt and is undeterred by accusations that she is being selfish or foolhardy. "So far, I haven't met a person who decided to have a child without some selfish motivation in it. I don't feel that I stand out in any way apart from other people who have decided they want to be parents." In fact, she adds, "I have had more time by myself to think and consider being a single mother than anybody I know."

Only two problems remain for Deborah. First, there is the delay caused by the litigation. "I am frightened that each month it becomes more difficult for me to get pregnant, especially since I have become forty," she admits. "I know that Sandra Irwin's intent is to keep me hanging on for as long as she possibly can, so that I cannot conceive this child." Second, there is the expense of raising her child alone. "My only real concern about having this child is the finances. Bill intended for me to have some financial backing so that I could have this child—not necessarily so that I would be comfortable my whole life, but enough to get my career going again. Sandra Irwin has demolished any possibility of my having money in the bank."

In life, Bill Kane was not a traditional father, and even Deborah admits that he often was not there for his children. "Bill was a difficult and unusual man, so it was hard for them," Deborah acknowledges. Everett says much the same thing. "He wasn't the ideal father. Most of the relationship that we had was because of my efforts and not his."

Those who never knew Bill Kane may wonder why those who loved him were so often willing to overlook his careless behavior. Perhaps some explanation can be found in Everett's assessment of his own relationship with his father. "I am grateful that in a tweaked world I had such a powerful, charismatic figure to develop me. I wish things had worked out differently, but when he was alive, he was a very interesting man to be around."

Remaining as difficult for his children in death as he often was in life, this unorthodox, absentee father chose as his final wish the desire to reach from beyond the grave to try fatherhood again. With each legal hurdle she clears, Deborah moves closer to fulfilling that wish. "I am sad that when I have Wyatt, Wyatt's father will not be around," Deborah says. "You have no idea how sad that makes me for myself and for Wyatt. But it should not keep Wyatt from being allowed to be born."[9]

CHAPTER 18

CONFLICTING CLAIMS
IN DONOR-ASSISTED BIRTHS

Remember the words to the old song "Just Molly and me, and Baby makes three"? Technology has not rendered those words obsolete, but it may be time to revise them. A modern couple with both male and female infertility factors might conceivably find themselves singing an updated verse like this one: "Start with Molly and me; add a laparoscopy; fertilize clinically/Donor gametes! Add a surrogate to the mix; now Baby makes six. Let technology fix/Our problem."

All of the moral dilemmas raised by technologically assisted conception are compounded even further when gamete donors are involved. My survey found that while 59 percent of those responding would try in vitro fertilization with their partner if they were unable to become pregnant after a year of trying, only 18 percent would try in vitro fertilization with a donor gamete.[1] Survey participants' willingness to use artificial insemination with donor sperm was viewed about the same as using a donor gamete with IVF.[2]

When the use of a surrogate is involved, however, survey participants were less willing to use that alternative, although 12 percent said they would consider it if the fetus she gestated were conceived with the couple's own egg and sperm.[3] In situations where the fetus would be genetically related to one partner only, slightly more said they would consider it if the relationship were with the father (6.5 percent) than with the mother (5 percent), but in neither case were many willing to involve a surrogate to gestate a fetus conceived with a donor gamete.[4]

Gamete donation provides a reproductive option for two primary groups: first, for infertile couples who want to have a baby, and second, for unmarried adults who want to have a baby without having a partner.[5] Public opinion on the use of non-traditional reproductive technology generally splits between the two groups. Among participants in my survey, while 90 percent approved of the use of nontraditional reproductive technology by married couples without children, approval dropped sharply to 37 percent if the couple were unmarried, even if their relationship were stable. Even fewer approved of a single person using the technology (only 29 percent), and the lowest approval ratings were for gays and lesbians, whether or not they were in a relationship.[6]

Should society be troubled when gamete donation is involved in assisted conception and birth (the "borrowing of the makings of a baby" that worried Arlette Schweitzer), or is it comparable to tissue donation, which society not only approves but even encourages (a "win-win situation" in Julie Johnson's words)? Or is it among those increasingly complex modern moral issues we see as sometimes right and at other times wrong?

We are most likely to approve whatever means will allow infertile couples to create families, yet even in those situations the use of donor gametes deserves closer public scrutiny. In about 25 percent of the cases, both male and female factors, or unknown factors, are involved in the couple's infertility.

As for the remaining 75 percent, the source of the infertility can be traced to one or the other, but not both partners. Although specialists are careful not to use language that suggests "fault" or "blame," most infertile couples struggle to avoid those feelings completely. Statistically, male factors are involved nearly as frequently as are female factors, and so, both husbands and wives know the guilt of being unable to accomplish their part in the reproductive process, and both husbands and wives know the resentment of being the fertile partner in an infertile marriage.

Each spouse brings a separate set of emotions to their

shared longing for a child, and to assume that providing a child will mean the same thing to each of them ignores these separate feelings and fertility factors.

Infertile couples initially go to doctors to be cured. When blocked Fallopian tubes can be opened or vasectomies can be reversed, the doctor really has "cured" the infertility so that the patient's reproductive system can function normally. If a laparoscopy must be used to retrieve the woman's eggs from her ovary or if the husband's sperm must be collected and concentrated, the doctor has assisted the couple's own reproductive capacity in ways not too dissimilar from fitting a patient with glasses or a hearing aid. Technology is used to assist the patient's own ability to see or hear, even though the doctor cannot cure the poor vision or deafness, just as technology is used to assist the patients' ability to conceive, even though the doctor cannot cure the underlying cause.

But when a donor egg or sperm is substituted for the gamete of the dysfunctional partner, the doctor has neither cured the problem causing infertility nor assisted the patient's own capacity to reproduce. Rather, he has replaced one of the partners with a proxy. Is this practicing medicine or merely sanctioning infidelity in the guise of technology?

Sanctioned infidelity for couples unable to bear and beget children together has historical precedents. In the first book of the Old Testament, an infertile wife invites her husband to have sexual intercourse with her handmaid, "that I may obtain children by her."[7] In some cultures, families allow a woman to have intercourse with her infertile husband's close relative, such as a brother, because of the importance attached to producing a family heir. By substituting artificial insemination or in vitro fertilization of a donated egg in place of sexual intercourse, fertility specialists remove the physical intimacy with the donor but do not alter the intent of the participants—to have someone serve as a sexual proxy for the infertile marriage partner. Nor do they alter the outcome—a child genetically related to only one spouse. This book shares several stories of people who have used family members as gamete donors in an effort to replicate the genetic contribution the infertile spouse might otherwise have made to the conception, or who have selected a donor similar in appearance and ethnic background to the infertile spouse. Since ours is not the first society to utilize donor gametes for infertile couples, should we accept the age-old practice as merely another infertility option that should be privately considered by a husband and wife, or does the practice have compelling public consequences that warrant regulation?

For Julie Johnson, who provided not only the gestational environment but also the egg fertilized by artificial insemination with her brother-in-law's sperm, her biological contribution to the birth of her nephew was insignificant. "To me, that doesn't even make a difference. I compare it to blood donation. When you give blood, you get it back. When you have a baby for someone else, your body hasn't really lost anything." She acknowledges, however, that her decision to become a surrogate and her satisfaction with that decision depend heavily upon the past and future family relationships. "It is embarrassing to me when people try to put some kind of halo on me for doing this. I wanted a nephew. It's not like I lost. I got a nephew. And my sister and brother-in-law got a child that they had been wanting for years." That is why she calls it a "win-win situation."

Julie is correct that the contribution of her egg as part of her natural cycle did not reduce the number of eggs available for her own fertility in the future. But for an egg donor who consents to the extraction of eggs, her natural monthly cycle is disrupted, not by pregnancy but by hormone therapy and the retrieval of multiple eggs. Since a woman is born with all the eggs she will ever produce and her body will not replicate the eggs she donates, she has not contributed a renewable resource like blood. These donors are given fertility drugs to stimulate their ovaries. They must undergo an extraction, surgically or by aspiration, which may be painful and may involve exposure to a general anesthetic. While these women may be spared the medical and emotional risks of pregnancy, the physical and fertility sacrifices they make are significant. An extremely controversial fertilization technique is being studied in England. Dr. Roger Gosden, at Edinburgh Medical School, is pioneering the retrieval of eggs from aborted female fetuses. If these eggs were fertilized in vitro and transferred to a woman for gestation, it would be possible for an aborted fetus to have offspring although she was never born![8]

For men donating sperm, there are no comparable medical risks or threats to future fertility.[9] However, both male and female donors may suffer unanticipated emotions about their decision, and those feelings may radiate beyond themselves to other members of their families. One egg-donor applicant admitted to a newspaper reporter that her own husband worried about the effect her decision to donate eggs might have on their future ability to have another child. "He's got that whole thing of it being part of me," she said.[10] A sperm donor confided to researchers, "I am technically his or her father but I am not allowed to be part of their life. At first I didn't think it would bother me . . . but I think about it more frequently now."[11] Because doctors prefer younger men's sperm, donors are generally eighteen to thirty-five years of age, and college campuses are a primary arena for recruitment. Most male donors are quite young and without children of their own when they agree to participate. Society must recognize that donors may come to view their decisions quite differently as they mature, marry, and begin their own families, yet little scientific study has been made of the emotional consequences that may result. Because extraction of eggs for donation is a relatively recent procedure, there has been even less opportunity to study the future emotional impact on female gamete donors. As in the case of sperm donation, which has been widely practiced for half a century, egg donation has been implemented with little reflection upon the future emotional cost to the donors.

Records surrounding donor-assisted conceptions are flawed by guesswork and self-deception.[12] Dora Vaux, administrator of the Repository for Germinal Choice, says, "Many people don't tell us when they get pregnant. They just drop out of the program. Sometimes we learn of the birth when they call back a year or so later and tell us they did have a baby and now they want a second one."[13] Although the Paces Cryobank and Infertility Services clinic in Atlanta attempts to maintain records, administrator Vicki Ofsa explains the difficulty: "We've run into situations where couples had insemination with a donor because the husband's sperm count was very, very low. Of course, we attempted to match the physical characteristics of the donor with those of the husband. After the birth, we called, and the husband told us, 'Well, we were going to call you, but the baby looks so much like me that I think it's my own child.' Of course, we have to attribute it to the donor, but it could have happened that by some miracle it was the husband's child, and if they want to believe that, it's fine—and is probably even healthier for the couple."[14]

The tendency on the part of the medical community to tolerate or even encourage husbands to believe that their own sperm, rather than that of the donor, fertilized the egg certainly complicates record keeping. In the past, doctors even mixed the donor sperm with the husband's sperm prior to insemination or encouraged the couple to have intercourse immediately following insemination to enhance the perception. Today's couples are more likely to have specific information about the male infertility factors, but the self-deception continues for some couples. Advancing technology makes it both harder to pretend that the husband fathered the baby (because male fertility factors are better understood) and easier (because computers and the nationwide sharing of donor sperm among banks have made it possible to match the physical characteristics, blood type, and ethnic origins of donor and husband so effectively that the baby will fit into the family without a visible clue to the genetic difference).

Mary Shearing, the postmenopausal mother of twins she gestated after donated eggs were fertilized by her husband's sperm, describes their search for a donor who not only resembled her physically but also had a mental outlook and athletic ability similar to her own, and believes one of the twins looks like Mary's husband, the genetic father of both twins, and the other twin "looks like me," although she made no genetic contribution to the twins' conceptions. Although Mary and Don have acknowledged the participation of an egg donor in the conceptions of their daughters, other couples may prefer to keep the donor-assisted conception that led to the wife's pregnancy between themselves and their doctor.

However privately the secret is held and however closely the baby resembles the infertile parent, the fact that the genetic contribution is from only one parent may have effects on the family, and that should not be ignored by either the couple considering the technology nor the fertility specialists proposing it. In her pioneering book, California psychotherapist Annette Baran tries to "open up that forbidden world" surrounding sperm donation to examine the impact on families. Her choice of title, *Lethal Secrets*,[15] reflects her assessment that the secrecy cloaking donor insemination has damaged relationships: within the family—between husband and wife, parent and child, and children with each other; beyond the family—by affecting the donor's relationships; and individually—by affecting the emotional well-being of each person touched by the assisted conception. She does not propose stopping the practice but rather urges an end to the secrecy.

Baran's research documents husbands who feel they have no right to deny their wives the experience of having a baby, even though they are opposed to the procedure,[16] as well as men who encourage secret donor insemination of their wives so that they will appear fertile.[17] She also reports long-term effects, such as cases of husbands who become weaker and more passive and distant from their children, wives who become stronger and assert a superior right to make decisions about the children, and children who perceive such differences in the roles played by their parents without understanding why.[18] We should anticipate similar results from egg-donor-assisted births, although gestation by the wife may allow a greater sense of participation that lessens some of the emotional alienation fathers in donor-assisted births feel.

The secrecy and sketchy record keeping make exact numbers impossible, but we do know that thousands of babies are born each year as a result of donor-assisted conceptions, and the numbers are continuing to grow. Among this number are uncounted successes, but gradually we are learning that a physically healthy baby matched to the appearance of the sterile parent and portrayed to the world as the natural child of the couple does not always end the emotional suffering of an infertile couple. Rather, only the form of the suffering and the people sharing the pain may have changed.

Those least deserving of an inheritance of emotional pain are the children. If society sanctions donor-assisted births, we must focus more attention on the responsibilities owed to the resulting children, even if it demands certain sacrifices from the adults participating in the donor conceptions.

When adults agree to maintain the confidentiality of donor identity, they relinquish something that belongs to none of them. Rather, they bargain away the unique genetic heritage that belongs to the child. The protection of strict confidentiality may benefit a donor who wants to avoid all moral and legal obligation to the child, or it may benefit the couple who prefers not to disclose publicly the fact of donor assistance, but the child is the one who bears the cost of their protection. Forever taking away a child's access to genetic ancestry amounts to parental larceny, and the clinics that facilitate such agreements are coconspirators in the thefts.

Among those who participated in my survey, there was strong support for making genetic information about the donor available to children born with donated egg, sperm, or embryo. 78 percent said that information should be available, only 8 percent said it should not, and 11 percent were undecided.[19] However, responses to the question of whether the donor's identity should be made available to donor-conceived children were mixed. More felt that it should be than believed that it should not, 40 percent as compared to 31 percent, but 26 percent were undecided.[20] Based on survey responses, protecting donors from later disclosure of their identity has significant public support, although the majority either questions the practice or believes it should be changed to allow children access to that information at an appropriate time.

The Center for Surrogate Parenting in Los Angeles, California, has an egg-donor program, and none of their donations is done anonymously. Dr. Hilary Hanafin observes, "In the infertile world, many more couples are saying, 'I want to choose the donor' or 'I want to meet the egg donor.'" Although the insistence on confidentiality of identity is lessening, it remains the norm. "You have to understand the pain of these infertile couples. They just want a baby to hold. Even if they know the baby really looks like the donor but all their friends say the baby looks like them, they have a real hope that secrecy about the donor assistance will make the bonding with them better, and will lessen the anxiety and grief. And it does work for some people." Based on her own experiences, however, Dr. Hanafin strongly believes that "the long-term benefit of openness will outweigh the immediate comfort of not having to confront the genetic contributive to the child."[21]

A sperm bank in Oakland, California, decided in 1983 to offer an opportunity for identity release of donors willing to participate. "We pioneered the idea of making at least the potential for a recipient to be able to identify the biological donor," says the director of the Sperm Bank of California, Barbara Raboy. "I believe we will begin to see other banks starting to do it, because we have found that it is a very popular request."[22] In their program, the potential for identification depends on delivery of data, such as Social Security number and other statistical information about the donor to the biological offspring, after age eighteen, if it is requested in writing by the offspring.[23] Because the program has only existed since 1983, no offspring have reached the age to request disclosure.

Most clinics maintain strict confidentiality concerning the identity of donors. The California Cryobank maintains records of the donors' identities but leaves it up to the individuals involved to decide whether donor and offspring should ever be introduced. "While we are not opposed in principle to breaking anonymity between the donor and the adult or near-adult child, we do strongly feel that it must be by mutual consent of both parties. We do not believe that the mother or the semen donor should be asked today how they might feel about such a sensitive and complex issue fifteen to thirty years from now," says Rhonda Wilkens, marketing director of the clinic.

Annette Baran thinks the donor's obligation goes beyond mere disclosure of identity. She believes a child born as a result of a donor-assisted conception "must be accepted as having two genetic parents who are important to him; they contribute to his identity and self-concept. They connect him to his biological and historical past and provide him with information that is vital to his health and well-being." She sees the role of the sperm donor as a lifelong responsibility, not in a legal or financial sense, but as the representative of half of the child's biological inheritance, and she advocates personal contact between donor and offspring at an appropriate age.

If Baran's proposal were put into practice, we would have to reconsider the number of genetic offspring a single donor should have. The current recommendations by the American Fertility Society are meant to prevent accidental inbreeding and genetic incest that might result if one donor begets too many children. Baran's recommended limit of three offspring relates to the donor's capacity to meet the psychological needs of the resulting children, without overburdening his own family.

The limit recommended by the American Fertility Society is fifteen, but there is no legal limit. Even reputable sperm banks may construe the recommended limit to allow more than fifteen total offspring by one donor. While the Atlanta sperm bank does follow the recommended limit with respect to a particular locality, they would continue to supply physicians in other metropolitan areas with sperm if the local limit were met and donor specimens remained available.[24] Certainly a donor might change his residence and participate in the program of a different sperm bank, and since each facility maintains independent, confidential records, prior donations might go undiscovered. Some other reasons for concern: computers link possible donor specimens that are shipped nationwide; couples of childbearing age are often in highly mobile careers and may relocate with donor offspring to a region where unknown genetic siblings live; and during the college years, when romantic attachments are likely, donor offspring are apt to reside outside the locality of their conception. These realities, coupled with the fact that the limitation of offspring is at the ethical discretion of the particular sperm bank, could result in the sort of incestual accident that the limitations are intended to avoid, although the odds remain slight.

The publicity surrounding the prosecution of a fertility specialist in Vienna, Virginia, for perjury and fraud in connection with his medical practice, documents one case of a single man who fathered excessive numbers of offspring. During the trial of Dr. Cecil B. Jacobson, prosecutors concluded that the doctor may have provided the semen used to conceive over seventy children born to couples treated at his clinic over a twelve-year period. Even more disturbing is evidence from DNA testing that refutes Jacobson's claim to have found a donor who was "a perfect match" for one patient's husband. In fact, the government's evidence showed that the doctor had never used another donor.

Scandal has touched even highly respected fertility clinics. In 1995 the Center for Reproductive Health of the University of California at Irvine was charged with giving the eggs of women treated at their clinic to other women without the donors' knowledge or consent.

Couples place enormous trust in fertility specialists when they allow artificial insemination or in vitro fertilization with anonymous donor gametes. And, of course, there is always the possibility that human error could occur. In 1986 a woman gave birth to a mixed-race daughter after having been inseminated with what was supposed to have been sperm deposited by her same-race, cancer-patient husband. She sued the laboratory where the sperm was stored and the doctor who had done the insemination, claiming she had received the wrong semen. Both the doctor and the laboratory paid financial settlements to the woman, without admitting liability. Her husband died prior to the settlements.[25]

In a Dutch case that received worldwide attention, a couple used IVF to conceive twin boys, but at birth one baby was blond, like his parents, while the other baby was dark. Gossip circulated through the couple's village accusing the mother of infidelity. When DNA testing confirmed that the husband is not the biological father of the dark twin, the fertility clinic that had performed the couple's IVF admitted "a deeply regrettable mistake," apparently caused by the use of the same instrument in their IVF that a technician had used previously in a different IVF. The clinic presumes that the sperm of a man from the Caribbean island of Aruba was transferred by the instrument to one of the woman's eggs, resulting in the fertilization of two of her eggs by two different men, one of them her husband and the other a stranger of a different race. Although the couple love both sons, the careless handling of sperm by the prestigious University Hospital at Utrecht fertility clinic has exposed this family to social isolation, fears that the biological father may assert some claim, and worry that their sons will face unequal opportunities throughout their lives.[26]

In a different case, the trust Cynthia Hallvik placed in her infertility clinic may have even more grave consequences for her and her family. When Cynthia and her husband were unable to conceive, they decided to try donor insemination. When no pregnancy resulted after a series of inseminations with the anonymous donor's sperm, they chose to adopt and are now the busy parents of a daughter and a son.[27]

In 1991, eight years after the initial inseminations, Cynthia was scheduled for a surgical procedure. "I went in as a precaution to give my own blood, and at that time, through the donation of blood presurgery, it was tested [including a test for the AIDS virus]," she explains. "It came back positive." While the donor insemination years before had not resulted in a pregnancy, it had infected her with the AIDS virus. "We didn't tell the kids for a year, because my husband and I had so much going on to adjust our own thoughts about it. It was pretty hard to tell them."

Nearly all of the fifty-three women who received sperm from Cynthia's donor have been located, but only she and one other woman have tested positive. The donor died in December of 1993.

"At the time of the inseminations, we were told that the donor was a student from UCLA and that his basic characteristics were similar to my husband, as far as weight and height and that kind of thing. That was what we were concerned about then. I was just thinking how much I wanted a family." Although Cynthia agrees that AIDS awareness was not then what it is today, she believes she was inadequately warned of the possible risks: "Even in 1983 it could have been stated to me that there was a slight possibility that STDs [sexually transmitted diseases] or whatever could be transmitted, but none of that was addressed."

Cynthia has found the courage to speak publicly about her condition because she wants other women to be aware of the possibility of HIV infection before they consent to insemination. Furthermore, she wants to alert other women, like herself, who were inseminated before HIV screening of semen became common practice, that they should be tested. Cynthia does not condemn the practice of sperm donation itself, but she does advocate stronger regulation of clinics and greater awareness among women considering the procedure.

She offers this advice to other infertile couples: "I think people should take a really good look at the possibility of not having families, rather than thinking that is the only way they can have meaning in their lives. There are other options out there, and women need to be really clear on that." She pauses and laughs softly before adding, "When you don't get pregnant, there is the possibility that God is trying to tell you something."

Only a few states require semen testing for AIDS, and there are no federal regulations, but today virtually every reputable clinic has implemented AIDS testing as a part of their donor-screening process, whether the clinics are motivated by ethical standards or fears of legal liability. Even so, Cynthia Hallvik's warning is essential to couples considering donor insemination: "Just make darn good and sure that the clinic or the physician you are dealing with has taken precautions!" she urges.

The medical screening of donors before they are accepted into reputable programs is stringent. In fact, the risks of transmitting genetic and sexually transmitted diseases through donor sperm are far less than in normal conceptions. "We test them for everything that we can. Their family histories have been reviewed and they have been tested for genetically and sexually transmitted diseases," says Vicki Ofsa. And she adds, "You don't test somebody you are going to marry. Yet the ladies coming in and using a donor specimen have the benefit of that extensive testing."[28] The elimination of potential sperm donors for reasons having to do with family medical history, testing for genetic and sexually transmitted diseases, and sperm quality narrows the number of actual donors at reputable clinics down to only about 5 to 15 percent of those who apply.[29] As a result, donor-conceived offspring may face fewer risks of inheriting medical disadvantages from their biological fathers than babies in general. Rather than assuming that medical screening has occurred, couples must investigate the practices of their clinic or physician before consenting to the procedure.[30] Dr. Hanafin believes couples are taking more responsibility for ensuring that appropriate donor screening occurs. "Couples are becoming much better consumers and requesting much more information. They used to leave most of these decisions up to social workers and physicians."

Donor offspring may even enjoy certain intellectual advantages from their biological fathers, who are often recruited from universities and graduate schools. One sperm bank goes even further. The Repository for Germinal Choice in Escondido, California, was founded in 1963 specifically to provide sperm for donor insemination from men of recognized intellectual achievement. Although the program has gained a reputation as the "genius" sperm bank, it also claims to seek men having "physical and mental health, longevity, and a sociable personality." Unlike other sperm banks that recruit among students, this bank says of its donors: " 'Above average' is not good enough. Each donor excels in his field," and adds, "These men invariably have high intelligence . . ."[31] Couples who use sperm from this facility are often suspected of wanting not just a baby but rather a "superbaby."[32]

While we can evaluate the medical heritage of donor offspring, it is much more difficult to assess the psychological consequences of intentionally introducing donor gametes in the creation of families. We must not validate intentional choices by citing the unplanned imbalance in many families as a result of adoption or divorce. Yet many people do make that argument. Trying to do what is best for children that are members of blended families or broken homes imbalanced by unplanned divorces, deaths, or adoptions is a very different moral issue from justifying the use of a donor to create a child with the planned intention to raise it in a situation similar to that found in blended or broken homes. Recognizing that children suffer emotional difficulties relating to divorce or adoption is not to criticize single or adoptive parents who have provided loving and supportive homes in spite of those difficulties. Rather, it is simply to acknowledge that such circumstances are less than ideal and that few parents would intentionally choose them for their children.

Without using divorce and adoption as a justification for donor-assisted conceptions, we may look to those situations for guidance in evaluating their impact on the lives of children who are separated from their biological roots. Most of us know of adopted children who have searched throughout their lives for their biological origins, despite having happy adoptive homes. Too many of us know the tensions among divorced parents, stepparents, and the children who must cope with the added emotional challenges present in such blended families, despite the best efforts of everyone. This personal knowledge alerts us to the kinds of emotional problems a donor-conceived child might face and should cause us to ask whether it is responsible to intentionally subject a child to a life defined from conception by those sorts of emotional challenges.

If we determine that the emotional risks to children conceived via donor assistance are worth taking, the adults who decide to assume those risks for these children bear special responsibilities. Foremost among those decisions is deciding whether and when to tell a donor child the unusual means of conception.

People generally agree that it is best to tell adopted children of their origins. Researchers report that even in families in which the information is withheld, the children are likely to have "a sense of being different from others in the family, or an awareness of a secret in the family about them. Once they learn they [are] adopted, a lot of confusion in their lives [is] resolved."[33] Despite the general consensus about disclosing adoptive origins, secrecy still surrounds donor arrangements.

At the Atlanta sperm bank, Vicki Ofsa urges the couples to "go home and come to a mutual decision—not so much about telling anybody else but about what they are going to tell the child." She believes about half the couples tell the child of the donor conception and half do not. "Some couples just don't want to tell, and that's their right, too. They don't have to tell a child, because legally on the birth certificate the husband is down as the legal father."[34] The marketing director of California Cryobank, one of the nation's largest donor-sperm repositories, believes few of their clients disclose the use of donor sperm in the wife's pregnancy.[35] At another of the nation's largest sperm banks, Dr. Joseph Feldschuh, medical director of the Idant Laboratory in New York, actually advocates against disclosing the donor conception to the child. "It adds to division between the man who raised the child and the child. It adds an uncertainty. It adds a way of interpreting your entire life's experience in a different way."[36]

The secrecy in many families has been so complete that not only have researchers been unable to evaluate the effect of nondisclosure on the children but the children themselves may never learn the possibility that donor conception played some role in their family relationships. A few donor offspring have come forward as adults to describe the poisonous effect secrecy has had on their lives,[37] but since it is impossible to balance their experiences against descriptions from donor offspring in families in which the effect of the undiscovered secret was positive, we are left with only a fragment of the picture.

There is no doubt about the emotional toll keeping a solemn secret exacts by threatening to reveal itself in unguarded moments or unanticipated circumstances. That emotional baggage must complicate the development of trustful, nurturing relationships among all members of the family. Even without the research data to support it, the old maxim "Honesty is the best policy" sounds like good advice.

Experts agree. Annette Baran says, "Universal human needs for genealogical and historical connections are the same for people everywhere, no matter how they were conceived or gestated. The understanding of who we are, where we came from, and whom we connect with in our past must not be sacrificed in the name of the new era of scientific bioengineering."[38] As Dr. Hanafin reasons, "The adults can make an informed choice, but the child they are planning to conceive can't. In order to protect the child, we need to have open records access to information, and if the adults are not comfortable with that, they should ask whether they should be doing the procedure."

Many parents seek confidentiality because they fear that the gamete donor may later claim a place in their child's life, either by seeking legal custody or by stealing a bit of the child's affection from the parents. The highly publicized custody battles between surrogates and the couples with whom they contracted, as well as those between biological and adoptive parents, have only heightened such fears.

Single parents especially fear losing or having to share custody of the child with the gamete donor. My survey results reflect that the public attitude toward donor-assisted conception within unconventional families is viewed less favorably.[39] Yet, more and more single women are deciding to be parents.

Katherine Ward[40] was in her early thirties, with no partner in sight, when she began to think about having a baby. "It really was a ten-year process, but eventually it became clear to me that if I waited for everything to be perfect that I might have to wait too long. People talk about vocations and having a calling, and I felt very, very strongly that what I was supposed to do next was allow myself to give birth to this child. I really felt an intense spiritual calling to do that."

By the time she resolved to proceed, she was nearly forty years old and had carefully researched donor conceptions in an effort to do what was best for her future child. "I talked to a lot of people who had been adopted and didn't know who their biological parents were, and I read a lot. I didn't want to set up a situation for my child to feel a sense of loss or wondering, by not being able to know who its biological father was." She knew of no sperm banks that allowed donor offspring access to information about the donor, so Katherine asked a friend if he would be willing to donate sperm for her insemination. "He was somebody that I liked and I trusted, and we had a good time together," she explains. "I asked if he would be willing to do this. His response was that he would be honored."

Katherine obtained a form agreement in which the donor

expressly relinquished all rights to the baby conceived from his sperm. However, because she believed it was important to preserve the link between her baby and its biological father, Katherine and her friend changed parts of the printed agreement. Today she explains what she intended to accomplish: "There is a real, clear difference between wanting someone to be an active parent—daddy—in the child's life and wanting someone to be willing to have a relationship when it is important to the child and have regular contact when it is important to the child, rather than being a daddy. This person was a friend. Of course he was going to know my child, see my child, have a relationship with my child. As it became more important to the child to relate to and have a male figure in its life, he would be available to the child." From all apparent indications, the donor shared her intentions.

Katherine says she sought no particular traits in the donor relative to appearance, intellect, or personality. Even though there were no health care professionals to screen the semen, and raw rather than frozen semen was used for the syringe insemination, Katherine did verify that the donor had tested negative for HIV. She adds, "He agreed for the period of time that I was inseminating that he would be celibate so that there would be no possibility of him being infected during the process." As for herself, she says, "I was aware for a year or more before I actually started getting pregnant that that is what I was preparing to do. I was taking care of myself. I quit smoking and drinking caffeine. I was a purist!" she laughs.

Although the donor underwent no psychological evaluations, Katherine attended to her emotional as well as physical well-being during her preparations for the pregnancy. "I did not attempt to get pregnant until I was at a psychological space in my life where it did not matter to me whether my child was a girl or a boy, whether that child was 100 percent perfect or was going to have special problems."

As it turned out, psychological testing of the donor might have spared both of them a lot of heartache. For, despite all her careful preparations, Katherine and her donor friend found themselves in court, battling over what his claims as the father of the baby girl they had conceived together should be. The court refused to terminate the donor's parental rights, as Katherine had requested, but the donor was awarded only one day of visitation a month, from 9:00 A.M. to 6:00 P.M., far less than the donor had asked for. Katherine warns, "When people tell me that they are using a friend, I just get sick. I tell them, please don't do that. You don't understand the kind of turmoil." Today she believes the risks of facing the legal agony she has endured outweigh the risks of the child growing up without knowing its paternal biological roots.

"I feel jealous on some level, of couples that had children right at the same time that we did. The first two years of our child's life, we were in utter chaos," Katherine says. "I almost feel like I have been deprived of some serenity that new mothers, new parents experience, because I had this legal battle injected into my life. I don't think anybody should have to go through that."

By the time Katherine's daughter was born, she had found her life's partner, and although her little girl has two parents, the family remains unconventional. "We are a lesbian family," Katherine explains. "I don't see myself as a single mother at all. I feel like a single mother is someone who has no help and is doing everything by herself. That's not what happens in our family. There are two of us to take care of this child. I probably get more support in mothering and parenting from my partner than a lot of men give to their partners because of assumptions about sex-role differences. We don't have those kinds of differences."

Katherine's partner, Hannah, has no legal claim as a parent, although their daughter calls both women "Mom." "In the custody case, I filed a motion as an intervenor for joint custody, but it was denied," Hannah says.

Katherine relates a story of how their daughter, Judith, handles having two moms. "Hannah had always taken Judith to swimming lessons, and I had never gone. Finally, one night I walked into the dressing room and our daughter came running over to me calling me 'Mom,' too. I could just kind of see the lightbulbs going off in the little kids' minds. One little girl asked me why my daughter had two moms. I told her, 'Just because she is very lucky.' That was all that was said about it."

The stress caused by the legal dispute has been hard for Hannah, too. She would also like to conceive and give birth to a baby. Before the legal conflicts with their daughter's donor, Hannah had asked him if he would donate sperm for her, so that Judith would have a sibling that shared a common genetic heritage through the donor. Her own plans for pregnancy have been postponed by physical problems brought on by the stress of litigation. As her health returns, Hannah struggles with her own decision about selecting a donor. She is certain that she would no longer want to arrange insemination with the sperm of an acquaintance, but she might consider a sperm bank that allowed the child future access to information about the donor, but not one that allowed the donor access to the child. "I guess I would like for my child to have the option, if it wants to know who the sperm donor was. I waffle about how important that is. I know there have been times at school when Judith has been faced with children saying that she doesn't have a father. She just says that she does." Although Hannah believes that raising her child in a loving, supportive atmosphere could alleviate most of the child's longing for a father, she worries that cutting off all that information from a child might create a stigma that would make life harder.

Although Hannah would prefer that her parental role had been recognized by the court, it troubles her less than it might others. She grew up in a household consisting of her father and stepmother, and a natural sibling and stepsiblings. She says of her family, "We were very close, all of us. I don't have that feeling of my stepmother not being my mother and of my stepsiblings not being my brother and sister. To me, there is nothing missing." She knows from experience that love within a family is not dependent upon blood relationships or legal recognition.

The litigation with their daughter's biological father has obviously forced both Katherine and Hannah to think very seriously about just what defines a parent. For both of them, it is a matter of meeting the needs of the child, rather than the needs of the adults. "I still think," says Hannah, "that the law should look at what is in the best interests of the child, regardless of who did what or whose sperm went into what jar or what egg touched what sperm."

Katherine never considered adoption because, she says, "I really feel like there was a soul ready to be born, and for some reason I was supposed to facilitate that." She also declined all prenatal testing. "Even if any of those tests would have told me there was something 'wrong' with this baby, I was certainly not going to abort it." Then, quietly, with thoughtful deliberation, Katherine confides, "I have been pro-choice for a long time. When I was nineteen years old I had an abortion. I was exercising my right not to procreate at that time. In my midlife, I have exercised my right to procreate. I definitely think that there have been generations before us who thought that because a woman was a lesbian, or a couple was lesbian, that they couldn't have children. I am really grateful that I am living at a point in time where I don't have that kind of consciousness or attitude about my lesbianism, that it does not prevent me from also experiencing motherhood."

A San Francisco attorney who has written on the subject for the Lesbian Rights Project describes the growing trend of artificial insemination among lesbians, which began about 1979.[41] It is hard to get exact numbers on this trend. Because some physicians and sperm banks decline to inseminate unmarried women, lesbian women have developed innovative approaches to accomplishing their donor-assisted pregnancies, ranging from self-help manuals to founding their own clinics.[42]

The practice in the gay community of asking friends to cooperate in self-inseminations has been reduced by the AIDS epidemic, but some women continue to take the risk, or attempt to minimize it as Katherine did. Others have avoided the mainstream medical community's bias against inseminating lesbians by lying. As with heterosexual couples seeking surrogates and donors, sometimes family members are involved. In some cases, a male sibling of one of the partners provides the sperm to inseminate the other partner, and a same-sex couple is able to continue both of their family lines in the child they plan to raise together.[43] The trend toward planned pregnancies by single women is not just growing among lesbians, however.

When Oprah Winfrey hosted a panel of single mothers, the audience cheered an unmarried schoolteacher on the panel who had chosen to have a baby by insemination when she declared that the things she considered important for her child were love, self esteem, and the receiving and giving of trust, more than having two parents to provide those things.

Although the audience was generally enthusiastic in its support of the panelists' views, one female audience member disagreed. "My point is that every child has the right to a father and a mother," she said, and she challenged the panelists, all of whom had come from two-parent families: "Imagine your lives without your fathers. I'm sure some of you probably have a good argument [for choosing to become a single mother], but I personally can't imagine my life without my father, even though it wasn't always peaches and cream. The reason it takes two people to make a baby is because that's the way it's supposed to be."[44]

Unfortunately, statistics show that many children are not growing up in homes with both a mother and a father present. About 22 percent of American children live with a single parent, and contrary to common perceptions, many of these households are headed by fathers.[45] Even among families of married couples, the children they are raising are often not the offspring of the husband and wife together. According to a

1992 report by the Population Reference Bureau, one in three Americans is a member of a stepfamily, and projections predict that the number will rise to one in two by the turn of the century. Divorce rates are rising, marriage rates are falling, and some single women trapped by those trends are deciding they are unwilling to forgo motherhood while they wait for a male partner who may never come along.

Nearly everyone is aware of the escalation in birth rates among unwed mothers, but most people are surprised to learn that the largest percentage increases are among white, employed, and college-educated women. The number of unmarried women with one or more years of college who gave birth nearly doubled from 1982 to 1992,[46] and among never-married mothers in managerial and professional occupations the birth rate more than doubled.[47] In response to a 1990 nationwide poll, one-third of the three thousand women who were asked whether they would consider having a child out of wedlock if they were single and nearing the end of their childbearing years answered that they would.[48]

The nonprofit organization Single Mothers by Choice has been in existence throughout this period of changing social mores and was founded in 1981 by psychotherapist Jane Mattes. Its members are women who decided to have or adopt a child, knowing they would be the sole parent, at least initially. Their brochure explains the viewpoint of many of their members, typically career women in their thirties and forties, and the language mirrors the shift in social attitudes. "Most of us would have preferred to bring a child into a good marriage," the brochure reads. "However, while we have a lifetime to marry, nature is not so generous in allotting childbearing years. Single motherhood is ideally for the woman who feels she has much to give a child and has adequate emotional and financial resources to support herself and her child."[49]

There is no comparable trend among unmarried men, although many men view their roles in the conception and birth of their children much differently than the roles their own fathers played. The director of the Fatherhood Project at the Families and Work Institute, a private research organization, pointed out to *The New York Times* that thirty years ago almost no fathers attended the birth of a child, but today more than 90 percent are present.[50] A single man who wants to conceive a genetic child must obtain the cooperation of not only a gamete donor but also a surrogate to gestate the fetus, and Hilary Hanafin admits that many of the surrogates she has worked with would be unwilling to assist in that situation. "Most of these women become surrogates, at least in part, because they feel a great empathy with the infertile woman. They see themselves placing the baby they are carrying in the arms of another mommy, and psychologically it would be much more difficult to help a single man." She continues, "It is very important for a surrogate to be able to place a child in a home where she feels she will never need to worry about the baby, and that is why most of them prefer traditional couples." However, the center has helped four gay couples arrange surrogate births, and while those cases have gone fine, they remain the exception among surrogacy arrangements.[51]

The use of donor gametes may sometimes seem like an assault on traditional values, just as excessive pride (or what one adoptive mother called genetic narcissism) may sometimes play too large a part. But there are also unselfish reasons why people have chosen donor-assisted conceptions in their family planning. For example, parents who carry the gene for an inheritable disease may choose to substitute donor gametes for their own in order to spare their children the risk of inheriting the disease. Commonly, infertile partners may choose to use donors not only because they want to have children themselves, but also to allow fertile partners to have genetic offspring. "Is it so unnatural for any woman who wants and loves children but cannot bear them to want and love the child of the man she loves?" asked one infertile wife who supports genetic surrogacy.[52] Finally, the fertile spouse may turn to a donor out of love for his or her own family, to carry on the family line. "It was very important to me to carry on the female side of my family. I really wanted to have a grandchild for my mother. My grandmother, my mother, and I were all three only daughters in our families, and I wanted to have a daughter, too. It was tough to end that strain, that line," explains one woman.[53] The wisdom of their decision to involve someone other than their spouse in the conception of a child may be open to debate, but we should not automatically assume that the primary motivation in all cases is a selfish desire by fertile partners to create a genetic reflection of themselves.

If society determines that there are morally acceptable reasons to tolerate, or even encourage, the responsible practice of donor-assisted conceptions, and if the trend toward open records grows, can current laws defining "parents" accommodate the new roles of gamete donors and surrogates? Courts generally become involved after an agreement has been breached. Nearly all parties enter into their arrangements intending that only two legal parents will claim the child (or, in the case of a single mother by choice, that she alone will be the baby's parent). The lawsuit erupts when one or more of them no longer want to honor that original agreement. The court is then left to sort out their angry claims in an effort to rebuild a family for the baby, basing the court-imposed family upon a traditional, two-parent model. Some experts argue that forcing a legal recognition of two parents in these situations is an outmoded approach to the realities of assisted conception and birth.

Doctor-lawyer Bruce Wilder suggests that the law recognize three legal parents in certain situations when the participants cannot agree about traditional, two-parent roles. He believes this makes particular sense when three different people provide egg, sperm, and gestation. "Just as society has to some extent accepted, and just as our law has dealt with, situations where children are born out of wedlock, our society and our law should be able to accommodate the rare three-parent circumstance without any major upheaval in our body of legal precedent."[54] He argues that our old laws developed when only two people could share in the creation of a baby, but today we may have "a totally different kind of reproduction and it is appropriate to ask if law which determines parenthood should not, by the creation of new rules, adapt accordingly."[55]

Another writer also suggests that the law take into account the three separate elements that contribute to the birth of a child but in such a way that only two people are left with a legally recognized parental claim. He recommends determining parental rights based upon who has "contributed between them two out of the three elements necessary to the procreation of a child: either two gametes, or one gamete and the pregnancy." Under his proposal, a genetic surrogate who contributes both the egg and the gestation would always prevail over the wife of the couple she agreed to assist.[56]

The better resolution of these disputes among adults who have changed their minds, it seems, is the simple solution of holding them to the agreement they made at the time of conception, unless it is not in the best interest of the child to enforce their agreement. Proposals like the two summarized above are more concerned with the needs of the adults than with the well-being of the child, and if society is to accept donor- and surrogate-assisted births, the role of the courts should remain for these babies what it is for all children: determining the best interests of the child. The adults have the power to protect their own interests at the time they make their agreement, and if they fail, they should suffer the emotional consequences rather than harming the child their agreement brought to life.

A different question arises from agreements that avoid a two-parent family from the moment of conception. It is not necessarily in the best interests of the child for courts to enforce those agreements that deprive a child of its mother or father because the single parent (or same-sex couple) prefers to eliminate the role of the donor. Open records would at least allow a child to trace his or her genetic heritage, but perhaps society should insist on more. Perhaps single men and women who seek a sexual proxy to assist in the conception should also be expected, by law or by the encouragement of social opinion, to find a second proxy. After all, we impose legal obligations on both the mother and the father when unplanned pregnancies occur out of wedlock, without requiring the couple to marry. Since our laws have determined that it is in the best interests of the baby to recognize the legal obligation of both father and mother in those cases, it would be consistent to require the designation of a person of the same gender as the donor before releasing the donor from his or her legal obligation to the child.[57] In effect, this parent-proxy would serve as a legal guardian, benefitting the child by contributing lifelong emotional support and acting as a substitute role model for the absent parent in the child's home. If death or some other calamity befell the single parent and no custodial guardian had been named, the child would be assured of a familiar adult to assume guardianship. Many single mothers are already doing this in an informal way with the help of brothers or friends, but the benefits to the child would be better ensured if the practice were formalized. In past generations, when it was not automatically assumed that both parents would survive until their children became adults, the designation of godparents was more than a matter of mere ceremony. A revival of the significance of that role might serve babies born into single-parent families well once again.

Katherine Ward wanted her baby to know its father, although she did not want to share custody or parental rights. The agreement she and the donor attempted to craft failed when the donor began to claim a larger role as Judith's father than their preconception agreement had envisioned. When Katherine responded by asking a court to terminate all the donor's parental claims, the judge, feeling that what she wanted was not in her baby's best interests, refused to terminate the father's rights. Ironically, Katherine became ensnarled in the legal dispute over parental rights because she had respected the importance of protecting her unborn child's ability to know its biological father, and he might have enjoyed a greater role in Judith's life if he had been content with the preconception agreement.

All of us should be troubled by the idea of empowering one parent to eliminate the presence or identity of the other parent from the life of his or her child. The fact that natural parents may sometimes die before birth or that unmarried mothers may be unable to identify their children's fathers are not sufficient reasons to intentionally inflict those circumstances on a child. If the trend of donor-assisted conceptions for single parents is going to continue, we must find a way to encourage gender balance and security in the lives of the children, without causing single women, or even men, to act unsafely or illegally in order to avoid sharing the parental rights to children they prefer to raise alone.

Although Katherine is satisfied with the legal outcome of her own situation, she counsels other women to avoid the risk of legal fees, emotional and physical stress, and the possibility of an unacceptable legal outcome by using an anonymous donor. Her current support of donor anonymity is understandable, but her original respect for the future rights of the child is the practice society should attempt to encourage among women considering donor-assisted conceptions. The judge's actions in Katherine's case show that courts applying existing laws can honor the original intentions of the adults without sacrificing the child's relationships with both genetic contributors; however, such an outcome is far from assured and the costs in dollars and suffering are too great for society to take much comfort in the outcome of that single case.

The majority of states now recognize certain rights in persons other than parents, such as visitation rights of grandparents or custody rights of stepparents if the biological parent dies. Similar recognition could be extended to the person designated on the birth certificate, without elevating the rights of this proxy to the same level as those of the single parent. Designation by will of a different person to be the child's custodial guardian could allow single parents to continue the family unit involving stepparents or same-sex partners, but the proxy parent, or modern-day godparent, would also be there to provide emotional stability and continuity for the child. If proxy parents acquire some newly created legal status in our society, we must provide special protection to designated guardians so that people like Hannah, who are truly parents in the emotional and psychological sense, are not forced to relinquish custody to someone outside the family.

Whatever moral and legal strategies we develop, neither the single parents nor society in general wants to mark these children as different or to deprive them of the emotional supports necessary for healthy lives. The biological necessity for both a mother and a father may no longer be reflected in many American homes, but we risk a great deal when we tamper with our traditional view of that environment as the healthiest place to raise our children. Like Katha Pollitt's warning against exposing children to more "disposable relationships" in their lives,[58] another commentator believes, "[T]he bonds between people, though they change, require more than a casual fidelity on the part of successive generations."[59]

Society is right to worry about the suffering caused by the unexpected emotions participants in assisted conceptions may subsequently have. However, perhaps we should be more frightened by the prospect that widespread acceptance of the practice can also steal the emotion away from participants. A male audience member asked Oprah Winfrey, "I wonder what kind of a man would want to father a child and not take any more part in the nurturing or the care of it."[60] And as if to answer him, a sperm donor appearing on *Dateline NBC* told the reporter that he never thinks about the children who may have been born as a result of the sperm he contributed. "I really don't have any thoughts about that whatsoever," he says. "I basically view it as a way to make a little extra money on the side."[61] Contributing the gametes for the creation of a new life should never be reduced to a careless commercial transaction.

Although men and women are routinely paid for providing eggs and sperm for infertile couples to use, my survey results suggest that the public may actually oppose the practice. When asked if the sale of gametes should be prohibited by law, 68 percent said men should be prohibited from selling sperm, 69 percent said women should be prohibited from selling eggs, 69.4 percent said couples should be prohibited from selling embryos created from their egg and sperm, and 71 percent said third parties (such as clinics, physicians, or brokers) should be prohibited from selling sperm, eggs, or embryos.[62] If such sales were prohibited, clinics using gamete donation would be compelled to locate qualified individuals willing to provide eggs and sperm without receiving any compensation, or clinics would have to ask infertile couples to locate their own gamete donors. Even though gamete donations by family members and friends are increasingly common, requiring couples to provide their own donors in all cases would involve a significant change in current fertility practices.

One clinic has developed a practice they call egg sharing. Women who need in vitro fertilization but cannot afford the procedure provide their healthy eggs to other women being treated at the clinic who are in need of eggs. In return, the recipient of the eggs pays for two-thirds of the cost of the donor's in vitro procedure. The study conducted by the clinic concluded that this could be a cost-effective option,[63] but the economic coercion seems obvious. During the scandal surrounding the University of California at Irvine, enormous bitterness was expressed by one couple who never succeeded in having children when they learned that another woman had twin daughters with their stolen eggs. The potential for similar emotional suffering by women who participate in the egg-sharing program without achieving a pregnancy for themselves appears likely, whether or not they are specifically told of the outcome of the procedures using their donated eggs. Even if their own in vitro procedure succeeds, it seems reasonable to suspect that some of the donors will feel they paid for their baby's conception through the loss of a child they will never know. Dr. Hanafin's avoidance of selecting surrogates who need the financial incentive should serve as a warning against linking financial need with a request to donate eggs.

Today there are thousands of children born each year as a result of donor inseminations, and generally the sperm comes from an anonymous donor screened by the clinic or physician. Annette Baran found that among the husbands she studied, "To most of these men, that sperm was emotionally equivalent to infidelity. Intellectually they know that the sperm came in a test tube and was administered in an impersonal, technical way. However, their gut feelings, based on irrational, illogical considerations, were strong and disturbing." In other words, despite all the medical trappings surrounding the process, these husbands recognized the donors as their sexual proxies. Perhaps that is neither irrational nor illogical but rather more emotionally honest than the fertility specialists are willing to admit. After all, the artificial delivery of the sperm does not change the fact that each man's wife will share her genetic traits with those of another man.

Julie Johnson is grateful that the counselor from the Resolve support group warned them of the special bonding that often occurs between the surrogate and the man whose child she is carrying. Because they were prepared in advance, Julie, her sister, and her brother-in-law were able to interpret those feelings in a way that did not jeopardize their relationships.

Dealing with his complicated emotions toward the surrogate he and his wife used for the birth of their child was more difficult for one man. "Here was this very attractive, very intelligent woman . . . and she was bearing my child," he explains. His words reveal the contrast between the clinical situation and his instinctual responses. "I am happily married. I don't want anything mucking that up. It's just that way down in the older brain where sex and reproduction are connected, we get into some pretty delicate territory," he admits.[64]

In 1934 a doctor wrote: "What husband or wife, no matter how intense their longing for an heir, will consent to an injection of strange semen? Thank God that most people still have that much tact, decency, and moral feeling."[65] Soon after those words were written, however, couples were consenting to the very thing he predicted was too abhorrent for society to ever accept. Today technology allows the implanting of "strange" eggs as well. In the past two decades, so many taboos have been pushed aside by technological intervention in human reproduction that society has lost clear parameters for decent behavior. We are left to exercise our fundamental rights of procreation without the moral values we inherited from our parents, but this childbearing generation has not had time to evolve new guidelines appropriate to the possibilities of today.

Traditionally, churches assisted their members in setting guidelines, and 77 percent of the participants in my survey described themselves as religious.[66] However, only 36 percent knew the official position their church had taken with regard to most of the new reproductive technologies,[67] and less than 1 percent characterized their opinions as being always in agreement with those of their church.[68] An even more surprisingly small 34.5 percent said they were influenced in the decisions made in their everyday lives by what their churches say they ought to do.[69] Based on these responses, it appears that the traditional role of churches in setting the moral direction for their members provides only limited guidance today, and that may very well explain the lack of consensus about many of the reproductive options now available.

Even so, new moral values will eventually evolve. As we move through this process, clinical surroundings must not distort the moral landscape, nor should legislators and judges map our course. The moral appropriateness of donor assistance in family planning demands the thoughtful consideration of everyone, and well-intentioned professionals must not overwhelm the common sense and individual consciences of the families pondering their reproductive options. We must respect the value of our own inner voices that whisper to each of us what is right and what is wrong after we have listened to all the words spoken by others. If we do that, we are unlikely to betray future generations.

If you desired a child and you (or your partner) were unable to become pregnant after over a year of trying, would you use

- In vitro fertilization with donor egg or sperm?
- Artificial insemination with donor sperm?

Should reproductive technologies involving gamete donors be covered under health insurance, for example:

- In vitro fertilization with donor egg or sperm?
- Artificial insemination with donor sperm?

Would you be willing to pay higher health insurance premiums to cover the costs of extending coverage to include reproductive procedures involving donor egg and sperm to all policyholders?

Would you be willing to pay higher taxes so the government could assist in the payment of costs associated with donor technologies?

Should reproductive treatments involving donor gametes be prohibited by law, for example:

- In vitro fertilization with donor egg or sperm?
- Artificial insemination with donor sperm?

Should the sale of gametes be prohibited by law, for example:

- Sale of embryo by couple whose egg and sperm created it?
- Sale of egg by woman?
- Sale of sperm by man?
- Sales of egg, sperm, or embryo by third parties?

Who should be eligible to use nontraditional reproductive technology in order to have a child, for example:

- Married couples without children?
- Married couples with one child?
- Married couples regardless of other children?

- Heterosexual couples who are not married but who have a stable relationship, without children?
- Heterosexual couples who are not married but who have a stable relationship, with one child?
- Heterosexual couples who are not married but who have a stable relationship, regardless of other children?
- Any heterosexual couple who desire treatment?
- Heterosexual single persons without a current partner?
- Gay or lesbian couples without children?
- Gay or lesbian couples with a child or children?
- Gay or lesbian single persons without a current partner?

Should children born as a result of the use of donor egg, sperm, or embryo have available at their request the identity of the donor?

Should children born as a result of the use of donor egg, sperm, or embryo have available at their request genetic information about the donor?

Do you know the official position of your church regarding assisted conceptions and pregnancies?

In the decisions you make in your everyday life, are you influenced by what your church says you ought to do?

CHAPTER 19

THE STORY OF DOLLY LAMB

She was a beautiful baby, just as her mother had been, and like other births achieved with technological assistance, Dolly's birth was seen by those who were involved as a scientific miracle. Unlike most other technologically assisted births, however, Dolly's birth attracted the attention of the whole world. Until moments before the announcement, it was generally believed that cloning, if it were ever successful, would not be accomplished for decades. A group of scientists at the Roslin Institute outside Edinburgh, Scotland, changed everything when they revealed on February 22, 1997, that they had cloned Dolly from a single adult cell.

Of course, Dolly is a lamb and not a human baby. Predictions of human cloning are still guarded, but the fact that a fellow mammal has now been cloned makes human clones a realistic possibility in the foreseeable future, if society does nothing to stop it.

This is how the Scottish scientists cloned the lamb they named Dolly. They used a cell from the mammary glands of an adult sheep, which material provided the sophomoric inspiration for naming the newborn lamb after country-music legend Dolly Parton. The mystery that had previously stumped scientists was how to cause an adult cell to act like an embryonic cell, capable of dividing to create not just other specialized cells of the same type but all kinds of cells necessary for a whole animal—heart, brain, bones, and everything else. The Scottish team, led by Ian Wilmut, starved the cells in such a way that they reverted from the specialized status they possessed when they were taken from the ewe's udder to the universal potential present in the embryonic state of cell division. Next, the nuclei were removed from sheep oocytes, or eggs, and a single, starved mammary gland cell was placed alongside a single oocyte. Using a pulse of electricity, the scientists first caused the paired cells to fuse, merging the adult sheep's DNA into the altered egg. A second electrical pulse initiated the embryonic process of cell division that eventually created Dolly. Even after devising the process that led to their ability to clone Dolly, the team of scientists succeeded only after two hundred seventy-seven attempts.

The adult sheep from whom the mammary gland cell was taken, and whose DNA is shared with Dolly, is often referred to as her mother, but she and Dolly are really identical twins born years apart. The DNA they share resulted when the ewe was conceived. Biologically, it is more accurate to see the ewe's parents as the parents of Dolly. The classic scene from the movie *Chinatown*, in which Faye Dunaway tells Jack Nicholson that her daughter is her sister is an admission of incest, but cloning presents a similar biological confusion. Is the adult who has a baby through cloning himself or herself the parent or the elder identical twin of the child?

Laboratory-created identical twins are nothing new. Scientists have already manipulated early-stage embryonic cells to create multiple identical siblings in animals, but only with cloning can adult material be used to create an embryo with identical DNA. This possibility raises many interesting questions for scientists. For example, will the adult cell that was tricked into returning to an embryonic stage capable of creating every kind of cell retain traces of its true adult age, so that the resulting baby will mature at an accelerated pace and eventually catch up with its older, identical twin in the aging process? Will the medical history of the adult be repeated in the cloned baby, with the onset of disease occurring at the same stages in their lives? How different will intelligence and personality be, depending on differences in the educations and experiences of the adult and the clone? Will the adult and cloned identical twins, born years apart, share the extrasensory communication described by many conventional identical twins? The questions suggested by the technology are endless.

In media interviews, most scientists responded to the news of the cloning with shock and opposition to its use for human births. The director of the National Institutes of Health, Dr. Harold Varmus, testified before a congressional subcommittee that he found the idea of cloning humans "repugnant," and he predicted most scientists would reject pursuing such research. He told the subcommittee that he was of the opinion that cloning humans would answer no important scientific questions.[1] Such an opinion lacks imagination, and if he were truly unable to formulate any questions to arouse his scientific curiosity, he need only have looked to the editorial pages of newspapers for ideas.

Many of the people responding publicly to the news predicted megalomaniacs motivated by vanity to clone themselves or a society motivated by hero worship to clone athletic or intellectual superstars in order to pass their talents to another generation. These predictions echo many that were made when artificial insemination, surrogacy, and cyropreservation were introduced to the public.

Political reactions were essentially negative. The British Ministry of Agriculture, which had provided 65 percent of the funding for the research that led to Dolly's birth, gave notice that its support would not continue. The ministry spokesperson indicated that the ministry was concluding the financing it had provided for the previous eight years because the theoretical idea on which the research was based had now been proven and commerce could provide future funding for the research. At the same time, the fifteen-member European Union, of which Great Britain is a part, asked a scientific committee to investigate whether further regulation of genetic manipulation is necessary. Human cloning is already banned by the European Union. In the United States, President Clinton asked a bioethics advisory commission to investigate the implications of the news. Congress had already banned federal funding of research using human embryos, but private funding is not prohibited, and there are no specific bans on human cloning.

The 191 member-nations of the assembly of the World Health Organization declared: "The use of cloning for the replication of human individuals is ethically unacceptable and contrary to human integrity and morality." Resolutions passed by the assembly establish standards respected by scientists worldwide.

So far, the research has been used for animals. In agriculture, animals with better quality meat or greater yields of milk could be cloned to improve production from fewer livestock. In scientific research, identical laboratory animals could be cloned to improve the reliability of test results. In conservation, endangered animal species could be cloned. Dr. Wilmut emphasized at the time of Dolly's birth that his team did not intend for the technology they had pioneered to be used for human cloning.

Despite the reactions of politicians and scientists, limiting cloning to animals may be difficult. Dr. Hilary Hanafin recalls that when she first came to the Center for Surrogate Parenting she was contacted by a couple who asked if the center could assist them in having their own embryo implanted in a surrogate. "I told them that I did not know what they were talking about. At that time we were only doing surrogacies with artificial insemination," she remembers. "Within about eighteen months of their telephone call, we were doing IVF surrogacies, and now more than half of our surrogacies are IVF. Even today, I have such a clear recollection of talking with that couple, and the experience has taught me never to assume that any reproductive technology will remain unavailable once we know how to use it.[2]

One of the problems with regulating biotechnology, even if we determine that it should be done, is that the research can take place in private laboratories without complicated or expensive facilities. Most scientists agree that once the cloning process is understood, research could be conducted surreptitiously by those willing to ignore government prohibitions.

Another problem with regulation may be that many people do not want the process banned. Dr. Hanafin says the center has not discussed whether cloning might some day be offered as a reproductive option for their clients, nor is she familiar with the details of the technology, but she says, "I cannot foresee its use anytime soon, but I am not initially appalled by the idea. I can imagine times for which its use might be positive."

The Repository for Germinal Choice, known as the "genius" sperm bank, sees no role for itself with cloning in the near future, but spokesperson Anita Neff predicts that eventually human cloning will occur. "It will happen, whether we like it or not," she believes. "How it will be used, I don't know." Neff bases her opinion on what she has seen regarding attitudes toward donor sperm. "Often the people who criticize what we do are those who have never had to deal with being unable to conceive a child of their own. When I ask these people to put themselves in the place of people who cry every month over their inability to get pregnant, sometimes that makes them see what we do differently. I would predict that as we begin to see the good and bad uses for cloning, then people will put a more human face on the technology, and they will decide whether it should be used."[3]

Mary Shearing realizes that she and her husband Don were criticized for their use of technology in her own postmenopausal pregnancy when she was fifty-two, so she tries to keep an open mind regarding cloning. Even so, she says, "I'm like most people. I have visions of an evil scientist surrounded by test tubes, laughing evilly about having cloned himself. I'm sure there are positive uses for the technology, but I have trouble seeing it as something good." Upon reflection, Mary concludes, "If it had been financially available, as well as technically possible, Don and I might have considered cloning, although it is hard to imagine anything better than using the donor we did."[4] For other postmenopausal women, cloning a baby from their own or their husband's DNA might be more acceptable than using the eggs of a donor. Mary acknowledges, "You do worry when you use a donor that the donor might try to claim your baby, and cloning would avoid that."

Arlette Schweitzer, the mother who was the surrogate for her daughter and son-in-law, also struggles with criticizing technology when her family benefited from its use, but she opposes cloning. "It is very frightening to think of what could be unleashed with this power," she believes. "I know it seems I am only 'for' what we did . . . [but] in our case I just 'sat on the nest' for Christa. These were her and Kevin's babies, not mine. Nothing really strange took place except the medical intervention of transplanting embryos."[5] Arlette says she would never have considered being a surrogate for her daughter if Christa had been unable to provide the eggs, since "borrowing" donor gametes troubles her. For other women whose ovaries do not produce eggs and who are reluctant to use donor gametes in the creation of their families, cloning babies from both spouses' DNA may seem a morally appropriate way to have children of their own.

Guy and Terri Walden, the parents of three children born with Hurler's Syndrome, have broadened their acceptance of many technologies over the years, so they did not rush to condemn cloning as they once might have done. They discussed the possible uses by families like theirs, but Terri eventually decided, "Today, after what we have gone through with Nathan, we would try to help any child after God created it, and we would be willing to use technology to do that, but we would leave the creation itself to God." Guy agrees. "If the technology could be used to ameliorate disease, then there might be positive uses, but the uses for commercial or vain purposes probably outweigh positive possibilities," he thinks.[6]

Cynthia Hallvik, who is HIV positive as a result of artificial insemination with anonymous donor sperm, has religious reservations about cloning. "It is hard for me to say whether we would have considered it at the time I was inseminated, since we could not have known then that I would contract AIDS." Today she and her husband love their two adopted children, but the experience has taught her that birth parents do not always reveal the whole truth about their babies. "Adoptive parents don't always know what they are dealing with," Cynthia says. "While you might pass genetic problems to your own clone, at least you would know what [genetic history] you have." Without approving of the technology, Cynthia knows personally two reasons why someone else might prefer cloning babies from their own DNA rather than being ambushed by uncertain risks.[7]

Bree Walker is certain cloning has no place in human reproduction, an opinion related to her own experiences in dealing with public attitudes toward ectodactyly, the genetic condition transmitted to her from her mother and by Bree to her own children. "The height of hubris is for individuals to believe we need an exact replica of ourselves. People will attempt to design perfection in their own eyes instead of in God's eyes," Bree fears. "It is not a far leap to believe that if cloning were to become acceptable, it would be used to weed out all of those things that we fear or that disgust us."[8]

Although Bree and Terri Walden both accept the use of technology to make their children's lives better, they also emphasize the special value of each life, and both mothers worry that technology may be used to devalue the lives of children that are different. "I really believe in the specialness of an individual and how that individual came to be. That is God's creation," Bree believes, "and it should not be Man's creation." Terri relates the same idea when she describes what Nathan, despite his disease and his brief life, accomplished in changing the lives of the other members of their family. "He got us to the love," Terri explains. "He gave us such freedom, such love in our faith." Nancy Becker Kennedy, who credits quadriplegia with having brought a positive result to her life, agrees. "The accommodation of different people is important to the rest of us, not just for the people who need the accommodation. If cloning is used to reproduce in search of perfection, it is crazy. Not realizing the importance of adversity is a major problem in this country. We want everything to be perfect. I even have trouble with the use of in vitro because it seems to allow money to determine whose reproductive problems are solved instead of asking each of us to accept the adversity in our lives," she adds.[9]

Nancy makes another point about using cloning for human reproduction. "I think Americans are avoiding a sense of community, emphasizing independence rather than interdependence. If you can clone your offspring, isn't that carrying independence to the extreme, at the expense of the whole community?" she asks. This comment may have particular relevance for lesbian couples like Katherine and Hannah, or single women choosing to conceive a child with donor sperm. Because of their concerns that the donor might claim future parental rights as the biological father of their children, cloning a baby from their own DNA might be a tempting reproductive option. In a way never before possible, cloning does offer a woman an independent way to have a baby.

While vanity is often assumed as the primary reason for choosing to clone a child, egocentric motives may be less influential than commonly believed. Anita Neff remembers past predictions that sperm and embryos would be frozen and stored for future use, and she comments, "People are not that egotistical. In fact, less people are storing sperm than was initially anticipated. They thought men going into the military and other men facing risks would store sperm, but people have remained fairly conservative about it."

Most of us have things about ourselves that we wish were different. Since cloning creates an identical twin, people may decline to replicate what they regard as their own imperfections. From her experiences working with couples in surrogacies and donor egg conceptions, Hilary Hanafin agrees. "Most people want a better version of themselves. If I were to create a clone of myself, I would want her to be five feet seven inches tall," Hilary jokes.

The birth of a lamb named Dolly brought cloning out of the world of science fiction and into the real world. Knowing the speed at which other assisted reproductive alternatives have entered common practice, we cannot assume that human cloning will be shunned by all people. Among the circumstances described in this book, there are several for which cloning might have offered a powerful alternative to families. As only one example, imagine the temptation a new bride (with encouragement from the groom's parents) might feel when the young man lay dying from a fatal accident, if it were possible to clone his DNA before removing him from the life-support equipment.[10] The young widow could raise a son who was the twin of the man she had loved, and his parents could have a grandchild to fill the void created by their son's early death. In such a situation, as well as many others, the people who might consider using cloning would not be the megalomaniacs described in media accounts of possible abuses. Rather, they would be more like the thoughtful people who are now using the current nontraditional means for having babies, motivated to accept technological assistance by their longing for families and their love for family members.

Cloning, however, magnifies many of the concerns surrounding the other issues in this book, and it presents unique risks to the well-being of the cloned baby, particularly the psychological risks of meeting expectations unlike those imposed on other children. At the very least, scientists must devote adequate years to the study of long-term physical effects on cloned animals before ever considering use of the technology for humans. During that time, the rest of us must search our minds and hearts to determine whether any baby should be asked to enter life facing the unique challenges of having been cloned.

CONCLUSION

In the beginning pages of this book I challenged readers to thoughtfully consider all of the viewpoints in the chapters that followed and, with the benefit of those diverse opinions, reach their own conclusions. By now, readers have probably done that, so I will use this final chapter to share some personal comments about the conclusions I have made as a result of researching and writing this book.

When the five-year deadline for the destruction of unused embryos approached in Britain and many couples failed to contact clinics regarding disposition of the embryos they had created, a spokesperson from the government's Human Fertilization Embryology Authority commented on their neglect or inability to face a difficult decision. "You can't force people to make a decision," the official said, "but by default they have decided." By remaining silent, the couples allowed their embryos to be destroyed according to law, and whether the destruction occurred as a result of silence or authorization did not matter to the doomed embryos. One essential point I have tried to make in writing this book is that refusing to face a decision has consequences all the same.

I began my research believing that we needed legislation to regulate many of the reproductive practices occurring in this country. Gradually I moved away from that opinion for several reasons. I believe that the politicians we are sending to Washington and the state capitals tend to reflect two extremes. The conservatives think we citizens are so unable to conduct our lives appropriately that they enact regulations to tell us what to do. The liberals think we are so unable to conduct our lives wisely that they enact programs to rescue us from our own mistakes. Each of these political approaches ignores an essential part of the Constitution. The Founding Fathers included both the right to make our own decisions and the responsibility to assume the consequences of the decisions we make. We seem to have lost confidence in this dual aspect of our national character, choosing either to emphasize regulation to limit bad choices or social programs to relieve bad consequences. Rather than asking politicians to apply one approach or the other to resolve the difficult moral dilemmas raised by expanding reproductive options, we should remind ourselves of the power each of us holds.

I interviewed many people for this book, and often I disagreed with their conclusions. Yet despite any disagreement, I came to feel an affection and respect for them that I hope is apparent to readers. I find cause for optimism in the careful deliberation and genuine concern people felt for the babies, however diverse their ideas may be.

Many of the moral dilemmas raised by technologically assisted or unorthodox reproductive choices involve religious beliefs, but we are a nation that includes people of many faiths. Religious people disagree about these issues, even people who share a common faith. Nancy Becker Kennedy taught me a lesson in tolerance with her simple observation that "God may be speaking to them differently than He speaks to me." I have no doubt that people must look to their personal religious and moral values when making individual reproductive choices. But because our national religious and moral values are so diverse, I am equally certain that we cannot draft legislation to relieve individual Americans of their responsibility to decide according to their own consciences.

The influence of those who are in their childbearing and begetting years may seem to control reproductive practices in the future, but, in fact, each of us shares in deciding how our social mores will shift to accommodate the new technology or to absorb the unorthodox into the mainstream. I have suggested throughout this book that the influence of families, coworkers, neighbors, volunteers, and each of us is more powerful than laws and warning labels. We cannot determine proper conduct by asking only what is legal and what is affordable. There are things we should be ashamed of doing, even if we can afford them and we break no laws by doing them. I distrust the advice of strangers who know nothing about me, but I listen to what friends and family tell me out of love and concern. They are the ones who remind me when to be ashamed. Cecelia Lyles described the power of everyday people when she urged communities to "start educating one another and reaching out to one another—not running in the house, closing the blinds, and saying it's not my problem." I believe we can accomplish more by speaking privately with those we know or reaching out to offer individual help to others in our communities than by passing laws to regulate such personal decisions.

Professional organizations have implemented guidelines to help their members avoid many of the abuses that occurred when technologies were new. The loss of all eight fetuses because Englishwoman Mandy Allwood refused to selectively abort might have been avoided in this country because of the American College of Obstetricians and Gynecologists' member guidelines that emphasize the need to counsel couples regarding the risks of multifetal pregnancies, including asking couples to consider forgoing fertility treatments. Many of the early abuses of the 1980s have not been repeated as a result of voluntary compliance with professional guidelines rather than enactment of mandatory regulations.

The right to bear and beget children, which has been recognized by the United States Supreme Court, is not a *biologically protected right*. When infertile couples who cannot afford treatments or same-sex couples argue that they are only seeking the rights of parenthood enjoyed by other American families, they ignore the countless Americans for whom no amount of money or legal changes can produce a biological child. Living with AIDS contracted from her anonymous sperm donor, Cynthia Hallvik touched me with her advice: "I think people should take a really good look at the possibility of not having families, rather than thinking that is the only way they can have meaning in their lives." Almost as powerful were the words of the woman who had endured five years of unsuccessful fertility treatments before deciding to "focus on what I have in life as opposed to what I don't have, and on what I missed those five years by wanting something I didn't have." Perhaps society exerts subtle pressures on childless couples to use all the available technologies. Certainly many childless women shared with me a sense that they were viewed as failures or tragic figures if they could not give birth, and a quarter of the people participating in my survey indicated their belief that "life is not complete unless you have a child." Not only the childless couples but also the rest of society may need to recognize the value of relationships that do not include children.

Another shift in attitudes that I would find appropriate involves adoption. I understand the enormous urge to continue the genetic family line into another generation and I do not believe that is narcissistic or selfish. However, if continuing that genetic link is not possible, I do not understand why a person desperate to be a parent would reject certain children awaiting adoption. My opinion is, apparently, unusual. While 80 percent of those taking my survey said they would adopt a healthy, same-race baby if they could not conceive after a year of trying, far fewer were willing to adopt babies or children that are older, physically impaired, troubled, or of a different race. Surprisingly, more were willing to adopt foreign-born children than were willing to adopt American children of a different race. If the primary reason for having children, as survey responses indicated, really is the desire to love and be loved by a child, I do not understand how a child's race or age would defeat the giving and receiving of love. People were least willing to adopt physically impaired babies and children, even though there are no assurances that our biological children will be born without physical impairments. The unwillingness to adopt these children seems to support Bree Walker's view that the crippling effect of physical impairment is society's attitude rather than the condition itself. I am saddened that people with an aching desire to parent cannot find a place in their hearts for children who are different.

When people learned that I was working on a book that dealt with the public consequences of private reproductive choices, one of the most common issues they raised concerned births by women already receiving public assistance.[1] Contrary to public perception, the average size of a family receiving Aid to Families with Dependent Children (AFDC) is smaller than it was thirty years ago, and most AFDC recipients have two children or less. The perception of welfare mothers having more and more children to increase their public assistance led some state legislatures to consider offering women incentives for having the birth control device, Norplant, inserted in their arms. Union County, North Carolina, funded a program to provide Norplant procedures for anyone in the county that had no regular doctor to implant the device for them, but no incentive was offered to induce women to consent. County Health Director Lorey White told me that by the beginning of the program's second year over 10 percent of the women they serve had requested implants. "These are done during our family planning clinics, and we are doing as many as we can. For a while we had a waiting list." In other words, poor women voluntarily took advantage of the procedure without any coercive inducement.[2] A study by the Alan Guttmacher Institute found that between one-third and one-fifth of poor women with unplanned pregnancies would have aborted if they could have paid for the abortion or if Medicaid funding were available. For these poor women, poverty left them with no economic alternative but to continue the unintended pregnancy. Most single mothers, already trapped in poverty, know that having another baby will not make their lives easier, even if they receive a few more dollars in public assistance.

A more realistic explanation for the growing number of children living in poverty is found in a study by the Robin Hood Foundation, reported in 1996. Researchers working independently compared adolescents who have their first baby at age seventeen or younger with girls of similar economic, social, and educational backgrounds who wait until they are twenty or twenty-one to have their first child. They found that the younger mothers were far more likely to raise their babies alone and to drop out of school, and while the income levels of the two groups were similar, the younger mothers were more dependent on public assistance. The babies of the younger mothers also suffered measurable differences, being 50 percent more likely to have low birth weight and, if they survive, being more prone to respiratory problems, mental retardation, dyslexia, and hyperactivity. As these children grow, they are two or three times more likely to become runaways, and the boys are nearly three times more likely to be imprisoned. These dismal findings are consistent with what a former White House policy adviser, William A. Galston, often cited: The children of Americans who finish high school, wait until age twenty, and marry before a child is born have only an 8 percent chance of growing up in poverty, he said. Children whose mothers do not do all three of these things before they are born face a 79 percent chance of growing up in poverty.

Poor women who are already struggling to survive within the welfare system are looking for ways to avoid making their lives harder, and they know that another baby to support is going to make their subsistence standard of living even more strapped. Unmarried teenagers who have never been responsible for maintaining a household are far more likely to imagine that public assistance will provide a good life for them and their babies. It is not greed that swells the welfare rolls with new babies each year but ignorance.

This book considers the impact of technology and unorthodox choices on human reproduction, and the birth of around 350,000 babies each year to unmarried teenaged mothers is not really connected to either of those causes. Many of the medical and social problems once the babies are born, and the strategies for resolving resulting problems, are the same, however. The good news is that in 1996 the National Center for Health Statistics reported that the birth rate for unmarried women dropped for the first time in almost two decades, and the teen birth rate declined for the fourth year in a row. Adding yet another positive note to the news, abortion rates are also declining. Commentators credit the increased awareness of the hardship of raising a child alone with bringing about the changing birth rates.

Offering sex education classes in our schools is one way to deliver this information to young people before they become sexually active, but in many communities implementing these classes has aroused controversy. I was surprised that the survey question receiving the highest agreement among participants was "Do you think sex education should be taught in America's schools?" to which 290 of the 310 participants answered "Yes!" Their opinions did not reflect support for only a limited curriculum teaching abstinence from premarital sexual activity, for when participants were asked whether students should be given information regarding birth control, 87 percent of them responded affirmatively.[3] From the survey responses to these and other questions, I believe there is strong public support for educating young people about many of the reproductive issues considered in this book.

When I asked people to participate in my survey to test public attitudes about reproductive issues, many of them were initially eager to record their opinions, telling me how strongly they felt about reproductive irresponsibility. After they had taken the survey, many of these same people told me they discovered that when they were forced to respond to specific questions, they were far less certain of their feelings. Nearly all of the questions elicited a large percentage of "undecided" responses.

My perception before I sampled public opinion had been that Americans were reacting to these issues in an emotional, superficial way, but that we had given little thoughtful consideration to the specific implications of changing reproductive practices. I believe that the survey responses support my initial perception.

I wrote this book because I think the babies, as well as all the rest of us, deserve more than decisions made by default, more than procedures and practices entering the mainstream merely because they can be done, without sufficient regard to whether they should be done. I hope that in private reproductive decisions, the archaic notion of conscionability will be revived, and choices will be made in accordance with good conscience. If that sounds judgmental, I do not mean for it to be. The people I met in the course of writing this book restored my confidence in the wisdom of common sense and the moral obligation prospective parents feel toward the babies they are planning. I believe the rapid expansion of technological and lifestyle options may have caused many of us to lose our moral headings, but if we regain that individualism about which Americans take such national pride, knowing that the impact of each one of us really does make a difference in this country, the responsibility for deciding reproductive matters can be entrusted to no one better than the families that will live with the consequences of their decisions.

APPENDIX 1
THE SURVEY

The instructions and questions are reproduced just as they appeared in the Survey Question Booklet that was given to each participant, but the separate answer sheet on which survey participants were asked to record their responses has not been reproduced in this appendix.

Do not write in the question booklet.

*INSTRUCTIONS: Answer by circling the correct response, placing an "X" in the appropriate blank, or filling in the blank line on the separate answer pages. You may omit any question you prefer not to answer or may answer "undecided" if that response is among the choices, but remember, this is **not** a test where answers are right or wrong but rather an opportunity for you to express your opinion. DO NOT WRITE IN THE QUESTION BOOKLET. When you have completed your answers, place your responses in the envelope you have been given (or in the slotted box) and return the question booklet to the person conducting the survey.*

Thank you for sharing your point of view.

For your information in answering the survey questions, the following definitions are provided:

Artificial Insemination: Depositing sperm into the vagina or uterus artificially.

Embryo: Stage of growth from the second to the ninth week following conception.

Fetus: Stage of growth following nine weeks in the uterus until birth.

Genetically related: Having received genes from; sharing common traits of heredity.

Gestate: To carry the fetus in the womb during its development.

In Vitro Fertilization (IVF): Medically assisting conception outside a woman's body; sometimes called "test-tube" conception.

Surrogate: A woman who gestates and carries an embryo to term with the intention of relinquishing the baby at birth; the baby may be genetically related (artificial insemination) or may not be genetically related (in vitro fertilization) to the surrogate.

1. *On the separate answer sheet, circle the letter corresponding to all of the following reasons that you think are important and appropriate reasons for choosing to have a child. You may circle as many reasons as you wish.*

    a. Having children is the reason people marry
    b. Spouse wants a child
    c. To carry on the family name and inheritance
    d. A child is important for a happy marriage
    e. To prove you are able to have a child
    f. Life is not complete unless you have a child
    g. Pressure from your parents
    h. Pressure from your friends
    i. You think you would be a good parent
    j. Your friends have children
    k. You feel selfish without a child
    l. You feel useless without a child
    m. All women should experience pregnancy and birth
    n. All men should experience fatherhood
    o. You have a strong emotional desire to have a child
    p. Your religion encourages you to have children
    q. You want to share the things you know with a child
    r. You want to love and be loved by a child
    s. You want grandchildren
    t. You want someone to take care of you when you are old
    u. You want to pass along your genetic history
    v. It is important to society
    w. It is important to some group (ethnic, racial, religious, etc.) of which you are a part

2. *From among the reasons that you have circled as being important and appropriate for choosing to have a child, select the*

three reasons that you think are the most important and rank them as "most important reason," "second most important," and "third most important." If you selected less than three reasons in answering question 1, rank only as many as you selected.

3A. Do you think everyone should have the right to have a child? (Circle your answer in the answer sheet.)

3B. If you think there should be any limits on a person's right to have a child, list what limits you think are appropriate.

4A. Do you think the number of children a person could have should ever be limited? (Circle response on answer sheet.)

4B. If you think there should be limits on the number of children a person should have, state the number of children you think proper and your reason or reasons for limiting that number.

5A. List three methods of birth control.

5B. List all methods of birth control you have used, if any.

6. If you desired a child and you (or your partner) were unable to become pregnant after over a year of trying, would you use any of the following alternatives for having a family? (On the separate answer sheet, find the corresponding letter and check one of the three responses for each lettered alternative.)

    a. Adopt a healthy, same-race baby
    b. Adopt a healthy, different-race baby
    c. Adopt a healthy, foreign-born baby
    d. Adopt a physically impaired baby
    e. Adopt a healthy, same-race older U.S. child
    f. Adopt a healthy, different-race older U.S. child
    g. Adopt a healthy, foreign-born older child
    h. Adopt a physically impaired U.S. child
    i. Adopt a troubled or abused U.S. child
    j. Try in vitro fertilization with your partner
    k. Try in vitro fertilization with donor egg/sperm
    l. Try artificial insemination with donor sperm
    m. Try drugs or surgery to correct a medical problem

n. Use a surrogate mother to gestate an IVF embryo created from you and your partner

o. Use a surrogate mother to gestate an embryo genetically related to the male partner only

p. Use a surrogate mother to gestate an embryo genetically related to the female partner only

q. Accept infertility and redirect your desire to have a child to other pursuits

7A. *On the separate answer sheet, find the letter corresponding to each of the following reproductive technologies and answer whether you believe costs should be covered by health insurance.*

a. In vitro fertilization with your partner

b. In vitro fertilization with a donor egg/sperm

c. Artificial insemination with donor sperm

d. Drugs or surgery to correct medical problems

e. In vitro fertilization with a surrogate

f. Artificial insemination with a surrogate

7B. *Would you be willing to pay higher health insurance premiums to cover the costs of extending coverage to include nontraditional reproductive technologies for all policyholders?*

7C. *Would you be willing to pay higher taxes so the government could assist in paying for nontraditional reproductive technologies?*

7D. *If you would be willing to pay higher premiums or taxes, state (on the answer sheet) in dollars and cents how much more you would be willing to pay each year.*

8. *On the answer sheet, find the corresponding letter for each of the following and answer who you think should be eligible to use nontraditional reproductive technology in order to have a child. (In answering this question, assume the persons described are financially able to pay their own costs for the procedure.)*

a. Married couples without children

b. Married couples with one child

c. Married couples regardless of other children

d. Heterosexual couples who are not married but who have a stable relationship, without children

e. Heterosexual couples who are not married but who have a stable relationship, with one child

f. Heterosexual couples who are not married but who have a stable relationship, regardless of other children

g. Any heterosexual couple who desire treatment

h. Heterosexual single persons without a current partner

i. Gay or lesbian couples without children

j. Gay or lesbian couples with a child or children

k. Gay or lesbian single persons without a current partner

9A. *Would you consider freezing your egg/sperm if you were facing a situation that might damage your ability to produce healthy egg/sperm in the future?*

9B. *If you and your partner had frozen eggs, sperm, or a fertilized egg (embryo), what should happen to the frozen eggs, sperm, or embryo if*

a. one of you died?

b. both of you died?

c. you divorced?

10. *Whether or not you personally would utilize any of the following reproductive technologies, find the corresponding letter on the answer sheet and respond as to each one whether you think it should be prohibited by law.*

a. In vitro fertilization with partner

b. In vitro fertilization with donor

c. Artificial insemination with donor

d. Surrogate mother to gestate embryo genetically related to both parents but not to surrogate

e. Surrogate mother artificially inseminated with father's sperm

f. Surrogate mother to gestate mother's egg fertilized with donor sperm

11A. On the answer sheet, find the corresponding letter and answer whether you believe any of the following should be prohibited by law.

a. Experiments on unimplanted embryos conducted to gain knowledge to assist traditional pregnancies

b. Laboratory growth of embryo cells for medical use

c. Research to enable creation of an artificial womb

d. Sale of embryos by couple whose egg and sperm created it

e. Sale of egg by woman

f. Sale of sperm by man

g. Sales of eggs, sperm, or embryos by third parties

h. Fee by surrogate for gestating a fetus

i. Fee by third parties for arranging surrogacy

11B. Have you read newspaper or magazine accounts of the Baby M case or other cases involving disputes between the surrogate mother and the couple with whom she contracted?

11C. In a dispute between the surrogate mother and the couple with whom she contracted, the following factors might be considered. On the answer sheet, rank them in the order of importance you feel they should have in resolving the dispute, using "1" for the most important, and so on, through "6" for the least important.

a. Terms of the agreement they signed

b. Genetic ties of the claimants to the baby

c. Maternal feelings of the surrogate mother

d. Paternal feelings of the father

e. Maternal feelings of the father's wife (whether or not she is genetically related to the baby)

    f.   Economic abilities of the claimants to provide for the baby

12. *On the answer sheet, circle the characterization that best describes your views about abortion.*

13. *Would you choose to terminate your pregnancy if tests on the fetus indicated it was abnormal?*

14. *Would you approve of laboratory use in research for possible cures of diseases or defects which involves*

    a.   unimplanted embryos from IVF procedures?
    b.   aborted fetuses?

15. *Would you approve of the medical use in the treatment of diseased or disabled living persons of cells or tissue from*

    a.   unimplanted embryos from IVF procedures?
    b.   aborted fetuses?

16A. *Should mothers who deliver babies damaged by the actions of the mother during pregnancy be punished by law?*

16B. *If you believe a mother should ever be punished when it can be shown that her actions during pregnancy damaged her baby, find the letter corresponding to each of the following actions and indicate whether you believe the mother should be punished.*

    a.   Using illegal drugs during pregnancy
    b.   Using alcohol during pregnancy
    c.   Drinking coffee during pregnancy
    d.   Smoking during pregnancy
    e.   Continuing to work in an environment unsafe to the fetus
    f.   Refusing medical treatment for herself which would have benefited the fetus
    g.   Failing to obtain prenatal care
    h.   Cleaning a cat's litter box during pregnancy

    i.   Attempting to self-abort
    j.   Failing to eat a well-balanced diet during
        pregnancy
    k.   Failing to get adequate rest during pregnancy
    l.   Exposing herself to X rays during pregnancy

16C. What do you believe should be done to or for mothers who damage their babies as a result of their actions during pregnancy?

17A. Some judges have imposed mandatory birth control as a part of a woman's sentencing. Do you think this is ever appropriate?

17B. If you think there are times when mandatory birth control as a part of the sentence is or might be appropriate, on the answer sheet find the letter that corresponds to each of the following crimes and indicate whether mandatory birth control should be imposed as to each particular crime.

    a.   Abuse of existing children
    b.   Failure to report abuse of existing children by
        someone else
    c.   Substance abuse during pregnancy
    d.   Neglect or abandonment of existing children
    e.   Practice of a lifestyle harmful to her child
    f.   Prostitution

17C. If you believe there are other occasions not listed above for which mandatory birth control is appropriate, list them.

17D. If you oppose or are troubled by mandatory birth control as a part of a woman's sentence, would you feel differently if the woman agreed to it as a part of a plea bargain?

17E. Would your answers to questions 17A–17D be significantly different if they related to the male parent?

18. As to each of the following questions relating to genetic screening, find the corresponding letter on the answer sheet and record your answer.

a. If you could have a test to screen for genetic diseases you carry which might be transmitted to your child, would you take the test?

b. Do you think you should be required to take such a test, for instance, in connection with the blood test for a marriage license?

c. If the genetic screening showed that you and your partner had a high probability of conceiving an abnormal child, would you choose not to have children?

d. If the genetic screening showed that you and your partner had a high probability of conceiving an abnormal child, should the government prohibit you from having children?

e. Would you (or your partner) become pregnant if there was a likelihood of your having an abnormal child, with the intention of testing the fetus for abnormality and aborting any abnormal child?

f. If the genetic screening showed that you and your partner were certain to have an abnormal child, would you choose not to have children?

g. If the genetic screening showed that you and your partner were certain to have an abnormal child, should the government prohibit you from having children?

h. If you conceived a child knowing of the high likelihood or certainty of abnormality, should you be excluded from receiving health insurance proceeds for the medical treatment of the child relating to the abnormal conditions?

i. Are you willing to pay higher health insurance premiums to cover the cost of extending health insurance coverage to pay the medical expenses of babies born with genetic defects, even when the parents knew of the high likelihood or certainty that such defects would occur?

    j. If you conceived a child knowing of the high likelihood or certainty of abnormality, should you be excluded from receiving government benefits for the child relating to the abnormality?

    k. Are you willing to pay higher taxes to cover the costs of government benefits for babies born with genetic defects, even when the parents knew of the high likelihood or certainty that such defects would occur?

19A. Recent years have seen higher numbers of low-birth-weight infants born severely disabled, often from their mothers' substance abuse or AIDS, and despite enormous sums of money spent to help these children, many will never grow up or be able to achieve minimal physical and/or mental levels of normalcy. Who do you think should bear the expense of caring for these babies?

    a. The federal government out of existing social programs

    b. The federal government out of new tax revenues

    c. The state governments out of existing social programs

    d. The state governments out of new tax revenues

    e. Hospitals by passing costs on to other patients

    f. Health insurance plans through higher premiums

    g. Charitable organizations and churches through greater member contributions

    h. Families of the children

    i. Other

19B. President Ronald Reagan urged enactment of a law known as the Baby Doe law, which prohibits hospitals that receive federal funds from withholding medically indicated treatment from severely disabled infants. Do you agree with the government's requirement that heroic medical treatments be administered to severely disabled babies?

19C. *The medical community acknowledges that in the past, severely handicapped infants have sometimes been allowed to die, even though medical technology could have been aggressively utilized to keep them alive. Do you think it is ever morally acceptable to withhold treatment from a severely handicapped infant?*

19D. *From among the following choices, select the one you think should make life-and-death decisions concerning treatment of severely disabled infants. On the answer sheet, select only one.*

    a. The parents with the advice of the treating physicians
    b. A hospital committee consisting of medical professionals
    c. A committee of medical, legal, and religious professionals
    d. The courts of law
    e. The government
    f. Other

19E. *If a determination were made to withhold medical treatment from a severely disabled infant with a life-threatening condition, would it ever be appropriate to administer a lethal injection to shorten suffering as inevitable death neared for the infant?*

20A. *Do you think sex education should be taught in America's schools?*

20B. *If sex education is taught, in what grades should it be taught? Circle as many grades as you think appropriate.*

20C. *Should students be given information regarding birth control by school nurses or sex education teachers?*

20D. *Should students be provided with birth-control devices by school nurses if the student requests it?*

20E. *Should students be directed by sex education teachers or school nurses to outside clinics for birth-control information and devices?*

21A. Do you believe welfare recipients have babies in order to increase welfare benefits? On the answer sheet, circle only one.

21B. Do you believe present welfare programs encourage unmarried pregnancies? On the answer sheet, circle only one.

21C. Do you believe present welfare programs contribute to the breakdown of the family unit? On the answer sheet, circle only one.

22. Select the one statement that best expresses your viewpoint regarding midwives and circle the corresponding letter on the answer sheet.

    a. Birth is a natural process and a pregnant woman should be attended by whomever she wants, including attendance by a midwife at a home delivery.

    b. Women should be allowed to use midwives who meet certain minimum levels of training and birthing experience.

    c. Women should be allowed to use midwives who meet certain minimum levels of training and birthing experience, as required and certified by the state.

    d. Unexpected complications may arise in childbirth, and for that reason only nurse midwives practicing under the supervision of a physician should be licensed.

    e. Modern technology makes it necessary for safe childbirth to occur in a hospital, where personnel and facilities are available for the mother and baby should a medical emergency arise.

23A. Should children born as a result of the use of a donor egg, sperm, or embryo have available at their request the identity of the donor?

23B. Should children born as a result of the use of a donor egg, sperm, or embryo have available at their request genetic information about the donor?

24A. Would you describe yourself as a religious person?

24B. Do you belong to any church?

24C. What is your religion?

24D. When you have decisions to make in your everyday life, are you influenced in your decisions by what your church says you ought to do?

24E. Do you know the official position your church has taken with regard to most of the new reproductive technologies covered by the questions in this survey?

24F. If your response to question 24E was "yes," then characterize how often your opinions as expressed in this survey agree with the official position taken by your church.

25. This survey has included questions about transplanting tissue from unimplanted embryos and aborted fetuses. Please answer the following questions about organ donations.

> a. Would you object to having your organs removed for transplantation after death?
> b. Would you favor a change in the law to presume you have consented to organ donation after your death unless you have declared your opposition to organ donation prior to your death?
> c. Would you favor a law requiring you to declare each time you renew your driver's license whether you wish to donate your organs?

26. If you have a personal comment or experience relating to one of the topics covered in this survey, please feel free to share it on the back last page of your answer sheet. If you would be willing to discuss it further with me, you may give your name, address, and telephone number in the spaces provided; however, you do not need to include that information if you prefer to protect your privacy.

**Thank You for Sharing Your Time and Opinions
in Response to This Survey.**

APPENDIX 2

SURVEY METHODOLOGY
AND RESULTS

With hindsight, I believe I was motivated to undertake a survey of public opinions about the reproductive issues explored in this book for two related reasons. First, I was curious to assess public awareness of the constitutional protections involving reproductive rights recognized by the Supreme Court. Whether people knew that they were invoking a constitutionally protected right was not particularly significant; I was curious to see whether they acknowledged certain fundamental rights in response to the questions I was asking. Second, I respect the common sense of the average person and believe that social strategies must rest upon a strong foundation of public support. If we are to develop successful ways to address the problems resulting from new reproductive possibilities, current attitudes and mores must be taken into account. These are the themes that the survey explores.

I did not hire a social scientist to draft the questions or a professional pollster to administer the survey, but I did attempt to prepare and conduct the survey in ways that would assure the highest level of reliability possible. My training and experience as both a teacher and a trial attorney have taught me how to prepare questions and present them in a manner that elicits specific information in an unbiased way. I am also fortunate to have a wealth of friends and acquaintances living in many different states who generously agreed to help me obtain a national sampling. I took advantage of those resources to obtain the most broad-based and fair sampling I could devise. For those of you interested in the methodology employed in the survey, see the following section, entitled "Survey Methodology." For those of you who are merely curious to compare your survey responses with those given by others, you may wish to skip ahead to the section of this appendix entitled "Survey Questions and Responses."

SURVEY METHODOLOGY

How the Survey Was Prepared

As a lawyer, I know how important the form of a question can be in eliciting particular results. During my research for this book, I was sometimes annoyed to see survey questions that were so leading and manipulative that the answers had no validity. It was my intention to draft questions for my survey that gave no suggestion of a preferred response among the choices available.

I also know that altering one detail in the framing of a question can change a person's answer. For that reason I tried to be very specific, and I would often ask a series of questions with a single element changed from one to the next. Using a series of similar questions was my substitute for interviewing each person individually, to ask, "Would your opinion be different if. . . ?"

Another thing I have learned is how the sequence of questions can influence the answers. I tried to arrange the survey questions in ways that would not encourage the subject of a preceding question to unintentionally influence the response to the next question. In some instances, however, questions were grouped so that participants were led through issues in a sequential way. For example, infertility alternatives were arranged in the sequence in which a couple might encounter them during treatment. Also, certain questions were grouped for clarity, so there could be no suggestion that an element of the question was obscured. For example, I placed the questions concerning use of cells and tissues from aborted fetuses near the question asking participants to characterize their attitudes toward abortion so that no one could say the survey concealed the connection between a woman's decision to abort and the subsequent therapeutic and experimental use of the material.

Because the survey was lengthy and answers were entered on a separate page, I selected a key word from the question and used it as a heading on the answer sheet to facilitate the marking of answers in the correct spaces. In one instance, I regret that my choice of heading may have caused some confusion. Questions 10 and 11 both ask whether certain things should be "prohibited" by law, and rather than repeating the same heading on the answer sheet, I used "Laws to Prohibit" for question 10 and "Laws to Regulate" for question 11. A few people wrote in the space reserved for comments at the end of the answer sheet that they found this confusing and then explained how they had chosen to answer. Most of these comments indicated they had responded to the term contained in the question rather than to the word "regulate," a term that might suggest something less than complete prohibition. Obviously, the questions themselves should have determined the answers, but I regret any confusion the heading on the answer sheet may have caused. But for that one concern, I learned of no other problems with the format. A few participants did comment about the length of the survey, and several observed that they found the specific nature of the questions challenging.

How the Survey Was Taken

People were given the written survey materials with as little spoken instruction as possible in order to minimize unintentional influences. I usually told them I was researching a book dealing with reproductive issues and that the survey was being given to people in order to sample public opinion. As a practical matter, no one was going to agree to take the survey unless they were told in advance at least something regarding the subject of the survey. I also told people that there were no right or wrong answers since I was surveying opinions, not giving a test. If people took the survey with them and returned it to me later, I asked them not to discuss their responses with anyone else, since I was sampling individual opinions rather than answers arrived at by committee. Participants included friends, acquaintances, and strangers. A space was provided on the answer sheet for people to disclose their names, addresses, and telephone numbers if they wished to do so, but most left those spaces blank.

When the surveys were returned to me, I entered responses by darkening spaces on separate tally forms. In this way, I separated both the identity of the person and the content of the question from the responses I tallied. Each tally sheet recorded the results from thirty surveys, and when all the sheets were completed, I compared the totals among the sets to see if any group of thirty displayed obvious differences that might suggest responses had been altered to support a particular viewpoint. This was especially important to me since others helped me administer the survey.

The friends and acquaintances who helped me broaden the geographic scope of the survey were instructed not to solicit participants from a similar group (such as asking only their neighbors, their coworkers, or members of a club or a class) and not to screen participants in any way that related to how they might answer survey questions. They were asked to seek a variety of ages, education levels, incomes, and other personal characteristics among those they solicited to participate. Finally, I asked them not to interpret the questions or otherwise make explanatory comments that might influence the responses. While to some extent I had to blindly trust the good faith of those who helped me administer the survey, I believed that the extensive breadth of the subjects covered by the survey would make it practically impossible for a person to distort all the results in ways preferred by that individual. Furthermore, most people took five or less surveys, so any attempt to influence the overall results would be minimal. In this way, I was able to sample the opinions of strangers from all across the country, and I am grateful to everyone who helped me expand the sampling. I also solicited my own group of participants from among friends, family, business acquaintances, and strangers. Some of these strangers circulated surveys among their own friends and acquaintances across the nation, and in this way a divergent group helped me administer the survey and minimized my imprint on the results.

When responses were returned to me, I numbered the answer sheets and recorded the manner of return by postmark or the name of the individual who had administered that survey, for the purpose of documenting the validity of the returns. Later, as I entered responses on the tally sheets, I noted whether the participants solicited by a single person responded in too similar ways, suggesting a biased selection of participants or an effort to distort survey results. I found nothing to suggest any intentional tampering, although there was a tendency for participants to fall within the same education and income levels as the person who solicited them. Although the personal traits were sometimes similar, the opinions were not, and due to the checks and balances I employed, I believe the integrity of the sampling is sound. I did not omit any of the responses that were returned to me.

Who Participated in the Survey

A total of 310 people participated. A few people were so determined to protect their identities that they did not complete all of the personal information at the top of the answer sheets, so total numbers of participants within the particular personal categories did not always come to 310. More women than men participated, 222 compared to 74. Men tended to be more self-conscious about their responses and indicated they found the questions more personal than women did.

I did not strive to reflect the statistical proportions of the general population among survey participants. Rather, I wanted

a strong sampling from every category represented in the per-
sonal-information section of the survey. As I compared the sets
of thirty responses, I evaluated whether the results were influenced significantly by the personal characteristics of the particular participants represented within that set. I was surprised
to discover that although the personal traits of the participants
might vary from one set of tally sheets to another, the overall
proportions of the responses were rather consistent. Although I
would have preferred to obtain larger samplings from certain
groups, I do not believe the survey conclusions would have been
greatly altered.

Among the eight designated age groups, participants were
represented as follows: 42 aged eighteen to twenty-four; 44
aged twenty-five to thirty; 40 aged thirty-one to thirty-five; 37
aged thirty-six to forty; 37 aged forty-one to forty-five; 65 aged
forty-six to fifty-five; 30 aged fifty-six to seventy; and 12 aged
seventy-one and older. Among participants who were not yet
sexually active or who were past their childbearing or begetting
years, they sometimes commented that answers to certain hypo-
thetical questions were based on what they believed they either
will do or would have done at that time in their lives.

Participants included those with children and those
without, specifically: 90 had no children; 53 had one child; 90
had two children; 45 had three children; 11 had four children;
4 had five children; and 1 had more than five children. Seventy
of the participants had never been married; 191 were married;
31 were divorced; and 14 were widowed.

Because of the length and written format of the survey,
people with less education tended to be reluctant to participate.
Unfortunately, this led to a disproportionate representation of
college-educated people, which in turn affected the income levels
represented among those taking the survey. Although I would
have preferred a sampling more reflective of the general population, all education and income categories are represented among
the participants, specifically: 1 participant completed elemen-
tary school; 4 completed junior high school; 37 completed high

school; 99 completed some college; 108 completed a college degree; and 53 completed a graduate degree. The annual family-income levels were as follows: 44 of less than $20,000; 55 of $20,000 to $35,000; 58 of $35,100 to $50,000; 62 of $50,100 to $80,000; and 74 above $80,000.

Participants came from 175 different zip codes, representing 17 different states. Dividing the nation into six different regions, 28 came from the Northeast; 96 came from the Southeast; 77 came from the North-Central states; 74 came from the South-Central States; 1 came from the Northwest; and 7 came from the Southwest.

The majority of participants, 274, identified themselves as white or Caucasian; 16 identified themselves as blacks or African-American; 4 as Asian; 1 as Indian; and 2 as Hispanic or Latino.

Participants were asked to describe their occupations rather than merely circling predetermined choices. Ninety-five different occupations were named, the most common ones being: 31 students; 31 housewives or homemakers; 18 retired persons; 15 teachers; 14 secretaries; 12 in sales; 8 artists; 7 accountants; 6 nurses; 5 stockbrokers; 4 who were unemployed, writers, self-employed, or counselors; and 3 attorneys. Also included were an animal technician, an antiques dealer, an embalmer, a brewery workers, a shoe repairman, teachers of dance, piano, and cosmetology, an editor, a gardener, an interior designer, a banker, and a mechanic. Two of each were travel consultants, engineers, flight attendants, ministers, pharmacists, or probation officers. Others identified themselves as being in management, 10; real estate, 3; retail, 4; education, 3; marketing, 4; and security. There were 5 executives and 1 executive assistant; 3 administrators; and 4 administrative assistants; an office coordinator; a project coordinator; and a staff assistant. There were business managers, 2; a product manager; a shop manager; and a fast-food assistant manager. Others described themselves by their occupation: insurance; investments; graphic design; the performing arts; government; tissue transplant; communications, 2;

customer service; clerical, 3; finance, 2; business instruments; mental health; and advertising. Finally, there were two claims examiners, a civil servant, a court service officer, and a cashier; there were a translator, a tax preparer, and a therapist; there were 3 receptionists; a library clerk and a program clerk; a paramedic, a factory worker, a professor, a housekeeper, an orthodontist, a laborer, and a disability specialist; and there were 3 who described themselves as mothers. The remainder of responses were: a professional; a paraprofessional; 3 who wrote GED in the space; and 2 who wrote "none" or "N/A." (In this enumeration, certain responses were combined, such as including practical and registered nurses together.)

Within the survey itself, participants were asked to identify their religion. Some people described themselves generally, such as Christian, while others stated a particular denomination, for instance, Baptist. Arranged alphabetically, their responses were: agnostic, 5; Assembly of God, 1; atheist, 2; "B," 2; Baptist, 43; Buddhist, 1; Catholic, 48; Christian, 26; Church of Christ, 1; "Cy," 1; Disciples of Christ, 2; eclectic, 1; Episcopalian, 15; Hindu, 2; Holiness, 2; Jewish, 8; Lutheran, 5; Mennonite, 3; Methodist, 36; Mormon, 1; N/A, 1; naturalist, 1; Nazarene, 2; none, 6; Pentecostal, 3; personal spirituality, 1; Presbyterian, 15; Southern Baptist, 5; Unitarian, 2; United Church of Christ, 1; United Methodist, 2; and Wicca, 1. Fifty-nine did not reply.

How Responses and Percentages Were Reported

Although 310 people participated in the survey, not everyone responded to each question. As a result, when all the responses to a given question are totaled, the sum is not always 310. I did not treat these omissions as "undecided" responses, since I have no way of knowing why the participant declined to answer that particular question. It may have been too personal; it may have been confusing; or it may have been an oversight, among other possibilities. In computing percentages, I always used 310 as

100 percent, since that was the full number of participants in the survey. In other words, if 31 people answered in a certain way, their opinions represent 10 percent of the total participants' opinions, even though among the remaining 90 percent there may have been some opinions that were not disclosed.

Survey Questions and Responses

1 and 2. Select from the following choices as many reasons as you think are important and appropriate for choosing to have a child. Rank in order of importance up to three from among your choices.

		Total selections	1st	2nd	3rd
a.	Having a child is the reason people marry.	21	0	4	1
b.	Because spouse wants a child.	49	4	5	7
c.	To carry on the family name and inheritance.	80	4	10	18
d.	Because a child is important for a happy marriage.	48	7	6	9
e.	To prove you are able to have a child.	8	0	1	2
f.	Life is not complete unless you have a child.	76	16	12	11
g.	Pressure from your parents.	6	1	3	0
h.	Pressure from your friends.	3	0	0	0
i.	You think you would be a good parent.	173	34	36	38
j.	Your friends have children.	12	1	0	1
k.	You feel selfish without a child.	10	2	1	0
l.	You feel useless without a child.	11	0	1	4
m.	All women should experience pregnancy and birth.	29	2	5	4
n.	All men should experience fatherhood.	24	0	1	4
o.	You have a strong emotional desire to have a child.	216	95	47	23

	Total selections	1st	2nd	3rd
p. Your religion encourages you to have children.	24	0	2	1
q. You want to share the things you know with a child.	203	28	58	54
r. You want to love and be loved by a child.	239	86	77	44
s. You want grandchildren.	73	2	3	13
t. You want someone to take care of you when you are old.	32	0	2	4
u. You want to pass along your genetic history.	42	8	4	7
v. It is important to society.	39	2	1	13
w. It is important to some group of which you are a part.	9	1	3	1

	Yes	No	Undecided
3A. Do you think everyone should have the right to have a child?	115	155	32

3B. If you think there should be any limits on a person's right to have a child, list what limits you think are appropriate.

Financial	86	Antisocial/unacceptable behavior	4
Mentally ill/deficient/ insane	56	Sex offenders	4
Ability to care for or to raise	45	Disease carriers	3
		Intellect	3
Child abusers	32	Love	3
Overpopulation/ zero growth	25	Sexual orientation/gay	3
Welfare	25	Parental rights to other children terminated	2
Retardation	22	Past abortions or illegitimacies	2
Genetic problems	21		
Emotional reasons	20	For the social good	2

Criminals/		"Unfit"		2
convicted felons	14	Because spouse might		
Drug abusers	14	abandon		1
Physical impairment	11	Character/morals		1
Medical reasons/health	9	Marital status		1
Age/maturity/too young	4			

	Yes	No	Undecided
4A. Do you think the number of children a person could have should ever be limited?	145	122	43

4B. If you think there should be limits on the number of children a person should have, state the number of children you think proper and your reason or reasons for limiting that number. Only 61 participants in the survey completed the space for the appropriate limited number, and most left the space for reasons blank as well. The reasons that were given generally repeated answers given to the previous question, and several wrote "same" or "see above."

Proscribed number of children:

1 (or 1 per parent)	7		
2	35	4	5
2–3	3	4–5	1
2–4	2	4–6	1
3	6	8	1

5A and 5B. List three methods of birth control. List all methods you have used, if any. *

Methods listed:

abstinence	diaphragm	IUD	patch	spermicide
cervical cap	douche	injections	pill	withdrawal
condoms	foam	Norplant	rhythm	

*Birth control is not within the content of the book, and this pair of questions was asked to determine how many people would include abortion as a method of birth control in a survey that asked about reproductive issues generally rather than a survey specifically addressing opinions about abortion. In my survey of 310 people, only 2 listed abortion as a birth-control method. Both were white males, a generation apart in ages, living in different regions of the country, and having different income levels and marital status. One described himself as opposed to abortion, the other as being pro-choice. Their surveys were administered by two different individuals who do not know each other. No women listed abortion as a birth-control method, and no one indicated they had used abortion as a means of birth control.

6. *If you desired a child and you (or your partner) were unable to become pregnant after over a year of trying, would you use any of the following alternatives for having a family?*

		Yes	No	Undecided
a.	Adopt a healthy, same race baby.	247	27	25
b.	Adopt a healthy, different race baby.	90	134	70
c.	Adopt a healthy, foreign born baby.	122	94	81
d.	Adopt a physically impaired baby.	36	175	81
e.	Adopt a healthy, same race older U.S. child.	150	72	73
f.	Adopt a healthy, different race older U.S. child.	57	161	72
g.	Adopt a healthy, foreign born older child.	72	141	88
h.	Adopt a physically impaired U.S. child.	39	174	75
i.	Adopt a troubled or abused U.S. child.	47	148	93
j.	Try in vitro fertilization with your partner.	182	70	42
k.	Try in vitro fertilization with donor egg/sperm.	55	165	61
l.	Try artificial insemination with donor sperm.	55	169	65

		Yes	No	Undecided
m.	Try drugs or surgery to correct a medical problem.	240	37	20
n.	Use a surrogate mother to gestate an IVF embryo created from you and your partner.	38	210	40
o.	Use a surrogate mother to gestate an embryo genetically related to the male partner only.	20	229	38
p.	Use a surrogate mother to gestate an embryo genetically related to the female partner only.	16	230	42
q.	Accept infertility and redirect your desire to have a child to other pursuits.	144	84	68

7A. Do you believe the costs of the following reproductive technologies should be covered by health insurance?

		Yes	No	Undecided
a.	In vitro fertilization with your partner.	165	100	35
b.	In vitro fertilization with donor egg/sperm.	78	155	63
c.	Artificial insemination with donor sperm.	76	154	65
d.	Drugs or surgery to correct medical problems.	245	40	19
e.	In vitro fertilization with a surrogate.	42	193	61
f.	Artificial insemination with a surrogate.	39	192	64

	Yes	No	Undecided
7B. Would you be willing to pay higher health insurance premiums to cover	46	196	61

*the costs of extending coverage to
include nontraditional reproductive
technologies for all policyholders?*

	Yes	No	Undecided
7C. Would you be willing to pay higher taxes so the government could assist in the payment of nontraditional reproductive technologies?	30	223	50

7D. *If you would be willing to pay higher premiums or taxes, state in dollars and cents how much more you would be willing to pay each year. (Although the question is conditioned upon a willingness to pay, others also responded. Not all of the answers were given in dollars and cents.)*

"?"	11	$120	1
"N/A"	22	$150	1
"No"	4	$200	8
"None"	14	$200 insurance/	
"0"	29	$300 tax	1
$1.50	1	$250	1
$10	3	$500	2
$13.50	1	"As needed . . ."	1
$15	1	"Can't afford"	1
$20	1	"Depends . . ."	2
$25	1	"Don't know"	3
$50	3	"Not willing"	1
$75	1	"Undecided"	4
$50–$100	2	"Whatever needed . . ."	1
$100	11	"X"	1

8. *Who do you think should be eligible to use nontraditional reproductive technology in order to have a child? (In answering this question, assume the persons described are financially able to pay their own costs for the procedure.)*

		Yes	No	Undecided
a.	Married couples without children.	280	14	9
b.	Married couples with one child.	231	48	23
c.	Married couples regardless of other children.	191	61	44
d.	Heterosexual couples who are not married but have a stable relationship, without children.	114	140	42
e.	Heterosexual couples who are not married but have a stable relationship, with one child.	107	147	42
f.	Heterosexual couples who are not married but have a stable relationship, regardless of other children.	99	152	45
g.	Any heterosexual couple who desire treatment.	89	160	47
h.	Heterosexual single persons without a current partner.	91	160	46
i.	Gay or lesbian couples without children.	64	197	36
j.	Gay or lesbian couples with a child or children.	62	198	38
k.	Gay or lesbian single persons without a current partner.	54	205	39

	Yes	No	Undecided
9A. Would you consider freezing your egg/ sperm if you were facing a situation that might damage your ability to produce healthy egg/sperm in the future?	184	85	35

9B. If you and your partner had frozen eggs, sperm, or a fertilized egg (embryo), what should happen to the frozen eggs, sperm, or embryo if one of you died? . . . both of you died? . . . you divorced? Sixty-four people who had answered question 9A "no" simply left the answer spaces for this question blank, apparently assuming they would never face such issues because they chose not to freeze the material in the first place. One even wrote "a, b, and c are reasons not to do it," and another wrote "It should not be used." Six wrote "N/A" in the space, and two wrote "none." Twenty-three wrote "undecided" or "?"

Several offered a common solution to all three situations. Sixty wrote "destroy" or other terms to that effect, 11 wrote "Donate," and 4 wrote "Keep." One wrote "save for 3 years" in each space, another wrote "It doesn't matter," and one wrote "Have the child in any case." The responses given by participants who considered each of the three circumstances and tried to describe a separate solution for each one are collected as follows:

. . . if one partner dies		. . . if both partners die		. . . if the partners divorce	
Decision by survivor	63	By will or heirs decide	17	As court decrees	8
Surviving partner use	1	Per written instructions	1	Negotiate	2
Heir decide	2	Destroy	80	By agreement/ mutual	11
Use it	11	Donate	25	To the mother	2
"Birth"	1	It depends	1	To the father	2
Donate	5	Keep	2	It depends	3
Keep	28	Undecided or "?"	5	Keep	7
Destroy	3			Do nothing	1
Do nothing	3			Undecided or "?"	6
It depends	7			Destroy	71
Undecided	4			Donate	10
Space left blank	2			To partner who wants to use	2

10. *Whether or not you personally would utilize any of the following reproductive technologies, do you think any of the following procedures should be prohibited by law?*

		Yes	No	Undecided
a.	In vitro fertilization with partner.	26	261	15
b.	In vitro fertilization with donor.	46	217	36
c.	Artificial insemination with donor.	45	217	37
d.	Surrogate mother to gestate embryo genetically related to both parents but not to surrogate.	74	171	55
e.	Surrogate mother artificially inseminated with father's sperm.	96	138	68
f.	Surrogate mother to gestate mother's egg fertilized with donor sperm.	94	143	65

11A. Do you believe any of the following should be prohibited by law?

		Yes	No	Undecided
a.	Experiments on unimplanted embryos to gain knowledge to assist traditional pregnancies.	128	131	44
b.	Laboratory growth of embryo cells for medical use.	135	128	40
c.	Research to enable creation of an artificial womb.	134	123	45
d.	Sale of embryos by couple whose egg and sperm created it.	215	58	29
e.	Sale of egg by woman.	214	63	26
f.	Sale of sperm by man.	211	62	31
g.	Sales of egg, sperm, or embryos by third parties.	221	56	27
h.	Fee by surrogate for gestating a fetus.	170	90	41
i.	Fee by third parties for arranging surrogacy.	190	69	42

11B. Have you read newspaper or magazine accounts of the Baby M case or other cases involving disputes between the surrogate mother and the couple with whom she contracted? (This question was asked in order to determine how familiar participants in the survey were with media accounts of nontraditional reproductive practices.)

274 answered "yes"; 37 answered "no."

11C. In a dispute between the surrogate mother and the couple with whom she contracted, the following factors might be considered. Rank them in the order of importance you feel they should have in resolving the dispute.

		Number of times ranked					
		1st	2nd	3rd	4th	5th	6th
a.	Terms of the agreement they signed.	214	31	9	7	8	13
b.	Genetic relationships of claimants with baby.	34	130	56	23	23	14
c.	Maternal feelings of surrogate mother.	18	17	46	65	46	84
d.	Paternal feelings of father.	9	21	54	89	71	26
e.	Maternal feelings of father's wife (whether or not she is genetically related to the baby).	10	17	41	65	70	72
f.	Economic abilities of claimants to provide for baby.	14	61	71	16	43	73

	Oppose abortion	Pro-choice	Undecided
12. *Which characterization best describes your views about abortion?*	78	198	31

	Yes	No	Undecided
13. *Would you choose to terminate your pregnancy if tests on the fetus*	132	58	117

*indicated it was abnormal? (This
question was included just to sample
whether responses to question 12
would dictate responses to any
other questions dealing with abortion.)*

14. *Would you approve of laboratory use in research for possible
    cures of diseases or defects which involves*

		Yes	No	Undecided
a.	unimplanted embryos from IVF procedures?	134	106	58
b.	aborted fetuses?	148	92	61

15. *Would you approve of the medical use in the treatment of diseased or disabled living persons of cells or tissue from*

		Yes	No	Undecided
a.	unimplanted embryos from IVF procedures?	148	91	63
b.	aborted fetuses?	161	85	57

	Yes	No	Undecided
16A. *Should mothers who deliver babies damaged by actions of the mother during pregnancy be punished by law?*	165	36	88

16B. *If you believe a mother should ever be punished when it
     can be shown that her actions during pregnancy damaged
     her baby, for which of the following actions should she be
     punished?*

		Yes	No	Undecided
a.	Using illegal drugs during pregnancy.	232	23	31
b.	Using alcohol during pregnancy.	142	74	69

c.	Drinking coffee during pregnancy.	34	198	56
d.	Smoking during pregnancy.	112	103	72
e.	Continuing to work in an environment unsafe to the fetus.	89	75	117
f.	Refusing medical treatment for herself which would have benefited the fetus.	152	59	74
g.	Failing to obtain prenatal care.	93	108	84
h.	Cleaning a cat's litter box during pregnancy.	28	191	65
i.	Attempting to self-abort.	155	72	58
j.	Failing to eat a well-balanced diet during pregnancy.	22	196	64
k.	Failing to get adequate rest during pregnancy.	19	203	60
l.	Exposing herself to X rays.	46	133	97

16C. What do you believe should be done to or for mothers who damage their babies as a result of their actions during pregnancy?

No response	67	Financial accountability	1
"Undecided" or "?"	32	Welfare ineligibility	2
"Nothing"	3	Depends on harm/ intent	17
Criminal prosecution	7		
Murder/manslaughter	1	"No way [for] . . . equality"	1
Drug abuse	1		
Sterilizing/restricting future pregnancy	41	Terminating parental rights/loss of custody	27
Community service, particularly working with children	23	Counseling/education	66
		Rehabilitation/therapy	17
		Financial/medical help	12
"Punishment to fit the crime"	3	Fines	11
		Close supervision	3
Watever law/court decides	3	Jail/prison/probation	30

	Yes	No	Undecided
17A. *Do you think imposing mandatory birth control as a part of a woman's criminal sentence is ever appropriate?*	252	21	28

17B. *If you think there are times when mandatory birth control as a part of the sentence is appropriate, for which of the following crimes would it be?*

		Yes	No	Undecided
a.	Abuse of existing children	263	15	19
b.	Failure to report abuse of existing children by someone else	108	121	68
c.	Substance abuse during pregnancy	229	24	47
d.	Neglect or abandonment of existing children	259	14	24
e.	Practice of a lifestyle harmful to her child	207	19	68
f.	Prostitution	191	50	56

17C. *If you believe there are other occasions not listed in 17B for which mandatory birth control is appropriate, list them.*

Mental disorders—illness, retardation, insanity, deficiency	26
Welfare—continuing to have children, fraud, abuse	25
Poverty—financially unable to support or provide for	20
Unstable—mentally, physically, emotionally	6
HIV-positive	5
Convicted murderer/murderer of a child	4
Serious genetic disease	3
Sex offender/molester	2
Health of mother in jeopardy/physically unable to care for	2
Prisoners convicted of violent crimes	2
Past abortions or illegitimacies	2
Any lifestyle harmful to the mother	1

Homelessness   1
Rapist   1
Severe child abuse resulting in death   1
Teenaged   1
Termination of parental rights   1
(Many of the choices listed involve status rather than conduct.)

	Yes	No	Undecided
17D. If you oppose or are troubled by mandatory *birth control as a part of a woman's sentence, would you feel different if the woman agreed to it as a part of a plea bargain?* *(Only 21 opposed mandatory birth control and 28 were undecided in response to question 17A, so apparently the conditional part of this question was generally ignored.)*	104	87	39

17E. Would your answers to questions 17A–17D be significantly different if they related to the male parent?

280 said "same"; 11 said "different."

18.	Yes	No	Undecided
a. If you could have a test to screen for genetic diseases you carry which might be transmitted to your child, would you take the test?	289	13	5
b. Do you think you should be required to take such a test, for instance, in connection with the blood test for a marriage license?	165	102	39

		Yes	No	Undecided
c.	If the genetic screening showed that you and your partner had high probability to conceive an abnormal child, would you choose not to have children?	169	29	106
d.	If the genetic screening showed that you and your partner had a high probability to conceive an abnormal child, should the government prohibit you from having children?	31	223	52
e.	Would you (or your partner) become pregnant under the likelihood of having an abnormal child, with the intention of testing the fetus for abnormality and aborting any abnormal child?	75	159	69
f.	If the genetic screen showed that you and your partner were certain to have an abnormal child, would you choose not to have children?	226	20	59
g.	If the genetic screen showed that you and your partner were certain to have an abnormal child, should the government prohibit you from having children?	41	215	50
h.	If you conceived a child knowing of the high likelihood or certainty of abnormality, should you be excluded from receiving health insurance proceeds for the medical treatment of the child relating to the abnormal conditions?	55	179	72

i. Are you willing to pay higher health
    insurance premiums to cover the
    cost of extending health insurance
    coverage to pay medical expenses
    of babies born with genetic defects,
    even when the parents knew of the
    high likelihood or certainty
    such defects would occur?   59   163   82
j. If you conceived a child knowing of
    the high likelihood or certainty of
    abnormality, should you be excluded
    from receiving government benefits
    for the child relating to the
    abnormality?   81   138   83
k. Are you willing to pay higher taxes
    to cover costs of government
    benefits for babies born with genetic
    defects, even when the parents knew
    of the high likelihood or certainty
    such defects would occur?   58   164   82

19A. *Recent years have seen higher numbers of low-birth-weight
      infants born severely disabled, often from their mothers' sub-
      stance abuse or AIDS, and despite enormous sums of money
      spent to help these children, many will never grow up or be able
      to achieve minimal physical and/or mental levels of normalcy.
      Who do you think should bear the expense of caring for these
      babies?*

		Yes	No	Undecided
a.	The federal government out of existing social programs.	146	89	57
b.	The federal government out of new tax revenues.	49	181	57
c.	The state governments out of existing social programs.	134	99	56

		Yes	No	Undecided
d.	The state governments out of new tax revenues.	47	183	55
e.	Hospitals by passing costs to other patients.	22	229	39
f.	Health insurance plans through higher premiums.	54	173	58
g.	Charitable organizations and churches through greater member contributions.	158	65	62
h.	Families of the children.	219	30	40
i.	(The space for suggesting other sources of funds was left blank in all but so few instances that results are not reported.)			

19B. *President Ronald Reagan urged enactment of a law known as the "Baby Doe" law, which prohibits hospitals receiving federal funds from withholding medically indicated treatment from severely disabled infants. Do you agree with the government's requirement to employ heroic medical treatments for severely disabled babies?*

Yes	No	Undecided
88	136	77

19C. *The medical community acknowledges that in the past, severely handicapped infants have sometimes been allowed to die, even though medical technology could have been aggressively utilized to keep them alive. Do you think it is ever morally acceptable to withhold treatment from a severely handicapped infant?*

Yes	No	Undecided
169	70	64

19D. *Whom do you think should make life and death decisions about treatment of severely disabled infants. Select only one.*

	Number of times selected
a. The parents with the advice of the treating physicians.	267
b. A hospital committee consisting of medical professionals.	16
c. A committee of medical, legal, and religious professionals.	8
d. The courts of law.	7
e. The government.	2
f. Other:	4

One chose "other" but did not describe who should decide.
One said "The parents with the advice of the treating physicians and their pastor."
One said "The parents and a medical committee."
One said "The parents and a committee of medical, legal, and religious professionals."

	Yes	No	Undecided
9E. *If a determination were made to withhold medical treatment from a severely disabled infant with a life-threatening condition, would it ever be appropriate to administer a lethal injection to shorten suffering as inevitable death neared for the infant?*	131	87	87

	Yes	No	Undecided
20A. *Do you think sex education should be taught in America's schools?*	290	9	6

20B. *If sex education is taught, in what grades should it be taught? Circle as many grades as you think appropriate.*

Grades 1–3	4–5	6–7	8–9	10–12
94	198	260	262	242

	Yes	No	Undecided
20C. *Should students be given informa-tion regarding birth control by school nurses or sex education teachers?*	271	16	14

	Yes	No	Undecided
20D. *Should students be provided with birth-control devices by school nurses if the student requests it?*	145	109	51

	Yes	No	Undecided
20E. *Should students be directed by sex education teachers or school nurses to outside clinics for birth-control information and devices?*	213	48	42

21A. Do you believe welfare recipients have babies in order to increase welfare benefits?

Often	Sometimes	Rarely	Never
127	126	29	10

21B. Do you believe present welfare programs encourage unmarried pregnancies?

Often	Sometimes	Rarely	Never
132	119	35	15

	Yes	No	Undecided
21C. *Do you believe present welfare programs contribute to the breakdown of the family unit?*	162	53	83

22. Select the one statement that best expresses your viewpoint regarding midwives. (I had originally intended to include in the book a chapter on delivery, which I subsequently eliminated. Although this question is not used in the book, it reveals interesting attitudes.)

a. Birth is a natural process and a pregnant woman should be attended by whomever she wants, including attendance by a midwife at a home delivery.   65
b. Women should be allowed to use midwives who meet certain minimum levels of training and birthing experience.   2
c. Women should be allowed to use midwives who meet certain minimum levels of training and birthing experience, as required and certified by the state.   71
d. Unexpected complications may arise in childbirth, and for that reason only nurse-midwives practicing under the supervision of a physician should be licensed.   93
e. Modern technology makes it necessary for safe childbirth to occur in a hospital, where personnel and facilities are available for the mother and baby should a medical emergency arise.   77

	Yes	No	Undecided
23A. *Should children born as a result of the use of a donor egg, sperm, or embryo have available at their request the identity of the donor?*	124	97	80

	Yes	No	Undecided
23B. *Should children born as a result of the use of a donor egg, sperm, or embryo have available at their request genetic information about the donor?*	242	24	33

24A. *Would you describe yourself as a religious person?*

238 answered "yes";   64 answered "no."

24B. Do you belong to any church?

231 answered "yes";   75 answered "no."

24C. What is your religion?
Arranged alphabetically, their responses were:
agnostic, 5; Assembly of God, 1; atheist, 2; "B," 2; Baptist, 43; Buddhist, 1; Catholic, 48; Christian, 26; Church of Christ, 1; "Cy," 1; Disciples of Christ, 2; eclectic, 1; Episcopalian, 15; Hindu, 2; Holiness, 2; Jewish, 8; Lutheran, 5; Mennonite, 3; Methodist, 36; Mormon, 1; N/A, 1; Naturalist, 1; Nazarene, 2; none, 6; Pentecostal, 3; personal spirituality, 1; Presbyterian, 15; Southern Baptist, 5; Unitarian, 2; United Church of Christ, 1; United Methodist, 2; and Wicca, 1. Fifty-nine did not reply to this question.

24D. When you have decisions to make in your everyday life, are you influenced in your decisions by what your church says you ought to do?

107 answered "yes";   189 answered "no."

24E. Do you know the official position your church has taken with regard to most of the new reproductive technologies covered by the questions in this survey?

112 answered "yes";   177 answered "no."

24F. If your response to question 24E was "yes," then characterize how often your opinions as expressed in this survey agree with the official position taken by your church.

Always	Often	Sometimes	Rarely	Never
2	38	57	20	7

(Twelve more survey participants replied to this question than said they knew the official position of their churches in response to question 24E.)

25.	Yes	No	Undecided
a. Would you object to having your organs removed for transplantation after death?	41	235	29
b. Would you favor a change in the law to presume you have consented to organ donation after your death unless you have declared your opposition to organ donation prior to your death?	135	126	47
c. Would you favor a law requiring you to declare each time you renew your driver's license whether you wish to donate your organs?	195	72	38

26. *The survey concluded with an invitation to share personal comments or experiences relating to the issues covered in the survey. Most participants did not write anything in the space provided, but some offered written comments or shared spoken comments when they returned their responses to me. Among those, several told me they had agreed to participate in the survey because they felt strongly about reproductive practices, but that they found that their broad generalizations had proved to be inadequate guidance in the face of the specific situations described in most of the questions. They said they appreciated the challenge and found the survey "thought-provoking," a term used by several participants. Teachers and others who had worked with young people often emphasized the urgent need to educate the youngsters who are having children far too early—before they become pregnant. A few participants who oppose abortion used the space to indicate that from their perspectives, some reproductive practices involve murder of an unborn child. Nearly all of the comments related to the reproductive practices of others rather than reflecting their personal insights into their own experiences.*

Notes

Introduction

1. Before defining "conscionable" as "in accordance with good conscience," my dictionary notes that use of the word is "now rare."

Chapter 1: The Story of Mary Shearing

1. Interviews with Mary Shearing were conducted on February 9, 1993, April 8, 1996, and April 11, 1997.

Chapter 2: Do We Have an Absolute Right to Have a Child?

1. When survey participants were asked whether everyone should have the right to have a child, only 37 percent answered with an unqualified "yes." Fifty percent thought not everyone should have that right, and 10.3 percent were undecided. (Responses to survey question 3A.) The reason most often selected as important and appropriate for choosing to have a child was "You want to love and be loved by a child," selected by 239 of the 310 people taking the survey, with the second most popular choice being "You have a strong emotional desire to have a child," selected by 216 people. In contrast, when they were asked to list reasons for limiting the right to conceive or the number of children someone should have, the most frequent responses involved financial ability, followed second by responses related to mental ability. The ability to love a child was mentioned by only 3 of the 310 participants. (Responses to survey questions 3B and 4B.) See Appendix 2 for a full description of the responses to survey questions 1–4.
2. Skinner v. Oklahoma, 316 U.S. 535 (1942).
3. It is amusing to note that the state legislators excluded some felonies from among those requiring sterilization, and one of the exceptions these politicians wrote into the law was the felony conviction for political offenses!
4. 1 Annals of Congress at 759, August 15, 1789.
5. Testimony of Robert Bork during his appearance before the Senate as quoted in *The Wall Street Journal*, October 5, 1987, p. A22.
6. Carey v. Population Services International, 431 U.S. 678 at 686, citing Doe v. Bolton, 410 U.S. 155 (1973).

Chapter 3: The Story of Laura Campo and Baby Theresa Ann

1. The interviews with Laura Campo were conducted on April 14, 1993, and April 28, 1997, with correspondence on March 22, 1995.
2. In re T.A.C.P., 609 So.2d 588 (1992).
3. In 1995 a nine-member policy-setting committee of the American Medical Association urged changes in state laws to allow organ donation by anencephalic babies like Theresa. The opinions of the AMA Council on Ethical and Judicial Affairs are regarded as constituting AMA policy. The committee conditioned its recommendation for use of these infants as live donors on the requirement that two experts diagnose the anencephaly and that the parents request that their baby be an organ donor.

Chapter 4: Parents' Rights, Public Concerns

1. In re T.A.C.P. at 594.
2. Although most anencephalic babies die within a week or less, that is not strictly true. See page 48 for the story of Baby K, whose mother has insisted on repeated medical intervention to keep her child alive.
3. Responses to survey question 19C.
4. Jeff Lyon, *Playing God in the Nursery* (New York: W. W. Norton, 1985), p. 292.
5. Survey participants were asked whether several sources should be used to pay the expenses of caring for low-birth-weight babies born severely disabled and with a limited likelihood of achieving normal physical and mental levels, and they responded as follows:

	Yes	No	Undecided
The federal government out of existing social programs	47%	29%	18%
The federal government out of new tax revenues	16%	58%	18%
The state governments out of existing social programs	43%	32%	18%
The state governments out of new tax revenues	15%	59%	18%
Hospitals by passing costs on to other patients	7%	74%	12.6%
Health insurance plans through higher premiums	17%	56%	19%
Charitable organizations and churches through greater member contributions	51%	21%	20%
Families of the children	71%	10%	13%

(Responses to survey question 19A)

6. Mary M. McCallum, *Atlanta Journal-Constitution*, November 1, 1991, p. A12.
7. Mary Jean Goode, *Atlanta Journal-Constitution*, November 4, 1991, p. A8.
8. A 1973 report in the *New England Journal of Medicine* described a study showing that 14 percent of the infant deaths in the special-care nursery of a large hospital were the result of withholding or withdrawing treatment (vol. 289, p. 890).
9. The number of times each of the six choices concerning who should make life-and-death decisions concerning the treatment of severely disabled infants was selected by survey participants is as follows:

The parents with advice of physicians	267
A hospital committee of medical professionals	16
A committee of medical, legal, and religious professionals	8
The courts of law	7
The government	2
Other	4

(Responses to survey question 19D)

10. Guest on Oprah Winfrey show aired January 29, 1992.

11. Bowen v. American Hospital Association, 476 U.S. 610 at 647 (1986).
12. The United States Supreme Court began the new year in 1997 hearing arguments in a pair of cases that challenged two states' prohibitions against doctor-assisted suicides. From opposite coasts, the cases of *State of Washington v. Glucksberg* and *Vacco v. Quill* (a New York case) reflected the majority of laws, since forty-four states make it a crime to help others hasten their own deaths. In 1994 voters in Oregon made theirs the first state to approve medical assistance for dying patients. The Oregon law allows medical personnel, under highly limited circumstances, to facilitate suicides for terminal patients who wish to die, but before the law could take effect it was blocked by a federal judge. Among the briefs filed in the pair of cases before the Supreme Court in 1997 were two taking opposite positions. The American Medical Association supported preserving the prohibition against doctor-assisted suicides, saying in their brief that the ban "helps ensure that patients will never lose the trust that must exist for the relationship between healthcare professionals and patients to flourish." The American Medical Student Association disagreed in their brief, saying, "Terminally ill patients who are competent and make a voluntary choice to hasten their death with the assistance of their physician should have the same right to control the time and manner of death as patients who refuse life-sustaining treatment." Perhaps the contrast indicated a generational shift in attitudes about the right to choose when one's own life should end.
13. Responses to survey question 19E.
14. Helga Kuhse and Peter Singer, *Should the Baby Live? The Problem of Handicapped Infants* (New York: Oxford University Press, 1985), pp. 99–110.
15. Lyon, *Playing God,* p. 213. See also Peter Singer, *Rethinking Life and Death: The Collapse of Our Traditional Ethics* (New York: St. Martin's Press, 1994).
16. Lyon, *Playing God,* pp. 237–40.
17. Matter of Baby K, 16 F.3d 590 at 596 (4th Cir. 1994).
18. In October 1994, two years after Baby K's birth, the United States Supreme Court refused to hear the case, thereby exhausting the hospital's legal appeals.
19. Maureen Hack, M.B., Ch.B.; H. Gerry Taylor, Ph.D.; Nancy Klein, Ph.D.; Robert Eiben, M.D.; Christopher Schatschneider, M.A.; and Nori Mercuri-Minich, B.S., "School-age Outcomes in Children with Birth Weights Under 750 g," *New England Journal of Medicine,* vol. 331, no. 12 (September 22, 1994): pp. 753–59.

Chapter 5: The Story of Lisa Landry Childress

1. The interview with Lisa Landry Childress was conducted on January 16, 1992. Her husband, Gary, was interviewed on August 30, 1995, and May 20, 1996.
2. The interview with Dr. Whitney Gonsoulin was conducted on January 23, 1992.
3. The primary goal of the Lisa Landry Childress Foundation is to further public awareness, particularly among young people, of organ and tissue

donation. Programs have been developed for implementation in school cur-riculums, youth programs, and church groups. The foundation may be con-tacted at 1-800-221-LISA (5472).

Chapter 6: Who Is the Patient? Balancing Maternal and Fetal Rights

1. The interviews with George Hughes were conducted on January 29, 1992, and May 26, 1995.
2. American College of Obstetricians and Gynecologists (ACOG), Technical Bulletin no. 136, "Ethical Decision-Making in Obstetrics and Gynecology," November 1989.
3. American College of Obstetricians and Gynecologists (ACOG), Committee Opinion no. 55, "Patient Choice: Maternal-Fetal Conflict," October 1987.
4. In re A.C., 533 A.2d 611 (D.C.App. 1987); vacated at 539 A.2d 203 (D.C.App. 1988); 573 A.2d 1235 (D.C.App. 1990).
5. Interview with Highland General Hospital spokesperson Marty Boyer con-ducted on July 26, 1994.
6. Even if she had consented, she would have had no assurance that her fetus would survive, for she was told that this particular surgery had been attempted only twice before, and that the fetus had survived in only one of the two attempts.
7. ACOG Bulletin no. 136 and Opinion no. 55.
8. Stallman v. Youngquist, 531 N.E.2d 355 (Ill. 1988).
9. Andrea Boroff Eagan, "Who Decides for Women?" *American Health,* vol. 9, no. 7, p. 43.
10. The interview with Cook County public guardian Patrick Murphy was con-ducted on May 9, 1996.

Chapter 7: The Story of Bree Walker and Jim Lampley

1. The interview with Bree Walker and Jim Lampley was conducted on Feb-ruary 23, 1993, followed by correspondence on September 23, 1996, and an interview with Bree on May 2, 1997.
2. Ibid.
3. *20/20* interview with Barbara Walters broadcast January 10, 1992.
4. Jean Seligmann with Donna Foote, "Whose Baby Is It Anyway?" *Newsweek,* October 28, 1991, p. 73

Chapter 8: The Dilemmas of Genetic Knowledge

1. Gregor Johann Mendel was an Austrian scientist and Roman Catholic priest who lived from 1822 to 1884 and formulated a system of heredity known as Mendelism based on the conclusions he drew from records of his breeding experiments with garden peas.
2. The interview with Betsy Gettig, genetic counselor, was conducted on March 4, 1993.
3. The interview with Dr. Paul Billings, physician and bioethicist, was con-ducted on March 2, 1993.
4. Her mother had breast cancer, and Lyndall's own cancers at that age were a

rare tumor of the muscle (embryonal rhabdomyoscarcoma) and a malignant bone tumor (osteogenic sarcoma).

5. Her youngest brother was diagnosed at seventeen with acute lymphocytic leukemia and osteogenic sarcoma, and at twenty-seven with adeno-carcinoma of the gastrointestinal tract. The older of the two brothers was diagnosed with osteogenic sarcoma at age twenty-four. In addition to her two different childhood cancers, Lyndall was first diagnosed with breast cancer at age thirty-one, and again at age thirty-four.

6. Lyndall's maternal grandparents had two children, both of whom died of cancer in their thirties. Lyndall's uncle had three daughters, one of whom died of cancer at age eight. Her other two cousins are in their late twenties and have never been diagnosed with cancer. The family is unaware of its medical history prior to her grandfather, and so on their medical-history chart he is seen as the source of the mutant gene.

7. The interview with Lyndall Southern was conducted on March 9, 1993, with correspondence on March 28, 1995, and April 12, 1997.

8. Lampley interview.

9. Responses to survey question 12.

10. Responses to survey question 18A.

11. Responses to survey question 18F.

12. Responses to survey question 18C.

13. Responses to survey question 18E.

14. Responses to survey question 13.

15. The interviews with Cam Knutson, genetic counselor, were conducted on March 4, 1993.

16. The interview with Nancy Becker Kennedy was conducted on March 2, 1993, and April 4, 1997.

17. *Count Us In: Growing Up with Down Syndrome,* published by Harcourt Brace in 1994, has won awards and has allowed Jason and his friend Mitchell Levitz to reach even more people with their positive message as they travel promoting their book.

18. The National Down Syndrome Adoption Exchange has not only been suc-cessful in placing children with Down syndrome, but also maintains a waiting list of willing adoptive parents.

19. The interview with Emily Perl Kingsley was conducted on March 4, 1993, with correspondence on March 17, 1995, and March 22, 1996.

20. Fifty-three percent felt it should be required, 33 percent felt it should not, and 12.6 percent were undecided. (Responses to survey question 18B.)

21. Responses to survey questions 18D and 18G.

22. Billings interview and materials he provided; Paul R. Billings, Mel A. Kohn, Margaret de Cuevas, Jonathan Beckwith, Joseph S. Alper, and Marvin R. Natowicz, "Discrimination as a Consequence of Genetic Testing," *American Journal of Human Genetics,* vol. 50 (1992): pp. 476–482, esp. p. 481.

23. The interview with Theresa Morelli was conducted on March 5, 1993, with correspondence on March 19, 1995.

24. Billings et al., "Discrimination," p. 480.

25. *California Cryobank News,* vol. 2 no. 1 (Spring 1992): p. 1.

26. Responses to survey questions 18C and 18F.
27. Responses to survey question 18H.
28. Responses to survey question 18I.
29. Responses to survey question 18K.
30. Walker interview.
31. Myk Cherskov, "Fighting Genetic Discrimination," *American Bar Association Journal,* June 1992, p. 38.
32. Responses to survey question 18B.
33. Charcot-Marie-Tooth atrophy, or peroneal muscular atrophy, causes muscles to waste halfway up the arms and legs, but progression is so slow that people with the disorder are rarely completely incapacitated, and sometimes the deterioration stops for no apparent reason. Although life expectancy is normal for people with CMT, this case, collected by Dr. Billings's team, exemplifies the sort of discrimination that faces people with genetic disorders that involve normal abilities and life expectancy. (Billings et al., "Discrimination," p. 481.)
34. Wes Jackson is the director of the Land Institute in Salina, Kansas, which studies natural plant life in order to better select and adapt cultivated crops to local ecologies. He authored *New Roots for Agriculture,* and this quote is taken from an article entitled "Listen to the Land," published in the *Amicus Journal,* Spring 1993, pp. 32–34.
35. It is beyond the scope of this book to discuss the morality of genetically altering plants and animals to satisfy questionable human research, but some of the experiments described in this chapter should suggest the ethical questions raised by current scientific practices, especially experiments unrelated to medical treatments or cures.

Chapter 9: The Story of Sara Collins

1. Sara Collins is a real woman and her story is real, but she asked that this pseudonym be used to protect her daughter and to help her put this troubled time in her life behind her. All quotes are from interviews conducted on May 4, 1994, and May 1, 1996.
2. The interview with prosecutor Tony Tague was conducted on August 23, 1994.
3. California passed a law making it a criminal offense for a drug addict to be within the state. In 1962 the United States Supreme Court held the California law to be unconstitutional because it imposed criminal prosecution for a medical problem, drug addiction, without any accompanying criminal activity, such as possession or use of drugs while in the state. Robinson v. California, 370 U.S. 665 (1962). In other words, defendants cannot be charged with mere status; there must be some accompanying criminal *activity.*
4. People v. Hardy, 469 N.W.2d 50 (Mich.App. 1991) at 53.

Chapter 10: Should We Criminalize Parental Conduct?

1. Seven percent answered "no," and 9 percent were undecided. (Responses to survey question 17A.)

2. When survey participants were asked whether certain behaviors would justify including court-ordered birth control as a part of a woman's criminal
   sentence, they answered as follows:

	Yes	No	Undecided
Abuse of existing children	85%	5%	6%
Failure to report abuse of existing children by someone else	35%	39%	22%
Substance abuse during pregnancy	74%	8%	15%
Neglect or abandonment of existing children	84%	4.5%	8%
Practice of a lifestyle harmful to her child	67%	6%	22%
Prostitution	62%	15%	18%

(Responses to survey question 17B)

3. When asked whether their answers regarding imposing mandatory birth
   control would differ significantly if the fathers were in court, 90 percent said
   their answers would be the same. Among those few who said they would
   answer differently if the defendant were the father, a disproportionate
   number were men. (Of the 3.5 percent who said they thought men should
   be punished differently, half were men, although men represented only 24
   percent of the survey participants.) (Responses to survey question 17E.)
4. Responses to survey questions 17B(a) and 17B(b).
5. When survey participants were asked whether they would feel different
   about including birth control in a woman's criminal sentence if she agreed
   to it as a part of a plea bargain, 33.5 percent said they would. Unfortunately, both those who approved and those who disapproved of mandatory
   birth control responded to this question, despite the conditional language of
   the question, so what was meant by their affirmative replies is muddled.
   Likewise, the 28 percent who said their feelings were the same, whether the
   birth control is imposed or agreed to, included both those who approve and
   those who disapprove of court-ordered birth control. (Responses to survey
   question 17D.)
6. People v. Zaring, 10 Cal.Rptr.2d 263 (Cal.App. 5th Dist. 1992) at 269:
   "Even if we were to assume arguendo that the safeguarding of the health of
   any yet to be conceived unborn child of appellant may properly be the subject of probation conditions, it is clear to us that other conditions, less
   drastic than an outright ban on pregnancy, could be used."
7. People v. Pointer, 199 Cal.Rptr. 357 (Cal.App. 1st Dist. 1984).
8. Quotes from Judge Howard Broadman were taken from the transcript of
   the Johnson case that he provided as a supplement to his interview, and
   from the interview conducted on February 10, 1995.
9. Sixth Circuit Court Judge Lynn Tepper appearing on CNN's *Crier & Company*, broadcast May 3, 1991.
10. Responses to survey question 17B(a); see note 2 above.
11. Responses to survey question 17B(e); see note 2 above.
12. The interview with public defender Jeff Kelly was conducted on Novem-
    ber 18, 1994.
13. Although he had repeated his urgent desire for castration in order to avoid

the risk of violating his parole and harming more children, McQuay did not immediately utilize the procedure when it became available.

14. This book deals with reproductive conduct by people who have chosen to carry their babies to term, and therefore conduct intended to abort the fetus is beyond the scope of the discussion.

15. According to a new study at Emory University headed by epidemiology associate professor Carolyn D. Drews, published in the April 1996 issue of *Pediatrics*, vol. 97, no. 4.

16. According to a study by researchers with the Western Australia Pregnancy Cohort in Perth, published in the October 1996 issue of *The Lancet*, vol. 348.

17. According to a study by Paul Buescher for the State Center for Health and Environmental Statistics reported in the *Infant Mortality Monitor*, a publication of the Governor's Commission on Reduction of Infant Mortality. Since 1988 birth certificates in North Carolina record whether the mother used tobacco during pregnancy, including the average number of cigarettes per day that she smoked.

Another study found that even if the mother refrains from smoking during the pregnancy but resumes doing so after the baby arrives, women who smoke at least a pack a day have children with twice the rate of extreme behavior problems, such as anxiety, disobedience, or conflict with others, and although the behavior problems decreased as mothers smoked less, they still exceeded those of nonsmokers' children. The research was led by Dr. Michael Weitzman, associate chair of pediatrics at the University of Rochester School of Medicine in New York State, based on data from a Labor Department survey of parents of 2,256 youngsters ages four to eleven. Fathers were not asked about their smoking habits in the Labor Department data.

18. According to a 1991 estimate by the National Institute on Drug Abuse.

19. Responses to survey questions 16B(a) and 16B(d).

20. The behaviors selected by survey participants as most criminally blameworthy during pregnancy, in order of selection, were as follows: using illegal drugs, 75 percent; attempting to self-abort, 50 percent; refusing medical treatment for herself which would have benefited the fetus, 49 percent; using alcohol, 46 percent; smoking, 36 percent; failing to obtain prenatal care, 30 percent; continuing to work in an unsafe environment, 29 percent; exposing herself to X rays, 15 percent; cleaning cat's litter box, 9 percent; failing to eat well, 7 percent; drinking coffee, 7 percent; and failing to get adequate rest, 6 percent. (Responses to survey question 16B.)

21. Amy E. McGrory, "Letters from Readers," *Glamour,* September 1991, p. 28.

22. Oprah Winfrey show broadcast July 25, 1991.

23. Michael Dorris, *The Broken Cord* (New York: Harper & Row, 1989), p. 165. Michael Dorris took his own life in April 1997, six years after the son about whom he wrote so powerfully was struck and killed crossing the street.

24. The interview with Dr. Claire Coles and Iris Smith was conducted on January 15, 1992.

25. Charleston, South Carolina, solicitor Charles Condon, quoted in an article by Henry Eichel, "S.C. Lawsuit Spotlights Debate on How to Treat Pregnant Cocaine Users," *Charlotte Observer,* January 31, 1994, pp. 1A, 5A.

26. The interview with Jack Mallard, chief assistant district attorney for the Cobb County Judicial Circuit in Marietta, Georgia, was conducted on August 13, 1991, immediately following his appearance at the American Bar Association Convention.

27. Ira J. Chasnoff, M.D., et al., "The Prevalence of Illicit-Drug or Alcohol Use During Pregnancy and Discrepancies in Mandatory Reporting in Pinellas County, Florida," *New England Journal of Medicine,* vol. 322, no. 17 (April 26, 1990): pp. 1202–6.

28. Eleven percent of the black women used drugs, 5 percent of the whites, and 4 percent of Hispanics.

29. Twenty-three percent of whites drank alcohol, 16 percent of blacks, and 9 percent of Hispanics. Twenty-four percent of whites smoked, 20 percent of blacks, and 6 percent of Hispanics.

30. Their survey was conducted at fifty-two hospitals across the country by Westat Inc. between October 1992 and August 1993.

31. Researchers from the National Institutes of Health examined responses from 42,862 households to a federal government survey taken in 1992. The response of welfare recipients are stated in ranges because they reflect five different welfare programs. Among those surveyed, 6.4 to 13.8 percent of welfare recipients admitted they were heavy drinkers, compared to 14.8 percent of those not receiving welfare; 3.8 to 9.8 percent of welfare recipients admitted to drug use, compared to 5.1 percent of those not on welfare; and 1.3 to 3.6 percent of those on welfare, compared to 1.5 percent of those not on welfare, admitted to drug dependency.

32. The interviews with Cecelia Lyles were conducted on January 16, 1992, and May 22, 1996.

33. Cecelia's story reflects the multiple harmful behaviors present in many teenaged pregnancies.

34. Cecelia is now working with the homeless, but she continues to work on a part-time basis with Outreach, Inc.

35. The researchers at Emory found an increased likelihood of giving birth to retarded babies even among relatively light smokers. About 35 percent of women who gave birth to retarded children reported smoking as few as five cigarettes a week during their pregnancies. Pregnant women with a pack-a-day habit were 85 percent more likely to give birth to a retarded child. Professor Drew believes these preliminary findings emphasize the need for further studies.

36. The AMA opposes legislation that criminalizes maternal drug addiction, believing that "criminal sanctions or civil liability for harmful behavior by the pregnant woman toward her fetus are inappropriate." The March of Dimes "opposes the criminalization of substance abuse by pregnant women and advocates treatment on demand for such women." The American

Nurses Association feels that "the threat of criminal prosecutions is counter-productive in that it prevents many women from seeking prenatal care and treatment for their alcohol and other drug problems." The American Society of Addiction Medicine has concluded, "Criminal prosecution of chemically dependent women will have an overall result of deterring such women from seeking both prenatal care and chemical dependency treatment, thereby increasing rather than preventing harm to children and society as a whole."

Chapter 11: The Story of Guy and Terri Walden

1. Several interviews with Guy and Terri Walden were conducted over a period of time beginning on October 28, 1991, and continuing through 1997. Terri continues to send cards to children with special needs and invites people who know a child deserving of a special birthday card to call her at 407-295-6193.

Chapter 12: Fetal Tissue Use and Sibling Donor Conception

1. Among the statements in support of lifting the federal-funding ban were the following: "The moratorium on fetal tissue transplantation research impedes important scientific investigations, including studies which impact on prevention and treatment of cardiovascular disease" (the American Heart Association). "The American Medical Association supports continued research employing fetal tissue obtained from induced abortions with the provision that ethical guidelines are observed" (the AMA). "The medical possibilities using fetal tissue are endless, for patients of all ages and for countless diseases" (the Arthritis Foundation). "No individual should be allowed to 'ban' scientifically sound, high-quality biomedical research which has passed the scrutiny of peer review and has obtained necessary human subject research clearance" (the National Multiple Sclerosis Society). "This issue is not about abortion. It is about responsibility to use tissue which exists towards research which may cure a host of devastating diseases" (the Juvenile Diabetes Foundation). "The current prohibition on federal support of this research harms the development of potential therapies and may be needlessly prolonging the suffering of thousands of Americans" (the Association of American Medical Colleges). "Fetal tissue research has a long scientific history of promising research results in the development of treatments that may save human lives and reduce suffering" (American Medical Women's Association). "There is no question that our progress in this very promising field has been slowed considerably, and may eventually be halted altogether" (the American Diabetes Association). "Lifting the moratorium on fetal tissue transplantation research is sound public policy, both morally and scientifically" (the Association of American Universities). "The ability to make use of fetal tissue could be critical to success in saving the lives of cancer patients" (the American Cancer Society).

2. Each of the four orders related to abortion in some way. In addition to lifting the fetal tissue ban, the President also ended the so-called gag rule that forbade most health workers at federally funded clinics from discussing

abortion with pregnant women, reversed the Reagan administration's refusal to aid international population-control programs, and ordered a review of the decision to ban the importation of RU-486, the French drug known as the "morning-after pill," which the two previous administrations had refused to allow researchers, as well as pregnant women, to utilize, despite promising medical applications having nothing to do with abortion.

3. Responses to survey question 12.

4. The interview with Anne Udall was conducted on February 5, 1992. She says, "An aide to one of the Senators told me after the hearing, 'The Senators are really moved by the fact that a colleague suffers from a disease that might benefit from lifting the ban.' "

5. Guy Walden interview.

6. When survey participants were asked whether they would approve of the medical use of fetal tissue in the treatment of diseased or disabled living persons involving cells or tissue from aborted fetuses, 52 percent answered "yes," 27 percent answered "no," and 18 percent were undecided. Approval dropped slightly when they were asked about laboratory use in research for possible cures of diseases or defects involving aborted fetuses, with 48 percent answering "yes," 30 percent answering "no," and 20 percent undecided. A review comparing how people viewed abortion with their feelings toward the use of fetal tissue in medicine and research revealed no particular patterns distinguishing the responses of those who characterized themselves as pro-choice from the responses of those who opposed abortion. (Responses to survey questions 12, 14B, and 15B.)

7. Barbara Culliton, "Grave Robbing," *Science,* vol. 186 (November 1, 1974): pp. 420–23.

8. The number of abortions did, in fact, decline during President Clinton's first term in office.

9. Stephen G. Post, "Fetal Tissue Transplant: The Right to Question Progress," *America,* January 12, 1991, p. 16.

10. Joan Samuelson's statement to Congress on April 15, 1991.

11. John A. Morris, Jr., M.D., Ph.D.; Todd R. Wilcox; and William H. Prist, M.D., "Pediatric Organ Donation: The Paradox of Organ Shortage Despite the Remarkable Willingness of Families to Donate," *Pediatrics,* vol. 89, no. 3 (March 1992): p. 411. At Vanderbilt University Medical Center, during a thirty-one-month period there were nineteen pediatric deaths appropriate as donors. Doctos failed to ask one family, but of the other eighteen families asked, all agreed and organs were successfully procured in every instance. According to the researchers, "These data suggest that families of pediatric patients are much more willing to agree to donation than the families of adult patients."

12. The American Bar Association Probate Section voted in 1991 to begin a campaign to encourage the counseling of clients regarding the ease of becoming organ and tissue donors.

13. Sixty-three percent of the participants in my survey said they would approve of a law requiring a declaration of donor status in connection with driver's license renewal, 23 percent said they would not, and 12 percent were unde-

cided. (Responses to survey question 25C.) They were not so broadly in favor of a change in the law to presume that a deceased person had consented to organ donation absent a contrary declaration, however, although 43.5 percent favored such a presumption. Forty-one percent disapproved of the presumption, and 15 percent were undecided. (Responses to survey question 25B.) Only 13 percent of the survey participants said they would object to having their own organs donated after their deaths, and a strong 76 percent said they would have no objection, with only 9 percent undecided. (Responses to survey question 25A.) These attitudes differ from their responses regarding the research and therapeutic use of fetal tissue. See note 6 above regarding responses to survey questions 14B and 15B.

14. Statement of Rev. Guy Walden and Terri Walden to Congress on April 15, 1991.
15. The interview with Joan Samuelson was conducted on January 21, 1992. Since that interview, Joan and her husband have divorced.
16. See note 10 above.
17. When *Time* magazine told the family's story, it reported that 47 percent of those polled answered "yes" to the question "Is it morally acceptable for parents to conceive a child in order to obtain an organ or tissue to save the life of another one of their children?" but 37 percent answered "no." Lance Morrow, "When One Body Can Save Another: A Family's Act of Lifesaving Conception," *Time,* June 17, 1991, pp. 54–58.
18. The interview with Dr. Stephen J. Forman was conducted on February 12, 1992.
19. The most popular reasons selected by participants in my survey had to do with loving and sharing, but significant numbers selected such reasons as wanting to carry on the family name and inheritance, 26 percent; wanting grandchildren, 23.5 percent; and wanting someone to care for them in their old age, 10 percent. (Responses to survey question 1.)
20. See note 17 above.
21. The interview with Lea Ann Curry was conducted on May 18, 1994, and April 11, 1997.
22. The acceleration of Lea Ann's pregnancies was affected by Natalie's illness, but their desire for a donor never affected their love for each daughter. "The donor match was secondary to the health of each of our girls," Lea Ann says, and she is quick to correct any misconception that her younger daughters were valued in terms of their status as a donor.
23. Jen M. R. Doman and Kenneth Miller, "Together Forever," *Life* magazine, April 1996, pp. 45–56.

Chapter 13: Winter Workshop

1. An evening workshop on infertility and grief was sponsored by Kinder-Mourn on January 25, 1993, to which the public was invited. A panel of bereaved parents was led by the Kinder-Mourn program director in a discussion of infertility issues and the ways in which they had coped.

Chapter 14: Complex Choices for Infertile Couples

1. Vatican doctrinal statement, "Instruction on Respect for Human Life in Its Origin and on the Dignity of Procreation," issued March 10, 1987.

2. Rev. Richard A. McCormick, John A. O'Brien Professor of Christian Ethics at the University of Notre Dame, quoted by Ari L. Goldman in "Vatican Asks Governments to Curb Birth Technology," *New York Times,* March 11, 1987, pp. A1, A17.

3. Responses to survey question 6M.

4. Responses to survey question 6J.

5. Among participants in my survey, only 8 percent thought in vitro fertilization with one's own partner should be prohibited. An even smaller 5 percent were undecided, but an overwhelming 84 percent said it should not be prohibited. (Responses to survey question 10A.)

6. Richard P. Dickey, M.D., Ph.D., "The Medical Status of the Embryo," *Loyola Law Review,* vol. 32 (1986): p. 335. Dr. Dickey was the director of the in vitro fertilization program of the Fertility Institute of New Orleans.

7. Peter Singer and Deane Wells, *Making Babies: The New Science and Ethics of Conception* (New York: Charles Scribner's Sons, 1985), p. 76.

8. The interview with Dr. Roman Pyrzak, director of the Andrology Laboratory Research and Development, was conducted on June 4, 1992.

9. Success/failure ratios vary from clinic to clinic, but the national average for successful implantation in IVF is between 13 and 21 percent.

10. The interview with Lisa Fagg was conducted on June 10, 1992.

11. The interview with H.W. was conducted on June 10, 1992.

12. Jessica Mitford, *The American Way of Birth* (New York: Dutton, William Abrahams Books, 1992), surveys the history and current impact of technology on the delivery of babies in this country.

13. When survey participants were asked whether they would consider freezing their egg/sperm if they were facing a situation that might damage their ability to produce healthy egg/sperm in the future, 59 percent said they would, 27 percent said they would not, and 11 percent were undecided. (Responses to survey question 9A.)

14. Bernard Dickens of the Toronto Law School at the 1984 American Society of Law and Medicine Congress in Boston asked his colleagues, "Is this a case of the gametes inheriting the estate or the estate inheriting the gametes?"

15. The Tennessee Supreme Court considered numerous articles, in which "medical-legal scholars and ethicists have proposed various models for the disposition of 'frozen embryos' when unanticipated contingencies arise, such as divorce, death of one or both of the parties, financial reversals, or simple disenchantment with the IVF process. Those models range from a rule requiring, at one extreme, that all embryos be used by the gamete-providers or donated for uterine transfer, and, at the other extreme, that any unused embryos be automatically discarded. Other formulations would vest control in the female gamete-provider—in every case, because of her greater physical and emotional contribution to the IVF process, or perhaps only in the event that she wishes to use them herself. There are also two 'implied contract' models: one would infer from enrollment in an IVF program that the clinic has authority to decide in the event of an impasse whether to donate, discard, or use the 'frozen embryos' for research; the other would infer from the parties' participation in the creation of the embryos that they had made an irrevocable com-

mitment to reproduction and would require transfer either to the female provider or to a donee. There are also the so-called 'equity models': one would avoid the conflict altogether by dividing the frozen embryos equally between the parties, to do with as they wish; the other would award veto power to the party wishing to avoid parenthood, whether it be the female or the male progenitor." Davis v. Davis, 842 S.W.2d 588 (Tenn. 1992).

16. An earlier five-judge panel had ruled that Danny Nahmani had the right to prevent Ruti from using the stored, fertilized eggs, but the 7-to-4 decision by the Supreme Court reversed the earlier ruling. After the couple's separation, Danny fathered two daughters with another woman during the disputed divorce proceedings.

17. Associated Press reports: "Couples Seek More Time to Save Embryos," July 31, 1996, p. A5, "Catholic Cardinal Backs Destruction of Embryos," August 1, 1996, p. A10; "British Clinic Begins Embryo Purge," *Fort Worth Star-Telegram,* August 2, 1996, p. A15.

18. Fagg interview.

19. Participants in my survey were asked whether they would approve of the medical use in the treatment of diseased or disabled living persons of cells or tissue from unimplanted embryos from IVF procedures, and 48 percent said they would, 29 percent said they would not, and 20 percent were undecided. (Responses to survey question 15A.) They were asked a similar question regarding laboratory use in research for possible cures of diseases or defects, and 43 percent said they would approve of such a use of unimplanted embryos, 34 percent said they would not, and 19 percent were undecided. (Responses to survey question 14A.)

20. When participants in my survey were asked whether certain uses of unimplanted embryos should be prohibited, 41 percent thought experiments conducted to gain knowledge to assist traditional pregnancies should be prohibited, 42 percent thought they should not and 14 percent were undecided. As for using unimplanted embryos to cultivate the growth of more embryo cells for medical uses, 43.5 percent thought the cultivation of embryo cells should be prohibited, 41 percent thought it should not be, and 13 percent were undecided. (Responses to survey questions 11A[a] and 11A[b]).

21. Despite the words of Manny's widow at the time of his death on June 4, 1994, six months later no insemination had been attempted. Beth J. Harpaz, "Couple Had Hoped for a Family; Procedure Keeps That Hope Alive," *Associated Press,* January 20, 1995.

22. Ibid. At that time, seven other cases of postmortem retrieval of sperm were known, and in none of the known cases had insemination actually been attempted.

23. The British public sympathized with Mrs. Blood, both offering donations to fund her legal appeal and issuing calls for retroactive amendment of the 1990 law blocking her insemination. Diana Brahams, "Widow Appeals over Denial of Right to Husband's Sperm," *The Lancet,* vol. 348 (October 26, 1996): p. 1164. Two years after her husband's death, on what would have been her husband's thirty-second birthday, she was given new hope when the British court of appeal upheld the Human Fertilization and Embryology

Authority, but returned the case with instructions that while the law does prohibit her insemination in Britain, the law might still determine that she is entitled under European Union law to be treated in another member country. After a rehearing, the Authority denied her application to export the sperm, citing the specific requirements Parliament had included in the law regarding the posthumous use of a man's sperm only with written consent following an opportunity for counseling and reflection upon the implications of such use. Not only was there no written consent for the posthumous use of his sperm, Stephen Blood was comatose when the sperm was extracted and unable to express his consent or refusal to the entire process. The Authority determined that Mrs. Blood should not be allowed to circumvent the requirements of British law by exporting the sperm.

24. Michael D. Lemonick and Alice Park, "The Sperm That Never Dies," *Time,* June 10, 1996, p. 69.

25. Doctors have since found that thalidomide has beneficial uses in the treatment of such diseases as lupus, leprosy, and the ulcers associated with AIDS, and the Food and Drug Administration is being asked to lift the ban.

26. Lucinda Finley, an expert on reproductive health law at the State University of New York, quoted by Robert Lee Hotz in "A Risky Fertility Revolution," *Atlanta Journal-Constitution,* October 27, 1991, p. D4.

27. Ibid., an unnamed woman quoted in the same article.

28. Interview with H.W.

29. The interview with Vicki Ofsa was conducted on June 4, 1992.

30. Christina Ruegsegger Veit, M.D., and Raphael Jewelewica, M.D., "Gender Preselection: Facts and Myths," *Fertility and Sterility* (American Fertility Society), vol. 49, no. 6 (June 1988): p. 939.

31. Pyrzak interview.

32. American College of Obstetricians and Gynecologists, Committee on Ethics Opinion no. 94, April 1991.

33. Joseph A. Califano, *Governing America: An Insider's Report from the White House and the Cabinet* (New York: Simon & Schuster, 1981), p. 70.

34. When participants in my survey were asked whether they would be willing to pay higher health insurance premiums in order to extend coverage for nontraditional reproductive technologies for all policyholders, 63 percent answered "no." Only 15 percent said "yes," and 20 percent were undecided. In response to a similar question regarding taxes, 72 percent said they would be unwilling to pay higher taxes in order to provide government assistance with the costs of the technology, only 10 percent were willing, and 16 percent were undecided. (Responses to survey questions 7B and 7C.) The inconsistency of their responses may be observed by comparing their answers to survey questions 7A(a)–7A(f) regarding which reproductive technologies they believed should be covered by health insurance.

35. Responses to survey question 7D.

36. Alice S. Whittemore, R. Harris, J. Itnyre, J. Halpern, and the Collaborative Ovarian Cancer Group, "Characteristics Relating to Ovarian Cancer Risk: Collaborative Analysis of Twelve U.S. Case-Control Studies," *American Journal of Epidemiology,* vol. 136 (1992): pp. 1175–1220.

37. Steven C. Kaufman, M.D., Robert Spirtas, DrPH, and Nancy J. Alexander, Ph.D., "Fertility Drugs and Ovarian Cancer: Red Alert or Red Herring?" *Journal of Women's Health,* vol. 4, no. 3 (1995): pp. 247–59.
38. The tragic experiences of women who took DES from 1941 through 1971, when illnesses and abnormalities in their offspring were finally linked to the drug, should serve as a warning.

Chapter 15: The Story of Arlette Schweitzer

1. The interviews with Arlette Schweitzer were conducted on July 8 and 16, 1992, and May 21, 1996, together with correspondence postmarked April 22, 1997.

Chapter 16: The Moral, Emotional, and Legal Complexities of Surrogacy

1. Survey participants were asked whether they had read newspaper or magazine accounts of the Baby M case or other cases involving disputes between surrogates and the couples with whom they had contracted to determine their familiarity with media reports concerning reproductive issues. Eighty-eight percent responded that they had read about such cases. (Responses to survey question 11B.)
2. Responses to survey question 11Ac.
3. William Plummer and Lynn Emmerman, "And Baby Makes Five," *People,* March 15, 1993, pp. 73–74.
4. Bruce Lord Wilder, M.D., J.D., *Defining the Legal Parent-Child Relationship in Alternative Reproductive Technology* (American Bar Association, Family Law Section, 1991), p. 7.
5. The interview with Karen Ferencik was conducted on October 22, 1991.
6. Phyllis Chesler, *Sacred Bond: The Legacy of Baby M* (New York: Time Books, 1988), p. 21, referring to a conversation with the author's friend Rita.
7. Johnson v. Calvert, 19 Cal.Rptr.2d 494 (Cal. 1993).
8. The baby-sitter analogy seems most applicable to gestational surrogacies in which the surrogate contributes no genetic material to the conception, as opposed to genetic surrogacies in which the genetic link remains.
9. Survey participants were asked whether they would use certain reproductive alternatives if they and their partner were unable to become pregnant after over a year of trying. Only 12 percent responded that they would use a surrogate to gestate an IVF embryo created from their own and their partner's egg and sperm, 68 percent said they would not, and 13 percent were undecided. If the embryo were related to the male partner only, an even smaller 6.5 percent said they would use a surrogate, 74 percent said they would not, and 12 percent were undecided. If the embryo were related only to the female partner, yet fewer, 5 percent, said they would use a surrogate, 74 percent said they would not, and 13.5 percent were undecided. (Responses to survey questions 6N–6P.) Later in the survey, participants were asked whether or not they would personally use certain procedures, should laws prohibit such use. Twenty-four percent said gestation of an embryo created from the egg and sperm of partners but gestated by a surrogate should be prohibited by law, 55 percent said it should not, and 18 percent were unde-

cided. Regarding artificial insemination of a surrogate with the male partner's sperm, 31 percent said that should be prohibited by law, 44.5 percent said it should not, and 22 percent were undecided. As for using a surrogate to gestate the female partner's egg fertilized in vitro by donor sperm, 30 percent said that should be prohibited by law, 46 percent said it should not, and 21 percent were undecided. (Responses to survey questions 10D–10F.)

10. *Newsweek* poll published January 19, 1987, p. 48.
11. Mary Beth Whitehead with Loretta Schwartz-Nobel, *A Mother's Story: The Truth About the Baby M Case* (New York: St. Martin's Press, 1989), p. 169. Mary Beth Whitehead named the baby Sara and continues to call her by that name, even though the Sterns call her Melissa (from which the initial "M" in the case name, Baby M, came).
12. Matter of Baby M, 537 A.2d 1227 (N.J. 1988).
13. Susan Squire's story "Whatever Happened to Baby M?" appeared in the January 1994 issue of *Redbook* magazine, pp. 60–64, 96. The story reveals that little of Mary Beth's animosity has subsided, and Baby M—who calls herself Sassy—must try to appease two sets of families, who each have very different values and goals for her.
14. Whitehead, *A Mother's Story,* p. 95.
15. Ibid., p. xv.
16. Elizabeth Kane, *Birth Mother: America's First Legal Surrogate Mother* (New York: Harcourt Brace, 1988), p. 290.
17. Barbara Kantrowitz, "Who Keeps Baby M?" *Newsweek,* January 19, 1987, p. 48.
18. The center is mindful of the sensitivity required in rejecting a couple and tries to convey the understanding that it is not judging them to be unsuitable parents but rather is suggesting that another program or another reproductive option might better suit the couple's needs.
19. Interviews with Dr. Hilary Hanafin were conducted on August 3, 1992, May 30, 1996, and April 24, 1997.
20. The comments of A.W. were made on April 6, 1991.
21. Participants in my survey ranked six factors for resolving disputes between the surrogate and the couple with whom she contracted in order of importance for determining who should receive custody of the baby, and the results of their responses are as follows:

	1st	2nd	3rd	4th	5th	6th
Terms of the agreement they signed	69%	10%	3%	2%	2.6%	4%
Genetic ties of claimants to the baby	11%	42%	18%	7%	7%	4.5%
Maternal feelings of the surrogate	6%	5.5%	15%	21%	15%	27%
Paternal feelings of the father	3%	7%	17%	29%	23%	8%
Maternal feelings of the father's wife (whether or not she is genetically related to the baby)	3%	5.5%	13%	21%	22.6%	23%
Economic abilities of the claimants to provide for the baby	4.5%	20%	23%	5%	14%	23.5%

22. Martha A. Field, *Surrogate Motherhood: The Legal and Human Issues* (Cambridge, Mass.: Harvard University Press, 1988), pp. 139–40.
23. Gary E. McCuen, *Hi-tech Babies: Alternate Reproductive Technologies* (Hudson, Wis.: GEM Publications, 1990), pp. 140–41, quoting G. Annas.
24. Thomas A. Shannon, *Surrogate Motherhood: The Ethics of Using Human Beings* (New York: Crossroads Publishing, 1988), p. 82, quoting G. Annas.
25. Justice Kennard writes: "Recent advances in medical technology have made it possible for the human female reproductive role to be divided between two women, the genetic mother and the gestational mother. Such gestational surrogacy arrangements call for sensitivity to each of the adult participants. But the paramount concern must be the well-being of the child that gestational surrogacy has made possible." Johnson v. Calvert, 19 Cal.Rptr.2d 494 (Cal. 1993) at 518.
26. Elizabeth Noble, *Having Your Baby by Donor Insemination* (Boston: Houghton Mifflin, 1987), p. 217, quoting Carole Anderson.
27. Kane, *Birth Mother,* p. 275.
28. In re Baby M at 1248.
29. American College of Obstetricians and Gynecologists, Committee on Ethics Opinion no. 88, November 1990. In connection with this opinion, the ACOG urges seven other guidelines to encourage a successful surrogacy: (1) use for infertility or other medical need, not mere convenience; (2) separate legal and medical representation; (3) oversight by nonprofit agencies; (4) plans for contingencies such as prenatal diagnosis of abnormality, termination of pregnancy, death or divorce, or birth of a handicapped infant; (5) written agreement; (6) surrogate as the sole source of medical consent; and (7) compensation of the surrogate unrelated to the successful delivery or health status of the child.
30. The *Newsweek* poll of January 19, 1987, indicated that 17 percent and 14 percent, respectively, said they did not have an opinion.
31. On January 19, 1995, a second son was born to Deirdre and her husband, Steve Sohmer, with the assistance of the same surrogate. Deirdre also portrayed herself in a television dramatization of her story.
32. In 1987 a twenty-four-year-old surrogate died of heart failure in the eighth month of the pregnancy. *New York Times,* December 13, 1987, p. 42.
33. ACOG, Opinion no. 44.
34. Responses to survey question 11A(h).
35. May/June 1991 issue of *Ms.*
36. Brian Oxman, "California's Experiment in Surrogacy," *The Lancet,* vol. 341 (June 5, 1993): p. 1468.
37. Responses to survey questions 11A(h) and 11A(i).
38. The interview with Julie Johnson was conducted on July 29, 1994.
39. Katha Pollitt, "When Is a Mother Not a Mother?," *The Nation,* vol. 251 (December 31, 1990): p. 846.

Chapter 17: The Story of Baby Wyatt

1. The interview with Deborah Hecht was conducted on March 13, 1995.
2. The interview with Everett Kane was conducted on March 12, 1995.

3. David Morgolick, "15 Vials of Sperm: The Unusual Bequest of an Even
   More Unusual Man," *New York Times,* April 29, 1994, p. B18.
4. The interviews with Sandra Irwin were conducted on March 5, 1995.
5. Specimen Storage Agreement of September 24, 1991.
6. Letter to Bill Kane's children dated October 21, 1991.
7. Hecht v. Superior Court (Kane), 20 Cal.Rptr.2d 275 at 290–91, citing
   Johnson v. Calvert, 851 P.2d 776 (1993).
8. The interviews with J. R. Nerone were conducted on March 17, 1995, and
   April 25, 1997.
9. Although Deborah Hecht has now been awarded access to the sperm, she
   has not conceived Bill Kane's posthumous child. The legal obstacles have
   been replaced with the fertility difficulties of conception past the age of
   forty.

Chapter 18: Conflicting Claims in Donor-assisted Births

1. When asked which of several infertility options they would try if they and
   their partner were unable to conceive after over a year of trying, participants in
   my survey responded that 59 percent would try in vitro fertilization with their
   partner, 22.6 percent would not, and 13.5 percent were undecided. Only
   18 percent said they would try in vitro fertilization if a donor gamete were
   substituted for their partner's egg or sperm, 53 percent said they would not,
   and 20 percent were undecided. (Responses to survey questions 6J and 6K.)
2. When asked if they would try artificial insemination with donor sperm,
   18 percent of survey participants said they would, 54.5 percent said they
   would not, and 21 percent were undecided. (Responses to survey question 6L.)
3. When asked if they would use a surrogate to gestate a fetus conceived with
   their own and their partner's gametes, 68 percent of survey participants said
   they would, 12 percent said they would not, and 13 percent were undecided. (Responses to survey question 6N.)
4. If the surrogate gestated a fetus conceived with a donor egg, 6.5 percent of
   survey participants said they would try that option, 74 percent said they
   would not, and 12 percent were undecided. If the surrogate gestated a fetus
   conceived with donor sperm, only 5 percent of survey participants said they
   would try that option, 74 percent said they would not, and 13.5 percent
   were undecided. (Responses to survey questions 6O and 6P.)
5. As will be discussed later, many unmarried women with lesbian partners
   have utilized sperm donation to conceive a child, and a few gay couples have
   utilized a surrogate to have a baby.
6. When survey participants were asked which persons should be eligible to
   use nontraditional reproductive technology in order to have a child, assuming they were financially able to pay for the procedure, they answered as
   follows:

	Yes	No	Undecided
Married couples without children	90%	4.5%	3%
Married couples with one child	74.5%	15.5%	7%
Married couples regardless of other children	62%	20%	14%

	Yes	No	Undecided
Unmarried heterosexual couples in a stable relationship without children	37%	45%	13.5%
Unmarried heterosexual couples in a stable relationship with one child	34.5%	47%	13.5%
Unmarried heterosexual couples in a stable relationship regardless of other children	32%	49%	14.5%
Any heterosexual couple who desires treatment	29%	51.6%	15%
Heterosexual single persons without a current partner	29%	51.6%	15%
Gay/lesbian couples without children	20.6%	64%	12%
Gay/lesbian couples with a child or children	20%	64%	12%
Gay/lesbian single persons without a current partner	17%	66%	12.5%

(Responses to survey questions 8A–K.)

7. Genesis 16:2 and 30:3.
8. Reported by William Tuohy of the *Los Angeles Times*, "Fertilization Method Controversial," *Charlotte Observer*, January 3, 1994, p. 2A.
9. Although this is generally accepted as true, a study at the University of Arizona in Tucson by a graduate student using worms to measure the toll resulting from sperm production suggests otherwise. "In the soil nematode, *Caenorhabditis elegans*, sex significantly reduces male lifespan. . . . This suggests that spermatogenesis, rather than oogenesis or the physical act of mating, is a major factor reducing lifespan in *C. elegans*. This contradicts the traditional biological assumption that large oocytes [eggs] are much costlier to produce than small sperm." Wayne Van Voorhies, "Production of Sperm Reduces Nematode Lifespan," *Nature*, vol. 360 (December 3, 1992): p. 456.
10. Jane Hansen, "At This Frontier, Giving and Receiving Are Equal," *Atlanta Journal-Constitution*, February 18, 1992, p. D1.
11. Barbara Noble, *Having Your Baby by Donor Insemination* (Boston, Houghton Mifflin, 1987), p. 147, referring to a donor confidence shared with Achilles.
12. A 1987 study by Congress's Office of Technology Assessment, quoted in *USA Today* on May 8, 1991, p. 14A, indicated that 172,000 women had undergone artificial inseminations that year and that 65,000 babies were the result. The Sperm Bank of California cites 15,000 to 20,000 births per year in their literature, but *Dateline NBC* reported 35,000 to 50,000 donor-inseminated births annually in their June 16, 1992, broadcast. It is obvious from such inconsistent reports that we simply don't know.
13. The interview with Dora Vaux was conducted on August 26, 1991, followed by an interview with Anita Neff, her successor at the Repository, on April 22, 1997.
14. Ofsa interview.
15. Annette Baran and Reuben Pannor, *Lethal Secrets: The Shocking Conse-*

quences and Unsolved Problems of Artificial Insemination (New York: Warner Books, 1989).

16. Ibid., p. 37.
17. Ibid., p. 50.
18. Ibid., p. 51.
19. Responses to survey question 23B.
20. Responses to survey question 23A.
21. Hanafin interview.
22. The interview with Barbara Reboy was conducted on July 15, 1992.
23. Excerpts from The Sperm Bank of California (TSBC's) Donor Identity Release Policy: "During the screening process, TSBC offers its donors the option of identity release. Upon meeting and completing the screening requirements, the donor is required to sign one of two contracts. One contract assures the donor complete confidentiality and prohibits TSBC from revealing his identity. The other contract authorizes TSBC to reveal the donor's identity under certain circumstances. These circumstances are: (1) the information can only be released to the offspring resulting from donor insemination; (2) the offspring must be at least 18 years of age for information to be released; (3) the offspring must petition TSBC in writing requesting the information. . . . The identity release policy is strictly a mechanism for the release of information from TSBC to your child. Your child is the only person who is eligible to receive this information. It is not a mechanism for the donor and recipient to meet or know each other; nor is it an arrangement for the offspring and the donor to meet. Information is not released to the donor pertaining to the identity of the recipient or the child. The policy simply allows for information release. The following identifiers will be released under the circumstances described above: first, middle, last name; permanent address; telephone number, social security number; driver's license number; date of birth; and place of birth."
24. Ofsa interview.
25. Associated Press, "Sperm Bank Mix-up Case Settled," *Atlanta Journal-Constitution,* July 31, 1991, p. A4.
26. Marlise Simons, "Different-Race Twins Spark Ethics Debate," *New York Times,* reprinted in the *Charlotte Observer,* June 28, 1995, pp. 1A, 5A.
27. The interviews with Cynthia Hallvik were conducted on July 26, 1994, and April 9, 1997.
28. Ofsa interview.
29. The Ofsa interview indicated 5 to 10 percent; California Cryobank materials report 15 percent in their program.
30. The American Fertility Society and the Centers for Disease Control make the following recommendations to doctors and sperm banks: First, use only frozen donor semen; second, quarantine the frozen semen pending test results, and test donors twice, at three-month intervals, as a means of detecting donors unknowingly infected shortly before providing sperm; and third, obtain donors' detailed medical genetic histories. The largest non-profit patients' rights group in this country, the People's Medical Society, suggests that couples avoid insemination by private physicians, unless the

doctor uses only certified sperm banks; that they review the testing and record-keeping procedures; and that they demand to see donor medical records (with identity obscured).

31. Brochure of the Repository for Germinal Choice and Vaux interview.

32. After one woman rejected their donor list in favor of sperm from the Repository for Germinal Choice, the Atlanta clinic staff became worried. "We wondered if her child turned out to be just as common as any of the rest of the kids in his class if she and her husband would be disappointed" (Ofsa interview).

33. Lois Ruskai Melina, *Making Sense of Adoption: A Parent's Guide* (New York: Harper & Row, 1989), p. 228.

34. Ofsa interview.

35. The interview with Rhonda Wilkins was conducted on July 9, 1992.

36. Dr. Joseph Feldschuh, medical director of the Idant Laboratory in New York, appearing on *Dateline NBC*, "Who Is my Father?," broadcast June 16, 1992.

37. Ibid. and Melina, *Making Sense of Adoption*.

38. Baran and Pannor, *Lethal Secrets*, p. 164.

39. See responses to survey question 8 in note 6 above.

40. Katherine and the other members of her family asked that these pseudonyms be used, but her story and the legal dispute with the sperm donor who assisted in the birth of her daughter are real. Their request for confidentiality, common among many donor-assisted families, is based upon the desire to protect the donor-conceived child from feeling stigmatized by the method of her conception.

41. Gena Corea, *The Mother Machine: Reproductive Technologies from Artificial Insemination to Artificial Wombs* (New York: Harper & Row, 1985), pp. 44–45, quoting attorney Donna Hitchens.

42. Katherine acknowledges that a great deal of written material was available to her within the gay community when she was considering insemination. This is in contrast to the experience described by Julie Johnson, whose sister learned of the possibility of self-insemination from a brief reference on a talk show before they attempted the procedure.

43. Baran and Panna, *Lethal Secrets*, p. 132.

44. The Oprah Winfrey show, "Single Moms and the Right to Be Single Moms," broadcast December 19, 1991.

45. Census Bureau statistics for 1992 reflect 1,472,000 fathers (14 percent) heading single-parent households, compared to 9,028,000 mothers (86 percent).

46. From 5.5 to 11.3 percent, according to the Census Bureau.

47. From 3.1 to 8.2 percent, according to the Census Bureau. Overall, the biggest percentage of out-of-wedlock births occurs among black women and women who have not completed high school, but these groups do not reflect the increasing percentages found among the more affluent and educated. Among unemployed women, the rate actually dropped during that same period of time.

48. Beth Weinhouse, "Just the Two of Us," *Redbook,* October 1991, p. 68, citing a poll sponsored by Virginia Slims.

49. Single Mothers by Choice, P.O. Box 1642, Gracie Square Station, New York, NY 10028.

50. James Levine, quoted by Dirk Johnson, *New York Times,* September 1, 1993.

51. Hanafin interview, May 30, 1996. The center has not assisted a single man, believing first that a two-parent family is important, and second that a heterosexual single man may be able to eventually conceive a child within a traditional family, while surrogacy may be a gay couple's only option for having a child.

52. Lori Andrews, *Between Strangers: Surrogate Mothers, Expectant Fathers, and Brave New Babies* (New York: Harper & Row, 1989), p. 216.

53. H.W. interview. This woman's mother took DES during her pregnancy, and thus it may have been the drug that ended the maternal line so important to this family.

54. Bruce Wilder, M.D., J.D., *Defining the Legal Parent-Child Relationship in Alternative Reproductive Technology* (American Bar Association Family Law Section, 1991). p. 18.

55. Ibid., p. 14.

56. Oliver O'Donovan, *Begotten or Made?* (Oxford, England: Clarendon Press, 1984), p. 46.

57. The Center for Surrogate Parenting requires couples to designate a guardian who has agreed to assume custody of the child if, for some unknown reason, the couple were unable to assume custody after birth. This protects the child from being orphaned at birth if the contracting couple die during the pregnancy and ensures that the child will have a parent. Only once has a death occurred during a surrogate pregnancy arranged by the center. The husband, whose sperm provided the couple's only genetic link to the baby, died, and his widow proceeded with the surrogacy agreement, grateful to have the opportunity to raise her deceased husband's child.

58. Katha Pollitt, "When Is a Mother Not a Mother?," *The Nation,* vol. 251 (December 31, 1990): p. 844.

59. Thomas A. Shannon, *Surrogate Motherhood: The Ethics of Using Human Beings* (New York: Crossroads Publishing, 1988), p. 90, quoting John A. Henley: "The point is not that artificial reproduction is 'unnatural' in a biological sense, but that the bonds between people, though they change, 'require more than a casual fidelity on the part of successive generations.' "

60. Winfrey show, "Single Moms."

61. *Dateline NBC,* "Who Is My Father?"

62. Participants in my survey were asked whether certain nontraditional reproductive options should be prohibited by law. Regarding prohibiting fees for certain donor-assisted practices, they answered as follows:

	Yes	No	Undecided
Sale of embryos by couple whose egg and sperm created embryo	69%	19%	9%
Sale of egg by woman	69%	20%	8%

Sale of sperm by man	68% 20% 10%
Sales of eggs, sperm, or embryos by third parties	71% 18% 9%

(Responses to survey questions 11A[d]–11A[g].)

63. As reported by lead researcher Barry Peskin, a gynecologist at the University MacDonald Women's Hospital in Cleveland, Ohio, September 18, 1996.

64. Andrews, *Between Strangers*, p. 77.

65. Noble, *Having Your Baby*, p. xiv; from the foreword by G. Annas, quoting Dr. Hermann Rohleder.

66. When asked if they would describe themselves as religious, 77 percent of survey participants answered "yes" and 20.6 percent answered "no." (Responses to survey question 24A.)

67. When asked if they knew the official position of their church regarding most of the new reproductive technologies, 36 percent of survey participants said they did and 57 percent said they did not. (Responses to survey question 24E.)

68. The foregoing question was followed by one asking those who had answered "yes" to indicate how often their opinions, as expressed in the survey, agree with the official position of their church. Among those answering, 1.6 percent characterized their opinions as always agreeing, 30.6 percent as often agreeing, 46 percent as sometimes agreeing, 16 percent as rarely agreeing, and 5.6 percent as never agreeing. Among all the participants who took the survey, this indicated that only .06 percent knew the position of their church and always agreed with that position, 12 percent knew and often agreed, 18 percent knew and sometimes agreed, 16 percent knew and rarely agreed, and 2 percent knew and never agreed. Of course, most participants had indicated in response to question 24E that they did not know their church's positions. (Responses to survey question 24F.)

69. Participants in my survey were asked whether they are influenced in the decisions they make in their everyday lives by what their church says they ought to do, and 34.5 percent answered "yes," while 61 percent answered "no." (Responses to survey question 24D.)

Chapter 19: The Story of Dolly Lamb

1. Associated Press, "Clone Tests on Humans Rejected," *Fort Worth Star-Telegram*, February 27, 1997, p. 5A.

2. The interview with Dr. Hilary Hanafin was conducted on April 24, 1997.

3. The interview with Anita Neff was conducted on April 22, 1997.

4. The interview with Mary Shearing was conducted on April 11, 1997.

5. Correspondence with Arlette Schweitzer postmarked April 22, 1997.

6. The interview with The Reverend Mr. Guy and Terri Walden was conducted on April 16, 1997.

7. The interview with Cynthia Hallvik was conducted on April 9, 1997.

8. The interview with Bree Walker was conducted on May 2, 1997.

9. The interview with Nancy Becker Kennedy was conducted on April 4, 1997.

10. See the stories of Emanuele Maresca and Anthony Baez, whose families had the sperm of each man extracted and frozen so that it could be used by their respective young widows for posthumous conceptions of the men's children. Page 195 of this book.

Conclusion

1. See responses to survey questions 21A–21C in Appendix 2 for the attitudes participants expressed toward welfare recipients and reproductive issues.
2. The interview with Union County health director Lorey White was conducted on February 19, 1993.
3. Participants in my survey were asked about what school nurses and sex education teachers should be able to tell students, and their responses were as follows:

	Yes	No	Undecided
Should students be given information regarding birth control by school nurses or sex education teachers?	87.4%	5%	4.5%
Should students be provided with birth-control devices by school nurses if the student requests it?	47%	35%	16.5%
Should students be directed by sex education teachers or school nurses to outside clinics for birth-control information and devices?	69%	15.5%	13.5%

(Responses to survey questions 20C–20E.)

When asked in what grades sex education should be taught, 30 percent marked grades 1–3; 64 percent marked grades 4–5; 84 percent marked grades 6–7; 84.5 percent marked grades 8–9; and 78 percent marked grades 10–12. (Responses to survey question 20B.)

Selected Bibliography

Books

Andrews, Lori. *Between Strangers: Surrogate Mothers, Expectant Fathers, and Brave New Babies.* New York: Harper & Row, 1989.

1 Annals of Congress. August 15, 1789

Baran, Annette, and Reuben Pannor. *Lethal Secrets: The Shocking Consequences and Unsolved Problems of Artificial Insemination.* New York: Warner Books, 1989.

Bonnicksen, Andrea L. *In Vitro Fertilization: Building Policy from Laboratories to Legislatures.* New York: Columbia University Press, 1989.

Califano, Joseph A. *Governing America: An Insider's Report from the White House and the Cabinet.* New York: Simon & Schuster, 1981.

Chesler, Phyllis. *Sacred Bond: The Legacy of Baby M.* New York: Time Books, 1988.

Corea, Gena. *The Mother Machine: Reproductive Technologies from Artificial Insemination to Artificial Wombs.* New York: Harper & Row, 1985.

Dorris, Michael. *The Broken Cord.* New York: Harper & Row, 1989.

Field, Martha A. *Surrogate Motherhood: The Legal and Human Issues.* Cambridge, Mass.: Harvard University Press, 1988.

Kane, Elizabeth. *Birth Mother: America's First Legal Surrogate Mother.* New York: Harcourt Brace, 1988.

Kingsley, Jason and Mitchell Levitz. *Count Us In: Growing Up with Down Syndrome.* New York: Harcourt Brace, 1994.

Kuhse, Helga and Peter Singer. *Should the Baby Live? The Problem of Handicapped Infants.* England: Oxford University Press, 1985.

Lyon, Jeff. *Playing God in the Nursery.* New York: Norton, 1985.

McCuen, Gary E. *Hi-tech Babies: Alternate Reproductive Technologies.* Hudson, Wis.: GEM Publications, 1990.

Melina, Lois Ruskai. *Making Sense of Adoption: A Parent's Guide.* New York: Harper & Row, 1989.

Mitford, Jessica. *The American Way of Birth.* New York: Dutton, William Abrahams Books, 1992.

Noble, Elizabeth. *Having Your Baby by Donor Insemination.* Boston: Houghton Mifflin, 1987.

O'Donovan, Oliver. *Begotten or Made?* Oxford, England: Clarendon Press, 1984.

Shannon, Thomas A. *Surrogate Motherhood: The Ethics of Using Human Beings.* New York: Crossroads Publishing, 1988.

Singer, Peter. *Rethinking Life and Death: The Collapse of Our Traditional Ethics.* New York: St. Martin's Press, 1994.

————, and Deane Wells. *Making Babies: The New Science and Ethics of Conception.* New York: Charles Scribner's Sons, 1985.

Weiss, Ann E. *Bioethics: Dilemmas in Modern Medicine.* Hillside, N.J.: Enslow Publishers, 1985.

Whitehead, Mary Beth, with Loretta Schwartz-Nobel. *A Mother's Story: The Truth About the Baby M Case.* New York: St. Martin's Press, 1989.

Wilder, Bruce Lord, M.D., J.D. *Defining the Legal Parent-Child Relationship in Alternative Reproductive Technology.* American Bar Association, Family Law Section, 1991.

Articles

Alexander, Leo. "Medical Science Under Dictatorship." *New England Journal of Medicine,* 1949.

Associated Press, "Clone Tests on Humans Rejected," *Fort Worth Star Telegram,* February 27, 1997, p. 5A.

Associated Press. "Sperm Bank Mix-up Case Settled." *Atlanta Journal-Constitution,* July 31, 1991, p. A4.

Billings, Paul R., Mel A. Kohn, Margaret de Cuevas, Jonathan Beckwith, Joseph S. Alper, and Marvin R. Natowicz. "Discrimination as a Consequence of Genetic Testing," *American Journal of Human Genetics,* Vol. 50 (1992): pp. 476–82.

Bork, Robert. "Testimony." *Wall Street Journal,* October 5, 1987.

Brahams, Diana. "Widow Appeals over Denial of Right to Husband's Sperm." *The Lancet,* vol. 348 (October 26, 1996): p. 1164.

California Cryobank News, vol. 2, no. 1 (1992): p. 1.

Chasnoff, Ira J., M.D., Harvey J. Landress, A.C.S.W., and Mark E. Barrett, Ph.D. "The Prevalence of Illicit-Drug or Alcohol Use During Pregnancy and Discrepancies in Mandatory Reporting in Pinellas County, Florida." *New England Journal of Medicine,* vol. 322 (1990): pp. 1202–06.

Cherskov, Myk. "Fighting Genetic Discrimination." *American Bar Association Journal,* June 1992, p. 38.

Culliton, Barbara. "Grave Robbing." *Science,* vol. 186 (November 1, 1974): pp. 420–23.

Dickey, Richard P., M.D., Ph.D. "The Medical Status of the Embryo." *Loyola Law Review,* vol. 32 (1986): pp. 317–36.

Doman, Jen M. R. and Kenneth Miller. "Together Forever." *Life* magazine, April 1996, pp. 44–56.

Drews, Carolyn D., C. C. Murphy, M. Yeargin-Allsopp, and P. Decoufle. "The Relationship Between Idiopathic Mental Retardation and Maternal Smoking During Pregnancy." *Pediatrics,* vol. 97, no. 4 (April 1996): pp. 547–53.

Duff, R. S. and A. G. M. Campbell. "Moral and Ethical Dilemmas in the Special Care Nursery." *New England Journal of Medicine,* vol. 289 (1973): p. 890.

Eagan, Andrea Boroff. "Who Decides for Women?" *American Health,* vol. 9, no. 7, pp. 42–43.

Eichel, Henry. "S.C. Lawsuit Spotlights Debate on How to Treat Pregnant Cocaine Users." *Charlotte Observer,* January 31, 1994, pp. 1A, 5A.

Goldman, Ari L. "Vatican Asks Government to Curb Birth Technology." *New York Times,* March 11, 1987, pp. A1, A17.

Hack, Maureen, M.B., Ch.B.; H. Gerry Taylor, Ph.D.; Nancy Klein, Ph.D.; Robert Eiben, M.D.; Christopher Schatschneider, M.A.; and Nori Mercuri-Minich, B.S. "School-age Outcomes in Children with Birth Weights Under 750 g." *New England Journal of Medicine,* vol. 331, no. 12 (September 22, 1994): pp. 753–59.

Hansen, Jane. "At This Frontier, Giving and Receiving Are Equal." *Atlanta Journal-Constitution,* February 18, 1992, p. D1.

Harpez, Beth J. "Couple Had Hoped for a Family; Procedure Keeps That Hope Alive." *Associated Press,* January 20, 1995.

Hotz, Robert Lee. "A Risky Fertility Revolution." *Atlanta Journal-Constitution,* October 27, 1991, p. 4D.

Jackson, Wes. "Listen to the Land." *Amicus Journal,* vol. 15, no. 1 (Spring 1993).

Johnson, Dirk, quoting James Levine, *New York Times,* September 1, 1993.

Kantrowitz, Barbara. "Who Keeps Baby M?" *Newsweek,* January 19, 1987, pp. 44–49.

Kaufman, Steven C., M.D., Robert Spirtas, DrP.H., and Nancy J. Alexander, Ph.D. "Fertility Drugs and Ovarian Cancer: Red Alert or Red Herring?" *Journal of Women's Health,* vol. 4, no. 3 (1995): pp. 247–59.

Margolick, David. "15 Vials of Sperm: The Unusual Bequest of an Even More Unusual Man." *New York Times,* April 29, 1994, p. B18.

Morris, John A., Jr., M.D., Ph.D.; Todd R. Wilcox; and William H. Prist, M.D. "Pediatric Organ Donation: The Paradox of Organ Shortage Despite the Remarkable Willingness of Families to Donate." *Pediatrics,* vol. 89, no. 3 (March 1992): pp. 411–15.

Morrow, Lance. "A Family's Act of Lifesaving Conception." *Time,* June 17, 1991, pp. 54–58.

Oxman, Brian. "California's Experiment in Surrogacy." *The Lancet,* vol. 341 (June 5, 1993): p. 1468.

Plummer, William and Lynn Emmerman. "And Baby Makes Five." *People,* March 15, 1993, pp. 73–74.

Pollitt, Katha. "When Is a Mother Not a Mother?" *The Nation,* vol. 251 (December 31, 1990): pp. 825, 840, 842–44, 846.

Post, Stephen G. "Fetal Tissue Transplant: The Right to Question Progress." *America,* January 12, 1991, p. 16.

Simons, Marlise. "Different-Race Twins Spark Ethics Debate." *Charlotte Observer,* June 28, 1995, pp. 1A, 5A.

Squire, Susan. "Whatever Happened to Baby M?" *Redbook,* January 1994, pp. 60–64, 96.

Stick, S. M., P. R. Burton, L. Gurrin, P. D. Sly, and P. N. LeSouef. "Effects of

Maternal Smoking During Pregnancy." *The Lancet,* vol. 348, (October 19, 1996): pp. 1060–64.

Tuohy, William, of the *Los Angeles Times.* "Fertilization Method Controversial." *Charlotte Observer,* January 3, 1994, p. 2A.

Van Voorhies, Wayne. "Production of Sperm Reduces Nematode Lifespan." *Nature,* vol. 360 (December 3, 1992): pp. 456–58.

Veit, Christina Ruegsegger, M.D., and Raphael Jewelewica, M.D. "Gender Pre-selection: Facts and Myths." *Fertility and Sterility* (American Fertility Society), vol. 49, no. 6 (June 1988): pp. 937–40.

Weinhouse, Beth. "Just the Two of Us." *Redbook,* October 1991, pp. 68, 70, 72, 74–76.

Whittemore, Alice S., R. Harris, J. Itnyre, J. Halpern, and the Collaborative Ovarian Cancer Group. "Characteristics Relating to Ovarian Cancer Risk: Collaborative Analysis of Twelve U.S. Case-Control Studies." *American Journal of Epidemiology,* vol. 136 (1992): pp. 1175–1220.

Case Citations

Bowen v. American Hospital Ass'n, 476 U.S. 610 (1986).

Carey v. Population Services International, 431 U.S. 678 (1977).

Davis v. Davis, 842 S.W.2d 588 (Tenn. 1992).

Doe v. Bolton, 410 U.S. 155 (1973).

Hecht v. Superior Court (Kane), 20 Cal.Rptr.2d 275.

In re A.C., 533 A.2d611 (D.C.App. 1987); vacated at 539 A.2d 203 (D.C.App. 1988); 573 A.2d 1235 (D.C.App. 1990).

In re T.A.C.P., 609 So.2d 588 (1992).

Johnson v. Calvert, 19 Cal.Rptr.2d 494 (Cal. 1993).

Matter of Baby K, 16 F.3d 590 (4th Cir., 1994).

Matter of Baby M, 537 A.2d 1227 (N.J. 1988).

People v. Hardy, 469 N.W.2d 50 (Mich.App. 1991).

People v. Pointer, 199 Cal.Rptr. 357 (Cal.App. 1st Dist. 1984).

People v. Zaring, 10 Cal.Rptr.2d 263 (Cal.App. 5th Dist. 1992).

Robinson v. California, 370 U.S. 665 (1962).

Skinner v. Oklahoma, 316 U.S. 535 (1942).

Stallman v. Younquist, 531 N.E.2d 355 (Ill. 1988).

Published Letters

Goode, Mary Jean. Letter to the Editor. *Atlanta Journal-Constitution,* November 4, 1991, p. A8.

McCallum, Mary M. Letter to the Editor. *Atlanta Journal-Constitution,* November 1, 1991, p. A12.

McGrory, Amy E. Letters from Readers. *Glamour,* September 1991, p. 28.

INDEX

fetal tissue use and, 32, 148–51,
157–58, 161–64, 175
genetic knowledge and, *see* Genetic
knowledge
low-birth-weight babies and long-term
disabilities, 51–52, 304
right to decide whether to treat, 38–39,
40–43, 47, 50–51
surrogacy and, 229–30
survey questions, 53, 112–13
survey responses, 35–39, 44, 101
withholding of treatment for, 35, 153,
268–69
Divorce, 277
cryopreservation of embryos, 189–94
survey responses, 194
DNA (deoxyribonucleic acid), 81
cloning, 290–98
institutions collecting samples of,
105–106
Dolly Lamb, 290–98
Donor-assisted births, 213, 215, 220–21,
244–87
agreements, 271–72, 279–80, 281
anonymous donor, 265, 282, 285
best interests of children, 268, 280–81
for couple carrying gene for inheritable
disease, 278–79
custody disputes, resolution of, 218,
220–21, 272–73, 279–82
disposable relationships, 283
donor identity, confidentiality of,
260–63, 270–71, 280–81
effects on the family, 219, 221–22,
239–40, 260–61, 270
egg sharing, 284–85
emotional implications, 12, 260–61,
283–84, 285
emotional problems of the children,
260–61, 269, 270
family gamete donations, 12, 284
friend as sperm donor, 271–75, 284
human error in, 265
impact on donor, 257–58, 283–85
infertile partner, 278
informing the child of means of
conception, 12–13, 260–61, 269–71
the law lagging circumstances of, 279–81
matching donor traits to infertile
partner, 12, 259–260
medical screening of donors, 267–68,
272

number of genetic offspring, limitations
on, 263–64
obligations and rights of donor, 263,
281–83
payment of donors, 284–85
personal traits of donor, 258, 268, 294
for postmenopausal women, 9–14,
259–60
psychological testing of donor, 272
records on, 258–59
self-deception and, 258–59
sexually transmitted diseases and,
266–67, 272
single parent, 271–78, 281–84
survey questions, 288–89
survey responses, 220, 254–55,
261–62, 271, 284, 286
Dorris, Michael, 133–34
Down syndrome, 38, 41, 91–93, 105
Drug abuse *see* substance abuse, prenatal
Drug exposure in utero, 36, 115–17, 142
Dutch, 265

Ectogenesis, 216
Ectopic pregnancy, 149
Ectrodactyly, 74–79, 102–103
Edinburgh Medical School, 258
Education, 304
about genetic disorders, 111
about harmful behaviors during
pregnancy, 69, 139
sex, 305
Eggs:
donation of, *see* Donor-assisted births
finite number of, 257
microsurgery on, 203
monitoring development of, 201
retrieval from aborted fetus, 258
sharing of, 284–85
Embryos:
freezing of, *see* Cryopreservation of
embryos
in vitro fertilization, *see* In vitro
fertilization
Emergency Medical Treatment and Active
Labor Act (EMTALA), 49
Emotional implications of use of fertility
technology, *see specific procedures*
Endocrinal problems interfering with
conception, 183
Endometriosis, 183, 187
Endoscopic fetal surgery, 68